THE GLOBAL

ENVIRONMENT

AND Joseph F. C. DiMento

INTERNATIONAL

LAW

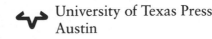 University of Texas Press
Austin

Copyright © 2003 by the University of Texas Press
All rights reserved
Printed in the United States of America
First edition, 2003

Requests for permission to reproduce material from this work
should be sent to Permissions, University of Texas Press,
P.O. Box 7819, Austin, TX 78713-7819.

⊚ The paper used in this book meets the minimum requirements of
ANSI/NISO Z39.48-1992 (R1997) (Permanence of Paper).

Library of Congress Cataloging-in-Publication Data

DiMento, Joseph F.
    The global environment and international law / Joseph F. C.
DiMento.—1st ed.
        p.   cm.
Includes bibliograpical references and index.
    ISBN 0-292-71620-6 (cloth : alk. paper)—ISBN 0-292-71624-9
(pbk. : alk. paper)
    1.   Environmental law. International.   I.   Title.
K3585 .D54 2003
341.7'62—DC21

                                                    2002012296

To
Donald N. Michael (in Memoriam)
and
Joseph L. Sax

I'm hopeful ... and this is important to us as a species ... we tend to do the right things when we get scared.

—Octavia Butler, novelist, *New York Times* interview, 1 January 2000

CONTENTS

PREFACE

Those who have followed the attempts in Rio de Janeiro, The Hague, Nairobi, Stockholm, Montreal, Kyoto, Buenos Aires, and Johannesburg to construct an international law of the environment have witnessed an intense, active, colorful, fascinating, and often confusing drama. They may have wondered whether the sometimes circuslike sessions involving heads of state and indigenous people and observers actually can produce what they understand to be effective law. Many legal specialists also question the contribution of the immense outpouring of instruments created to address global environmental degradation in the last several decades.

This book aims to answer the question "To what extent has international environmental law mattered?" I seek to do so in several ways. I summarize the history of the movement in law toward regional and global efforts to protect species, conserve resources, and stop pollution. I evaluate the effectiveness of efforts found in hundreds of treaties, customary laws, soft laws, and related international agreements. I describe the instruments that have been employed and the characteristics they share.

Some of the lawmaking techniques are new and innovative. They reflect experiments to organize hundreds of nations and thousands of cultures to confront unprecedented global challenges. International environmental law is a part of international law itself, but it also has been a major harbinger of change in global law generally. It has been a laboratory to test approaches to lawmaking and implementation that may be more generally applicable.

Two objectives come together in the newer international environmental law. One is substantive: slow down environmental harm, restore ecological health. The other is procedural: try to do so through cooperative activities that recognize and respect widely differing cultures and value systems. These are objectives to which I was first introduced by the people to whom I dedicate this work. Joseph Sax helped make the environment a subject of worldwide interest. Donald Michael helped policy-makers understand how social process can be structured to reach long-range goals.

I think that the topic is too important to be the domain only of specialists, so I have written for both professionals who are in dialogues about matters of fundamental importance to a law that works and for the citizen who wants to know how the law can better address global protection.

I aim to tell a story not well known by many concerned world citizens. In doing so I try to make competing legal frameworks understandable to people who often have rigid ideas about the role and potential of the law, to make social control and environmental policy comprehensible to legal scholars and practitioners, and to provide a framework for appreciating what can make the law effective.

International environmental law is an enterprise that often is misunderstood and too facilely maligned. In fact it has had considerable successes and, while facing daunting challenges, has an even greater potential.

Irvine, California, September 2002

ACKNOWLEDGMENTS

Many of the ideas set forth in this book evolved through conversations with colleagues in international environmental law and policy. Among the most important were those with Stefano Nespor, editor of *Rivista Giuridica Dell'Ambiente*, an environmental law journal. Stefano also introduced me to ELNI, the Environmental Law Network International. Helen Ingram pointed me toward a literature that is not in the mainstream of environmental law but should be. Gilbert Geis, as always, kept me working in as intelligent a way as I am able. Pamela Doughman contributed immeasurably throughout and centrally to the sections on the North American Free Trade Environmental Side Agreement. Suzanne Levesque, then a graduate student, summarized brilliantly a section of the literature. Reviewers for the University of Texas Press offered extremely useful suggestions. UCI librarians Kay Collins and Julia Gelfand assisted in bibliographic research. Carol Wyatt, Dianne Christianson, and Ben Yater of UCI provided typically flawless word-processing assistance. Deborah Newquist, my wife, and my no longer little ones Joseph and Allie created an environment that allowed me to make this small contribution to the environment. The National Science Foundation Division of Law and Social Sciences, the Canadian Government Research Council, the Global Peace and Conflict Studies program at UCI, and the University of California-Irvine Institute on Global Conflict and Cooperation funded underlying research for sections of the work and an international workshop that generated personal contributions of Byung-Sun Cho, Elizabeth DeSombre, Ronnie Lipschutz, Richard Matthew, Albert Mumma, Christopher Stone, Kilaparti Ramakrishna, Prue Taylor, and Tullio Scovazzi. Finally, my mother has never stopped supplying support in many ways.

ACRONYMS

BSEP	Black Sea Environmental Programme
CEC	Commission for Environmental Cooperation, under the NAFTA Environmental Side Agreement
CERES	Coalition for Environmentally Responsive Economies
CFC	chlorofluorocarbon, an ozone-depleting substance
CITES	Convention on the International Trade in Endangered Species
COP	Conference of the Parties
EC or EEC	European Economic Community
ECJ	European Court of Justice
EIA	environmental impact assessment
EMAS	Eco-Management and Audit Scheme of the European Union
EU	European Union
FAO	Food and Agriculture Organization
FCCC	Framework Convention on Climate Change
GAO	General Accounting Office, United States
GATT	General Agreement on Tariffs and Trade
GEF	Global Environmental Facility
GMO	genetically modified organism
ICJ	International Court of Justice
IGO	intergovernmental organization
INC	International Negotiating Committee of the FCCC
IPCC	Intergovernmental Panel on Climate Change
JPAC	Joint Public Advisory Committee of NAAEC
MARPOL	International Convention for the Prevention of Pollution from Ships and Its Protocol
MEA	multilateral environmental agreement
NAAEC	North American Agreement on Environmental Cooperation

NAFTA	North American Free Trade Agreement
NATO	North Atlantic Treaty Organization
NCP	noncompliance procedure
NGO	nongovernmental organization
ODS	ozone-depleting substance
OECD	Organization for Economic Cooperation and Development
POPs	persistent organic pollutants
TREMs	trade-related environmental measures
UNCED	United Nations Conference on Environment and Development
UNCLOS	United Nations Convention on the Law of the Sea
UNDP	United Nations Development Programme
UNEP	United Nations Environment Programme
USAID	United States Agency for International Development
WMO	World Meterological Organization
WTO	World Trade Organization
Y2Y	Yellowstone to Yukon Conservation Initiative

THE GLOBAL ENVIRONMENT AND INTERNATIONAL LAW

1. WORLDWIDE ENVIRONMENTAL QUALITY AND THE ROLE OF LAW

This chapter focuses on the need for international attention to global environmental challenges. It asks to what extent law is an appropriate vehicle to address the large number and variety of environmental and natural resource problems. The chapter sets the stage for later analyses of characteristics of an effective legal response.

MONDONIA

Dateline: The Pacific, 2030

The small island state of Mondonia was completely evacuated last week. An 85-year-old couple whose lives the media have been following daily became the last people to leave this lush tropical nation. The two were taken by helicopter from their lifelong home in the village of Susper. The airstrip that would have been their point of departure has not been in service for months, having been inundated by the rising waters of the Pacific Ocean.

Mondonia is the most recent of several small islands to be depopulated by the climate change that has resulted from what scientists forty years ago labeled the "greenhouse effect." The term refers to the increase in temperatures worldwide as the result of a variety of processes, most notably the burning of fossil fuels by humans.

At the turn of the century, Mondonia was the home of 50,000 people and a destination point for tourists who wished to experience the delights of tropical South Sea life. Now, one tenth of its earlier physical mass, with its splendid beaches washed away, it will be visited only by atmospheric scientists and the curious with high-powered boats. It stands as an eerie memorial to the excesses of contemporary industrial and consumer life.

Mondonia first felt the impact of global climate change twenty years ago when its modest production of foodstuffs began to drop, first by about 5 percent a year, then in much larger amounts as areas became flooded with salt water. Flash floods visited periodically. At the same time, sections of the country were in rare periods of drought, causing further erosion of the previously sustainable supply of crops. Exacerbating this problem was the intrusion of salt water into the country's main aquifer. Mondonia's small fishing take was eliminated when new species, foreign to the native population, replaced the fish that were a mainstay of the Mondonian diet. Migratory birds, forever an indicator of changing seasons, were seldom spotted. This was followed by reports of massive coral bleaching. About fifteen years ago, there was a spread of several infectious diseases previously not known on the island. Cases of encephalitis and cholera were reported in increasingly large numbers. Then a series of cyclones hit, though they had previously been very rare in the region.

There is neither a Susper nor a Mondonia, of course. But the story is not fiction; it is an extrapolation of the best science that exists to predict environmental conditions in the next several decades. Mondonia's story concerns the impacts of global warming.

TYPES OF GLOBAL ENVIRONMENTAL CHALLENGE

To begin this treatment of law and the world environment, I could have told stories about matters other than the greenhouse effect or climate change, taking what science knows today and projecting it to the not-so-distant future. I could have focused on the rapidly dwindling population of rhinos or tigers or elephants in the world. From 1970 to 1998 the rhinoceros population decreased from 65,000 to 11,000; from 1900 to 1998 the tiger population decreased from 100,000 to 5,000; elephant herds plummeted from 1.3 million individuals to about 600,000 in the decade after 1979.[1] The natural orangutan will be extinct in one decade if present patterns persist. I could have described the destruction of fish, quantifying the loss of specific species. In 1999, for instance, the biomass of spawning western bluefish was 13 percent of its 1975 level, and by 1999 60 percent of the world's fisheries were at or near declining points. In regard to regional catches, from 1986 to 1996 the number of fish species in the Black Sea dropped by about 75–80 percent. I could have chronicled the loss of sea turtles, four species of which—the loggerhead, the green leatherback, the hawksbill, and the Kemp's ridley—

now face extinction, or decimation of the rich resources, including deep-sea corals, of the high seas. I could have addressed the escalating number of skin cancers related to the ongoing destruction of the protective ozone layer. By 2050 the number of new cases of nonmelanoma skin cancer in the United States linked to the drop in protective ozone may be as many as 100,000 a year (de Guijl 1995).

I could have drawn pictures of the cumulative effects of the loss of productive agricultural land (10 million acres each year).[2] I could have viewed agricultural land more critically and focused on what its development takes away or what accompanies its successful development; up to 5 million cases of acute poisoning occur from pesticides annually. Loss of forest and woodland in the period 1700–1980 is estimated at one fifth, down from 47 percent of the global area in 1700 to 38 percent in 1980. From 1990 to 1995, 65 million hectares of forest were lost. I could have listed the thousands of species that will not be knowable by future generations because they will have been systematically wiped from the earth's surface. According to the *Global Biodiversity Assessment,* since 1600 extinction has occurred at 50 to 100 times the average estimated natural rate. Furthermore, the extinction rate is expected to rise between 1,000 and 10,000 times the natural rate.[3]

Problems of water quantity, distribution, and quality are also enormous. Daily there are 25,000 deaths attributable to poor water quality and waterborne diseases. One fifth of the world's population is without a safe drinking water supply and a full 50 percent lacks access to a safe sanitation system (*Global Environment Outlook 2000*). One third of the world's coastal regions are in jeopardy, particularly from the development of infrastructure such as homes, commercial sites, roads, and sewers and from land-based pollution sources. Pollution and global warming have combined to destroy a quarter of the world's coral reefs. Tourism and oil spills (both from tankers and from fuel bunkers) threaten coastal areas in many regions of the world. Illegal transboundary movement of hazardous substances is rampant. A global estimate is lacking, but the value, if it were legally handled, is clearly in the billions of dollars. In one year alone tens of thousands of tons of ozone-depleting substances were smuggled, making chlorofluorocarbons (CFCs) the second most valuable smuggled contraband in Miami, following cocaine (*International Environment Reporter,* 4 August 1999, 648).

The first United Nations *Global Environment Outlook* (in 1997) summarized environmental trends by region, ranking them as "increasing," "remaining relatively stable," and "decreasing." Land degradation, forest loss and degradation, biodiversity loss and fragmentation of habitat, pollution and scarcity of fresh water are all increasing in at least half of the world's regions. Atmospheric pollution is increasing in two regions and remaining stable in the others. Urban and industrial contamination and waste is stable in half of the regions but worsening in the other half. The only trend labeled as green was for decreasing land degradation in North America. At the millennium, *Global Environment Outlook 2000*, although reporting in a different manner, saw similar challenges.

Ethnic and regional wars, hostilities, and military action also bring about air pollution related to the deliberate setting of oil fires, serious destruction of water systems, loss of habitat, and blocking of important flows in rivers by weapons and military vehicles. Although remarkably removed from the policy agenda in very recent years, the close-to-ultimate environmental destruction that would result from a nuclear confrontation has not been fully resolved.

All this degradation has occurred in a world populated now by about 6 billion people. Since 1960, the population doubled, and even though the rate of population growth has begun to slow, the increase from 6 billion to 7 billion will take eleven years. Within a half-century thereafter the number of people on Earth, each potentially a protector of the environment but each a consumer, each making an environmental impact, will be around 10 billion (*Economist*, 18 February 1996). The fastest-growing regions include parts of Africa that have the least developed environmental management systems.

The *Outlook* did cite some progress in international environmental developments: greater international cooperation and public participation, the emergence of private-sector action, and the emergence of legal frameworks, economic instruments, environmentally sound technologies, and clean production processes. Progress has been made in coordinating action to prevent further destruction of the ozone layer. Nonetheless, its damage continues.

Acid rain and transboundary air pollution are now found in many regions of the world. Energy-demand projections linked to economic development indicate an ever-increasing use of fossil fuels, with concomitant environmental challenges. Several regions continue to experience the accumulation of radioactive waste and the effects of past radioactive spills. Long-range transport of a variety of pollutants threatens areas once considered pristine, including the planet's poles.

It is necessary to differentiate the seriousness of global environmental challenges when focusing on world environmental problems with a view toward legal intervention. The alternative is to accept the position of systems breakdown resulting from the devastating effects of environmental problems such as global warming. Such warming goes hand in hand with desertification and ozone layer destruction that results in massive global health problems and decimation of species. In this scenario at the least, "changes in global bio-geochemical cycles and the complex interactions between environmental problems such as climate change, ozone depletion, and acidification may have impacts that will confront local, regional, and global communities with situations they are unprepared for. . . . The future might hold more . . . surprises" (*Global Environment Outlook* 1997, 3).

Global environmental challenges differ along several dimensions. Climate change is created by almost all nation-states or entities within those states and has global impacts. Other environmental challenges are created by regions of nation-states and have extraregional effects (e.g., disposal of untreated wastes within a river basin). Some involve illegal actions (e.g., destruction of oil fields and resulting air pollution, illegal trade in hazardous wastes, deliberate setting of fires to clear land). Global environmental change is aggravated by the intentional (in some places legal and some places illegal) actions of small groups of people or small numbers of nations (e.g., burning of the forests in Southeast Asia and the Amazon). The uncountable number of daily activities of significant percentages of the world population, nonmalicious actions of billions of people simply living their consuming lives (e.g., driving automobiles), also contributes to global environmental change. Other global environmental challenges result from not-so-innocent activities (e.g., dumping from cruise ships).

Global environmental problems may take years if not decades to register as unacceptable insults to human health. Examples include the effects of exposure to rays associated with destruction of the ozone layer or diseases related to climate change. Others manifest themselves immediately and in dramatic ways. Results of transboundary pollution can be macabre: In 1997 two Australians fell into the Yarkon River in Israel and died, not from drowning but from exposure to toxics. In the early 1990s several cases of encephalopathy were reported in Texas areas bordering Mexico. There were froglike babies with undeveloped brains and eyes on the sides of their heads. Some investigators linked these abnormalities to contamination by industrial wastes. The wastes also affect people who are forced to work in areas where the infrastructure is more primitive than in medieval times and to use water from putrid wells.

Some get their water delivered in barrels formerly used to store radioactive wastes.

In the terminology of jurisprudence, the actions that law needs to target are those of misfeasance, malfeasance, and nonfeasance. Law speaks of violations of norms within sovereign entities. Norms are to be enforced by sanctions and incentives. Other fields employ different terms for the behaviors that law seeks to control. In the language of political science they are both legal and illegal actions of individual nation-states, regions, single actors, and collective actors. Sociology characterizes some of the actions as organizational outputs, others are the work of elites, still others of individuals. Economists describe the macroeffects of individual or collective action and failure to internalize external costs (Haas 1990, ch. 1).

My focus is on global environmental problems in their many forms. Degradation of the great seas; destruction of the earth's protective systems; loss of biodiversity; depletion of life-sustaining resources; transport across borders, physical and ecological, of substances that injure and kill; the end of natural beauty and cultural traditions—all are problems and all are potential targets of law. In addition, I will maintain a focus on change, worldwide, in climate patterns and events and evolving legal responses to it.

THE LEGAL RESPONSE: MAJOR THEMES

As we shall see, the response to the Mondonia challenge of global climate change reflects a maturing understanding of what can be done through the law to protect the planet. Several important themes are marking the negotiations that have continued for more than a decade. To a certain extent the climate case builds on the experience of other multinational legal efforts. To some extent it is breaking new ground. In general in international environmental lawmaking there is a growing expectation that multinational negotiations should be transparent (a widely used term that means activities should be open and visible and understandable to interested people), accessible, responsible, and equitable. Reliance on economic incentives is evolving, although not trusted equally by all participants. There is also faith among many that corporate expertise and capabilities, advances in science and technology, and private investment will lead to desirable alternatives to the current international climate predicament. International efforts also emphasize a balance between cooperation and coercion, the recognition of state interdependency and sovereignty, the role of voluntary commitments and of environmental activists and the business sector, and the importance of information accessibility.

This book is about whether these strategies are sufficient for creating effective treaties and other international instruments. We now have three decades of experience with a modern international environmental law. A large number of approaches have been taken. In effect, there has been a natural experiment on what works well and what does not in the complex system of the physical and sociolegal environments. A voluminous literature exists regarding virtually all of the major initiatives. There is an evolving consensus about some approaches, and there are criteria for resolving matters where consensus does not now exist. Many studies, including those done specifically for this book, have tested alternative understandings across cases that range from atmospheric and ocean pollution to procedural initiatives. Scholars from many disciplines have generated a rich set of perspectives from which a rather comprehensive assessment of law's role can be made.

THE FUNCTION OF LAW AND ITS RELATIONSHIP TO OTHER INSTITUTIONS

Law aims to influence behavior in order to promote environmental quality. It works in parallel with other institutions. It also works according to dynamics that some theorists would not classify as institutional. Law interacts—sometimes effectively, sometimes awkwardly, sometimes counter productively—with other systems that seek to order behavior and achieve social control. But law is a distinctive institution.

A precise meaning of law is less self-evident in the international arena than in national domains. Neither is the import of international law on the global environment stage a matter of consensus. Some conclude that the world environment will be sacrificed in the absence of significant new international legal agreements. Other analysts hold that environmental quality can improve in spite of the law and that the law is almost irrelevant in achieving environmental goals. These critics include both those who look to nonregulatory mechanisms and market systems as alternatives to legal regimes and those who put great confidence in local efforts, including grassroots and nongovernmental (NGO) efforts.

What to include within the construct of law at the international level is not a simple choice. The number of instruments that indirectly affect the quality of the environment is gigantic. The boundaries between law and other institutions aimed at influencing individual and collective behavior to promote environmental quality internationally are both weak and permeable. More so than at the domestic level, characterizing an institutional response as a legal initiative is a matter of some subjectivity, although most analysts will conclude that a legal instrument will involve decisions regarding jurisdiction, sanctioning, and standard, rule, or norm formation.

Many disciplines, including law, political science, economics, anthropology, organizational theory, and others, assist in understanding law's contribution to protection of the environment at the international level. Traditionally when legal scholars bound international law they point to several standard sources. These are international instruments (treaties, protocols, conventions, agreements); customary law, the general principles of law recognized by civilized nations; judicial decisions; and the writings of scholars.

Views on the nature of what should be fostered in international law differ dramatically. Some scholars and policy analysts promote a law that would create supranational organizations with innovative and unprecedented powers, including trade sanctions and criminal sanctions imposed by a central agency or world organization (Koskenniemi 1996; Smith and Hunter 1992; Szasz 1992; Vicuna 1992). On the other end of the continuum are scholars (Blatter, n.d.; Holdgate 1996; Hurrell and Kingsbury 1992; Ingram and Fiederlein 1988; Kamieniecke 1993; Lipschutz 1996; Mumme 1993; Shabecoff 1996; Switzer 1994) who conclude that only through participatory efforts can international legal initiatives be successful. These initiatives need to be structured by law but undertaken at the local level or among selective environmental alliances in ad hoc ways that are aware of the particular circumstances of an environmental problem. "Civic environmentalism," "civil society," and "environmental governance" are among the terms used by those in this policy camp.

Other writers and theorists accept some elements from either pole but emphasize additional characteristics (Chayes and Chayes 1991; D'Anieri 1995; Downs, Danish, and Barsoom 2000; French 1994; Gehring 1994; Haas and Haas 1995; Jurgielewicz 1995; Keohane 1995; Koh 1997; Mulenex 1991; Ostrom 1990; Raustiala 1997a,b; Sand 1991b; Sands 1993; Stone 1993; Susskind 1994a,b; Weiss 1993; Wettestad 1999; Young 1991). These include open exchange of relevant information, a hierarchy of progressively applied liability rules, understandable dispute resolution processes, coordination among related agreements, and establishment of independent secretariats.

Flexibility in achieving implementation, inclusiveness of parties, the involvement of NGOs, the existence of clear relationships to existing institutions, and a reasonable economic and considerable political commitment are also recognized. Still other theorists emphasize clarity of communication within and about the legal instrument itself, the natural or physical characteristics of the environmental objectives, scientific consensus, and a low threshold for initial entry by interested parties (i.e., a modest commitment and modest infringement on sovereignty).

The list of explanatory factors is long. This range of opinion is understandable since there is limited empirical work on the ground to assess what legally seems to have made a difference in promoting international environmental quality.

There are many other reasons for disagreement about how international environmental law should be structured. Potential parties to international environmental agreements reflect a range of conflicting interests: the generally wealthy North versus the poorer South, industrialized versus developing nations, Europe versus the United States and Australia. Alliances are numerous and shifting. There are also different understandings of the goals of international environmental law: how can success be determined when studying effects that may take decades to manifest themselves across billions of people throughout the globe, on land, in the seas, and in the atmosphere?

Some measure success in empirical, concrete terms. Is the water drinkable and fishable? Is the air no longer dangerous to breathe? Have we stopped the decimation of species? Is the global average temperature stabilizing? Other benchmarks can be used (Young, Demko, and Ramakrishna 1996). The law might be said to have made a considerable contribution if the behaviors of those who affect environmental conditions are influenced positively. It has been successful, in the views of some analysts, when it fosters international cooperation or when it makes decision making on environmental matters more democratic and inclusive. Finally, both analytical and politically driven differences abound regarding the most efficacious ways of reaching agreed-on goals: what kinds of legal and other institutional changes should be attempted?

THE APPROACH OF THE BOOK

What kinds of environmental law work in what international situations? How should the world's nation-states organize themselves to create law aimed at stopping serious environmental degradation and at controlling the pollution created by multinational corporations, governments, organized criminals, unorganized groups, and individuals? To what extent should society look to nation-states, organized or individually, for greater environmental protection through law? How much should law be based on centralized rule-oriented control strategies, versus bottom-up participation, or economic incentives? For what set of challenges should legal design incorporate combinations of all of these approaches? This book uses these questions to structure a global assessment of law and the planet's environmental status and future.

It is facile to conclude that nothing works well in the international arena when evaluated by the standards of the most developed domestic legal systems. Some fairly sophisticated generalists in law and policy so conclude. Others grudgingly concede that in extreme situations there has been some marginal international progress that can be attributed to legal efforts. Whether these assessments are accurate and whether that is the most that can be expected from law are foci of this work.

I attempt to make the case here that our knowledge of the kind of law that makes a difference is considerable. We have had some impressive successes, including with ozone depleting substances and pollutants of the atmosphere, oil pollution, endangered species, pesticides and chemicals regulations and hazardous substances control. Just as important, we are learning how to structure international environmental law; we are identifying the conditions under which it is better to rely on conventional regulatory approaches, the circumstances when a focus should be on process and actions should be aimed at creation and dissemination of norms of environmental protection—before specific decisions are made on what is to be controlled, at what level, and under which institutional design. And we have learned about the important function of participation of those to be affected, from the individual to the giant multinational company, in the development of the law. Substantively we have slowed down some of the destructive actions of society on the environment, although not as effectively and as quickly as we need to. Procedurally, despite the involvement of different cultures, value systems, political systems, and needs, we are learning how to cooperate to the ends of environmental protection. We are doing so as the stresses on the global environment increase dramatically with population growth and economic development. It is clear that for some environmental challenges, initiatives including those of the law will find it very difficult to keep pace. The place of international law in the race, however, is not a mystery, and it is considerable, although erratic.

My aim is to add to the analysis of the efficacy of international environmental law and the policy directions that law should be taking. In the following chapters I first inventory, historically, the lawmaking activities of global and regional entities. This entails description of the institutions that make and implement the law. The meaning of law in the international environmental context is treated here. Cataloged are the main instruments of control and influence within the legal domain.

Chapter 3 then asks: who and what needs to be influenced by international environmental law? This question involves a presentation on sources of the challenges. I summarize first the actual and potential role that multinational enterprise organizations can take in solving the world's environmental problems. A major premise of the analysis is introduced: one cannot simply wish changes in human behavior that have not been manifest over decades or even centuries as a condition for international environmental strategy. Lawmakers cannot assume that large organizations are going to behave differently, although they are quite capable of saying they will do so. Contributions to global environmental quality of green or environmental management (eco-auditing, eco-labeling, green products and processes, green policies, environmental quality life cycle analysis) suggested or required by law are assessed.

Next is a look at individuals who degrade the environment and an inquiry into how law should target them. These include rogues, the poor, and the desperate. The spotlight then turns from them to the normal consumer. Here too lawmakers cannot assume that those who are or who constantly become more affluent will change their consuming behaviors because they recognize impacts on species or human communities other than their own.

The chapter addresses whether each of these individuals or groups, whatever its contributions to the environmental problem, needs to be targeted *by law*. Are other institutions likely to be more effective than law?

Chapter 4 focuses more sharply on some examples of international environmental law. Which have succeeded and which have been less than successful in adequately influencing behavior? In addition to global, generic, and comprehensive evaluations, several case studies are employed. Why have carefully and exhaustively drafted instruments sometimes not achieved their goals? Why have some nontraditional international approaches been so impressive?

Chapter 5 is based on an integration of the analysis in the first four chapters. This is in two parts. The first lays out expectations of conditions in which law will operate, including shared interests, science, and capacity and commitment of institutions public and private. The second part offers my recommendations. Which legal strategies might work better under what conditions? What factors will be present in successful attempts to protect this planet through the law?

According to Jacob Werksman (1996), the two main groups that study international institutions are lawyers and political scientists:

> Lawyers tend to concentrate their attentions on the formal end of the scale, on international institutions that are known as "international organizations." . . . The definitions and taxonomies of the political scientist, on the other hand, take us away from legal formalities . . . focusing their definition of an institution on the extent to which it affects state behaviour rather than the formal legal structure of the institutions . . . as "persistent and connected sets of rules and practices." . . . They may take the form of bureaucratic organisations, regimes (rule-structures that do not necessarily have organizations attached), or conventions (informal practices). (Werksman is quoting Haas, Keohane, and Levy 1993.)

I combine both traditions and those of organizational theory, sociology, and other disciplines to describe the function of law and to explain that function.

2. LAW TRYING TO SAVE THE EARTH: STRATEGIES, INSTITUTIONS, ORGANIZATIONS

This chapter addresses law as an instrument of international environmental protection. It first presents a short history of international environmental law. It then describes modern law by type: global, multilateral, and regional within the treaty regime; court-made law; and soft law. Then the analysis describes criteria that distinguish an instrument as law and relates the meeting of these criteria to international law's effectiveness.

The proliferation of treaties, conventions, and protocols on environmental protection regionally, from a transboundary perspective, and globally has been dramatic. In the last quarter-century nation-states have entered into more than 250 international environmental instruments. Overall, almost 1,000 instruments have at least one provision addressing the environment. To be sure, the actual number of major treaties in which the main focus is an environmental issue is smaller, but the number is significant because it communicates how the environment has been legally recognized internationally. A modest environmental law based on custom has also evolved, and the development of various forms of soft law has accelerated, such as in hortatory statements of the Biodiversity Convention and the Statement of Forest Protection Principles and in norm recognition. The growth of international environmental law led the United Nations to pass a resolution directing that both the Security Council and the General Assembly be kept informed of international environmental conventions.[1]

The widespread concern over global protection of the natural environment is primarily a recent phenomenon. Contemporary surveys consistently identify saving of endangered species, control of atmospheric pollution, and related phenomena as legitimate foci of public policy recognized by a cross section of people worldwide. Though general public concern was not evident even a few decades ago, the international focus is not a completely new one. Legal efforts to address problems of oceans, of endangered species, of migratory birds, of landscapes, and of other natural resources date back well into the 1800s.[2]

By the mid-nineteenth century, although the term "environment" was not yet part of the legal vocabulary, protection of nature was the subject of several international laws, treaties, and organizational efforts. Bilateral treaties such as the 1818 Convention Respecting Fisheries, Boundary and the Restoration of Slaves between the United States and the United Kingdom that addressed natural resources existed even before that time, but the objective was not protection, rather it was allocation of rights. In 1867 France and Great Britain entered into a convention relative to fisheries, and two years later Constance and Basle created a convention regulating fishing in the Rhine. Salmon fishing in the same river's basin was addressed in a treaty signed by Germany, Luxembourg, The Netherlands, and Switzerland in 1886. In 1891 an agreement was reached between the United States and the Government of Her Britannic Majesty for a modus vivendi in relation to fur fisheries in the Bering Sea, and an international arbitration over the catch of fur seals was settled between the United States and Great Britain in 1898.[3] By 1902 the second International Congress on the Protection of Birds had been held in Paris, with a focus on birds useful to agriculture.

The International Conference on Protection of African Mammals met in London in 1900. This was the first international agreement aimed at preserving wildlife in Africa. The signatories were France, Germany, Great Britain, Italy, Portugal, and Spain, all then colonial powers. The 1900 Convention was ambitious, although flawed when viewed a century later. It considered crocodiles, poisonous snakes, and pythons unworthy of protection; in fact, it declared that they should be destroyed (Lyster 1985) and that herds of lion, leopard, hyena, dog, and certain birds should be reduced. Its primary goal was to preserve supplies for trophy hunters and traders and dealers in ivory and skins. According to the preamble, the convention aimed "to prevent the uncontrolled massacre and to ensure the conservation of diverse wild animal species in their African possessions which are useful to man or inoffensive." Article 2, nonetheless, prohibited the killing of all specimens of species listed and "all other animals which each local government judges necessary to protect, either because of their usefulness or because of their rarity and danger of disappearance" and the killing of nonadults and females "when accompanied by their young" of "elephant, rhinoceros, hippopotamus, zebra other than mountain zebra, buffalo, antelope and gazelles, ibex and mouse deer." Some methods of killing, including by explosives, were outlawed. The convention also encouraged the establishment of nature reserves.

The Hague Conference on Natural Resources took place in 1906, and the International Conference for the Protection of Nature was held in Paris in 1909. In that year the United States and the United Kingdom entered into the Boundary Waters Treaty, which stated (in article 4) that water "shall not be polluted on either side to the injury of health or property on the other side" of the U.S.-Canadian border. Also in North America, the United States entered a convention with Mexico addressing equitable distribution of irrigation waters of the Rio Grande (1907). The Treaty for the Preservation and Protection of Fur Seals was drafted in this period, and the Consultative Commission for the International Protection of Nature was created in 1913. In 1916 attempts at protection of migratory birds were made in a convention.

The twenties saw the creation of the International Council for Bird Preservation (1922) and the International Office for the Protection of Nature (1929). In the thirties several nations entered a convention to preserve fauna and flora "in their Natural State." It aimed to promote the establishment of national parks and natural reserves, to preserve forest areas, to control "firing the bush on the borders of forests," to encourage "domestication of wild animals susceptible of economic utilisation," to protect species noted in an annex (which included gorilla, lemur, wolf, antelope, ibex, zebra, rhinoceros, and others), to regulate the traffic in trophies (including those of ivory and rhinoceros horn, eggs, and plumage), and to regulate types of hunting, including by airplane or by use of "dazzling lights, flares, poison, or poisoned weapons." [4]

Migratory birds and game mammal protection were the subjects of a 1936 convention. Four years later the Washington Convention on Nature Protection and Wild Life Preservation in the Western Hemisphere was made. In 1935 the Roerich Pact was created. It aimed "to preserve in any time of danger all nationally owned and privately owned immovable monuments which form the cultural treasure of peoples." [5]

The first international efforts to address whaling occurred in this period; it is surprising from a modern perspective that they did not receive popular attention. In 1931 the League of Nations adopted a convention to strengthen efforts to regulate the whale industry. It applied only to some types of whales, however, although it covered the waters of the world. The International Agreement for the Regulation of Whaling was signed in London on 8 June 1937, and an amending protocol was added the following year, in part, establishing a new sanctuary for baleen whales.[6] Then in 1946 the International Convention on the Regulation of Whaling was passed, and it entered into force two years later. It started with a somewhat internally inconsistent and clearly controversy-producing preamble: "Having decided to conclude a convention to provide for the proper conservation of whale stocks and thus make possible the orderly development of the whaling industry . . ."

A treaty on utilization of the waters of rivers shared by the United States and Mexico was made in Washington in 1944. In 1948 the predecessor to the World Conservation Union was formed as the International Union for the Conservation of Nature and Natural Resources. In Paris in 1950 the Convention Internationale pour la Protection des Oiseaux was drafted. Plant protection was the focus of a 1951 convention, and protection of fisheries of the North Pacific Ocean was the concern of a 1952 convention. Six years later the Geneva Convention addressed more generally "fishing and conservation of the living resources of the high seas." In 1954, in the midst of the Cold War, the International Convention for the Prevention of Pollution of the Sea by Oil was adopted. In 1958 it was followed by conventions on the Continental Shelf and on the high seas. The fifties also saw the making of the Food and Agricultural Organization Plant Protection Agreement for South-East Asia and the Pacific Region in Rome (1956). The Treaty Establishing the European Economic Community in Rome was entered in 1957, but at its beginning it did not contain any specific environmental provisions.

Treaty agreements, as I explain below, depend to a large degree on political links among nations: the cooperative actions promoted by the 1958 Convention for the Conservation of Shrimp between the United States and Cuba, which entered into force in 1959, were officially terminated two decades later. Despite the political tensions between the two nations, agreements concerning fisheries off the coasts of the United States were signed in Washington in 1977, transmitted to Congress, and entered into force in September of that year. The aim, taking into consideration discussions on the Law of the Sea, was "to establish a common understanding of the principles and procedures under which fishing may be conducted by vessels of the Republic of Cuba for the living resources over which the United States exercises fishery management authority as provided by United States law" (article 1).

In 1960 the Black Sea Fishing Convention became effective. The Antarctic Treaty became international law the next year (1961), and conservation of Antarctic fauna and flora was the subject of Agreed Measures of 1964. A liability convention was made in Brussels in 1963.

The Treaty Banning Nuclear Weapon Tests in the Atmosphere, in Outer Space, and Under Water entered into force in 1963, in Moscow. That same year a convention to protect the Rhine River against pollution was signed.

Dozens of other regional and multinational agreements were made in the sixties. The subjects ranged from tuna protection (1966) to detergent use. They included attempts to protect outer space and the moon (1967) and African natural resources (1968). The need to control oil pollution of the seas became evident internationally, and the International Convention Relating to Intervention on the High Seas in Cases of Oil Pollution Casualties was entered in 1969. Its protocol was added in 1973.

Along the way, both existing and new international organizations adopted policies aimed at regional and global environmental protection. An example is the World Bank, formerly highly criticized for economic development policies that were insensitive to environmental impacts. In 1980 the World Bank, along with other development banks, adopted a declaration aimed at introducing environmental factors into project consideration. It called for the creation of systematic environmental assessment and evaluation procedures for all development activities and support for projects that enhanced the environment and the natural resource base of developing nations.

INTERNATIONAL ENVIRONMENTAL LAW: A TAXONOMY

Most of those efforts were formal international agreements. Much contemporary understanding of international law is associated with written contracts among nation-states and among states and international organizations, that is, treaties. The main corpus of international environmental law is treaty based; however, the field also includes customary law and soft law, which I discuss later in this chapter. The institutions that make treaty law include world organizations (mainly the United Nations and multinational organizations such as the European Union) and nation-states through bilateral and multilateral agreements. Nation-states and multinational organizations also create customary law. Soft law is generally understood as emanating from international organizations. These distinctions, however, are not always clear. There is no constitution of international environmental law, and leading theorists and states do not speak with one voice or even with the same vocabulary about custom and soft law. Furthermore, distinctions continue to develop with the proliferation of instruments.[7]

From Stockholm to Rio de Janeiro and the Next Generation

Early international efforts were relatively uncoordinated. Modern international environmental law is commonly understood to begin with the Stockholm United Nations Conference on the Human Environment (1972), which was proposed by Sweden. At Stockholm 113 countries participated. (The Soviet Union and Eastern European countries boycotted the effort.) The roots of the Stockholm conference lay in recognition of regional environmental problems affecting northern Europe. The Scandinavians, particularly the Swedes, supportive of the U.N. since its formation, saw it as an institution that could help solve the acid-rain and other international environmental problems (Shabecoff 1996, 32). The conference issued the Declaration on the Human Environment, with 26 principles and 109 recommendations. It approved the creation of a new agency, the United Nations Environment Programme (UNEP), established soon thereafter in Nairobi. Some of the flurry of international environmental agreement-making that followed Stockholm was promoted by UNEP. For example, it fostered treaties on endangered species, regional seas, and marine pollution and dumping. It now has administrative responsibility for seven major conventions. Other international environmental instruments were generated through other institutions.

The first generation of efforts of modern international environmental law was characterized by articulation of general principles and frameworks for further action. Treaties generally called for monitoring, research, and exchange of information. A second generation focused on emissions reduction and technology changes and implementation and compliance. Compliance might be sought through dispute resolution and enforcement regimes, innovative economic instruments, or other forms of incentives. Strategies included providing for central international environmental funds, emission trading techniques, and differentiation of responsibilities for rich and poor nations. Edith Brown Weiss (1992, 11) noted at the culmination of that second generation: "Many of these agreements were thought to be impossible ten years ago; some were thought impossible as briefly as two years before they were concluded." A third generation of the law began its evolution roughly in the late nineties.[8] In more recent efforts environmental analyses are integrated into other cooperative efforts of nations, and information about and participation in decisions are more widely available to nonofficial actors.

Some modern treaties are global, some regional, and some limited to a small number of countries. They address the full range of media (air, water, land), pollution sources (industry, agriculture, municipal waste, and commerce), threats (exploitation of nuclear energy, disposal of hazardous material), and conservation of species as well as forest and desert resources. Some treaties focus on certain areas or places (Antarctica, the wetlands); others aim to organize interstate cooperation in facing environmental challenges. Many are framework conventions that articulate overall principles and objectives that will, if cooperation continues, be given form and effect in later treaties. Some call for national inventories, action programs, and reporting mechanisms. Most expect that member countries will adopt regulations, standards, and limits at the national level—rather than implementing through supranational authorities.

Momentum created by the Stockholm Convention led to the signing in 1982 of the long-debated and immensely complex United Nations Convention on the Law of the Sea (UNCLOS), which entered into force in 1994. It contains several environment provisions, most of which are found in part 12. It addresses land-based sources of pollution (article 207), seabed activities within national jurisdiction (article 208), seabed activities beyond national jurisdiction (articles 145 and 209), dumping (article 210), vessels (article 211), the atmosphere (article 212), duties to prevent pollution from use of new technologies and introduction of alien species, monitoring and environmental assessment, and conservation and management of marine resources.

The inventory of treaties can be divided among those that are fundamentally global or multilateral, where *multi* connotes many countries from many regions; those that are multilateral and regional; and those that are bilateral, or among a small number of nation-states. The taxonomy is not precise, however, since global treaties do not include all nation-states; regions are defined variously, depending on the environmental problem; and bilateral agreements often add additional parties over time. Table 2.1 lists major treaties of a large regional or global scope. The list is not exhaustive and grows yearly. Recent foci, for example, have been on the elimination of so-called POPs (persistent organic pollutants, such as DDT, PCBs, aldrin, endrin, and toxaphene), on efforts to promote safe international trade in genetically modified organisms (Cartagena, the Biosafety Protocol), and on access to information and public participation and environmental justice in environmental decisions (the Aarhus Convention).

TABLE 2.1. Treaties of the Modern Era of International Environmental Law[1]

Convention on Wetlands of International Importance Especially as Waterfowl Habitat (Ramsar, 2 February 1971) and amendment.

Convention on the Prohibition of the Development, Production, and Stockpiling of Bacteriological (Biological) and Toxic Weapons, and their Destruction (London, Washington, Moscow, 10 April 1972)

Convention Concerning the Protection of the World Cultural and Natural Heritage (Paris, 23 November 1972)

Convention on the Prevention of Marine Pollution by Dumping of Waste and Other Matter (London, Mexico City, Moscow, Washington, 29 December 1972)

Convention on International Trade in Endangered Species of Wild Fauna and Flora (CITES) (Washington, 3 March 1973)

International Convention for the Prevention of Pollution from Ships (MARPOL) (London, 2 November 1973)

Agreement on the Conservation of Polar Bears (Oslo, 15 November 1973)

Convention on the Protection of the Environment by the Nordic Countries (Stockholm, 19 February 1974)

Convention on the Prevention of Marine Pollution from Lead-based Sources (Paris, 4 June 1974)

Convention for the Protection of the Mediterranean Sea Against Pollution (Barcelona, 16 February 1976)

Convention for the Protection of the Rhine Against Chemical Pollution (Bonn, 3 December 1976)

Convention on the Prohibition of Military or Any Other Hostile Use of Environmental Modification Techniques (Geneva, 18 May 1977)

International Convention for the Prevention of Pollution from Ships, as modified by the Protocol of 1978 (London, 17 February 1978)[2]

Amendment to the Convention on the Prevention of Marine Pollution by Dumping of Wastes and Other Matter Concerning Settlement of Disputes (London, 12 October 1978)

Convention on the Conservation of Migratory Species of Wild Animals (Bonn, 23 June 1979)

Convention on the Conservation of European Wildlife and Natural Habitats (Berne, 19 September 1979)

Convention on Long-Range Transboundary Air Pollution (LRTAP) (13 November 1979)

Agreement Governing the Activities of States on the Moon and Other Celestial Bodies (New York, 18 December 1979)

Convention on the Conservation of Antarctic Marine Living Resources (CCAMLR) (Canberra, 20 May 1980)

Regional Convention for the Conservation of the Red Sea and Gulf of Aden Environment (Jeddah, 14 February 1982)

Benelux Convention on Nature Conservation and Landscape Protection and Natural Resources (Brussels, 8 June 1982)

United Nations Convention on the Law of the Sea (Montego Bay, 10 December 1982)

Convention for the Protection and Development of the Marine Environment of the Wider Caribbean Region (Cartagena de Indias, 24 March 1983)

Vienna Convention for Protection of the Ozone Layer (1985)

Single European Act (Luxembourg, 17 February 1986)

Convention on Early Notification of a Nuclear Accident (Vienna, 26 September 1986)

Convention on Assistance in the Case of a Nuclear Accident or Radiological Emergency (Vienna, 26 September 1986)

Convention for the Protection of the Natural Resources and Environment of the South Pacific Region (25 November 1986)

Protocol on Substances That Deplete the Ozone Layer (Montreal, 16 September 1987)

Convention on the Control of Transboundary Movements of Hazardous Wastes and Their Disposal (Basel, 22 March 1989)

Convention for the Prohibition of Fishing with Long Driftnets in the South Pacific (23 November 1989)

London Amendments to the Montreal Protocol (29 June 1990)

Protocol on International Convention on Oil Pollution Preparedness Response and Co-operation (London, 30 November 1990)

Bamako Convention (Bamako, 30 January 1991)

Convention on Environmental Impact Assessment in a Transboundary Context (Espoo, 25 February 1991)

Environmental Protection of the Antarctic Treaty (Madrid, 4 October 1991) and Annexes

Convention on the Protection of the Alps (7 November 1991)

Treaty on European Union (Maastricht, 17 February 1992)

Convention on the Transboundary Effects of Industrial Accidents (Helsinki, 17 March 1992)

Convention on the Protection of the Black Sea Against Pollution (Bucharest, 21 April 1992)

United Nations Framework Convention on Climate Change (New York, 9 May 1992)

North American Agreement on Environmental Cooperation (Washington, Ottawa, Mexico City, September 1993)

Biodiversity Convention (Rio de Janeiro, 29 December 1993)

United Nations Convention to Combat Desertification in Countries Experiencing Serious Drought and/or Desertification, Particularly in Africa (Paris, 14 October 1994)

Oslo Sulfur Protocol (1994)

Agreement for the Implementation of the Provisions of the United Nations Convention on the Law of the Sea of 10 December 1982 Relating to the Conservation and Management of Straddling Fish Stocks and Highly Migratory Fish Stocks (New York, 4 December 1995)

Kyoto Protocol to the United Nations Framework Convention on Climate Change (10 December 1997)

Rotterdam Convention on the Prior Informed Consent Procedure for Certain Hazardous Chemicals and Pesticides in International Trade (10 September 1998)

---

[1] For a more complete list see Sands et al. 1994.

[2] Since 1979 the International Maritime Organization has adopted 30 treaties covering the marine transport of oil. Among the best known is the Convention on the Prevention of Marine Pollution by Dumping of Waste and Other Matters (known as the London Dumping Convention). At first the convention created a blacklist of materials and a gray list that was less strict. In 1988 the convention was extended to cover the ocean incineration of waste. In 1996 a protocol rejected the gray and black list approach and prohibited the dumping of *any* waste or other matter unless listed in annex 1. Dumping of annex-1 materials requires a permit. Annex-1 materials include dredge materials, sewage sludge, fish wastes, certain vessels, inert material, natural organics, and some steel, concrete, and iron materials.

To any list of modern treaties addressing evolution of a sector of international law must be added the Vienna Conventions on the Law of Treaties. They govern the meaning of treaties and codify the customary law on the significance of treaties. Even for countries that have not ratified them, the Vienna Conventions are generally seen as a source of binding principles. Because the international personality of some organizations was recognized by the International Court of Justice there are in fact two Vienna Conventions on Treaties, one among states (1980) and another among international organizations or between a state and an international organization (1986).

The vocabulary of international law varies among nation-states. Some, such as the United States, distinguish treaties that require the advice and consent of the Senate[9] from executive agreements in which the president may bind a nation without the legislature's consent. The distinction has itself led to controversy over whether an instrument has actually been entered. A treaty must be signed and must be ratified. It then enters into force only for the ratifying parties once instruments of ratification are deposited by the requisite number of countries (although a few treaties, including some in the environmental arena, specifically extend some rights to nonparties). According to the Vienna Convention on the Law of Treaties, no minimum number is required for nations to enter treaties. The Vienna Convention also addresses the grounds for treaty termination (article 60-62), which include a state of necessity, impossibility of performance, a fundamental change in circumstances, a material breach by a party, and the development of new norms of international law.

The Ozone Regime

Among the best-known international efforts are those involving the problem of the degradation of the ozone layer. That situation led first in 1985 to the Vienna Convention for Protection of the Ozone Layer and soon thereafter, in recognition of the crisis nature of the problem, to the Montreal Protocol on Substances That Deplete the Ozone Layer (1987). The protocol, addressed as a case study in Chapter 4, defined the substances to be controlled, established precise quantitative restrictions on the use of chlorofluorocarbons (CFCs) and halons, and set a time-scale for reducing the production and consumption of such substances. It also defined the trade restrictions applicable to nonparties and gave developing countries a ten-year grace period for the implementation of the measure.

The ozone regime marked a major turning point in the consideration of the world's environmental problems. It was an implicit recognition that no nation, "no matter how powerful or isolated, could defend itself from global environmental threats by exercising its sovereign powers, even within its own borders." With some scientific license it was said that a "puff of CFCs from an aerosol foam can of shaving cream squirted in

Tokyo can contribute to dangers of skin cancer in Chile" (Shabecoff 1996, 114). The treaty was the first to establish cooperation in circumstances where it is impossible to determine the contribution of each country to an environmentally harmful effect (Scovazzi and Treves 1992, 33).

Rio de Janeiro

The next major milestone in modern international environmental law was the United Nations Conference on Environment and Development (UNCED) held in Rio de Janeiro in 1992. The so-called Earth Summit attracted more heads of government than had ever assembled in one place, 50,000 NGO representatives, and thousands of civil servants. Through its Declaration on Environment and Development, it affirmed the Stockholm Declaration and laid out twenty-seven principles to guide environment and development. It adopted the Convention on Biological Diversity, the Framework Convention on Climate Change, and the Statement of Principle on Forests. It also adopted Agenda 21, itself not a binding entity but rather a guide to implementation of the conventions and the articulation of principles of sustainable development. The 800-page, 40-chapter agenda addressed several themes: a bottom-up approach to environmental quality that would involve women, indigenous peoples, and others in a participatory approach to fostering cooperation; the need for open governance and for adequate information; the need for institutional coordination; and the use of both regulatory and market mechanisms to reach the goals of "fulfillment of basic needs, improved living standards for all, better protected and managed ecosystems and a safer, more prosperous future" (Preamble, ch. 1). Both environmental protection and economic development were to be sought through an emphasis on sustainability.

Agenda 21 established the United Nations Commission on Sustainable Development and the Global Environmental Facility (GEF). GEF began in 1990 as a three-year pilot program to assist developing countries with global environmental problems by providing funding for investments and technical assistance. Global warming, biodiversity, international waters, and ozone depletion are its foci. Later, the GEF was designated the interim operational entity for the financial mechanisms established under the Biodiversity Convention and the Climate Change Convention and the financing instrument for relevant activities under Agenda 21.

Agenda 21 articulated priority areas on which UNEP should concentrate. One specific objective is further development and implementation of international environmental law and coordination of functions arising from an increasing number of international legal agreements (ch. 38, 22). This goal focused on the possible need to coordinate activities of secretariats and to slow their proliferation. "Effective, full and prompt implementation" of legal commitments was called for. Agenda 21 exhorts states to establish efficient and practical reporting systems for full and prompt implementation of international law.

Regional, Multilateral, and Bilateral Agreements

Regional and multilateral activity has been common and widespread during this modern period. The North Atlantic Treaty Organization (NATO) has sponsored some instruments. Others are more modest in their number of parties, such as the Helsinki Accord that focused on the environment and the 1974 Convention on the Protection of the Environment that involved Denmark, Finland, Norway, and Sweden.

In 1992 scholars could identify 256 regional environmental instruments. They share many characteristics, but they also differ. Under the most developed, decisions are made at a supranational level, and the decisions have a binding effect on the national members. Member states and even citizens of member states may bring actions in a judicial forum or some other dispute resolution forum to address the action of another member state. Sanctions or other forms of redress are available if a member is found in violation, or not in compliance, with the regional requirements. Virtually all regions are represented (*Global Environment Outlook 2000*).

The North American Agreement on Environmental Cooperation (NAAEC, a case study in Chapter 4) committed Canada, Mexico, and the United States to environmental cooperation to monitor, counter the negative impacts of, and exploit the positive effects of free trade among the parties to NAFTA (North American Free Trade Agreement). The Convention on the Organization for Economic Co-operation and Development pledged many countries in Europe to do the same. The Convention on Long-Range Transboundary Air Pollution (Geneva, 13 November 1979) established a framework for cooperation among North American and European states to control and reduce transboundary pollution and to monitor and evaluate emissions to assess the effectiveness of earlier agreements. The Convention on the Protection and Use of Transboundary Watercourses and International Lakes (Helsinki, 17 March 1992) under the sponsorship of the Economic Commission for Europe is a framework treaty that provides that riparian states shall act to eliminate contradictions with the precautionary principle, the polluter-pays principle, and the principle of consideration for future generations. These are elements of soft law explained later in this chapter. The Convention on the Protection of the Environment by the Nordic Countries, which entered into force in October 1976, seeks to prevent environmental harm from discharges into waterways of the parties and the continental shelf of the contracting states, and incorporates a general concept of nuisance.

The Association of Southeast Asian Nations Convention on the Conservation of Nature would address ecosystem protection and endangered species trade controls. Also in Asia, in March 2001, the seven nations bordering the South China Sea signed a joint agreement for regional cooperation to address problems of climate change, overfishing, coastal development, and pollution. Elsewhere nations entered the Comprehensive Agreement for the Zambezi River Basin to encourage regional cooperation and to promote sustainable development. The treaty addresses environmental assessment, management, legislation, and supporting measures. Under the Declaration of Brasilia, Amazon Basin countries created two new commissions, one to conserve fauna and flora and the other to protect indigenous people.

The most advanced regional efforts are those of the European Union.[10] The EU is "unmatched as a manifestation of international law in both its substantive and procedural content and in bringing a wide spectrum of the international community into the international legal process" (Sands 1991, 2523). It has four main institutions. The Commission, based in Brussels, has representatives nominated by their national governments from each of the member states in varying numbers. The Council of Ministers is made up of representatives, most commonly ministers, in the field of interest (e.g., environment). The Parliament is popularly elected. The Court of Justice, described later in this chapter, has jurisdiction over European Union matters.

The most common forms of legislation in the European Union are regulations, which are directly and generally enforceable in member states, and directives. The latter are binding as to results on each member state addressed; however, individual nations can choose the form and method of implementation (EEC Treaty, article 189). Regulations are addressed to individuals, member states, and community institutions. Directives, after an act of transposition by national legislatures, are addressed to member states and, once transposed (or in some special circumstances even if not in a timely manner transposed) create legal rights for citizens.

As a follow-up to the Stockholm Conference in October 1972, the member heads of state or government built environmental policy into the European Union. Since then, more than 200 items of environmental legislation have been enacted. Before that date there were a few examples of regulation in the region in what would become known as environmental law. For example, in 1957 European nations entered the European Agreement Concerning the International Carriage of Dangerous Goods by Road, and eleven years later the European Community restricted the use of certain detergents in washing and cleaning products (1968).

The Single European Act of 1987 built environmental policy into the Treaty of Rome. The Treaty of the European Union of 1992 enhanced the union's authority and allowed majority voting on environmental legislation. It also introduced the concept of sustainable growth respectful of the environment. The Environmental Action Program, which lays out the EU's environmental principles and objectives, was updated and extended in 1977, 1983, 1987, 1992, and 1998. Implementation of the Fifth Program for the EU emphasizes coordination in which high environmental standards for almost all pollutant emissions, discharges, and wastes are combined with positive incentives for industry. The Maastricht Treaty, adopted in 1994, spells out a comprehensive agenda for sustainable, noninflationary growth demonstrative of environmental values and defined environmental principles in article 130R. These seek to preserve, protect, and improve environmental quality; to protect health; to ensure prudent use of natural resources; and to promote international measures to address regional and global environmental problems. Soft law principles, described later in this chapter, are also incorporated in article 130R.

EU directives and regulations now number more than 225 and cover a range of European environmental challenges, including protection of waters against pollution from agricultural sources, regulation of new municipal waste plants and municipal waste incineration plants, the Seveso directives (1 and 2) on the control of major accident hazards involving dangerous substances, noise pollution, conservation of wild fauna and flora, urban wastewater treatment, bathing water quality, and environmental impact assessment of public and private projects.

Among the most ambitious regional environmental law initiatives is the EU's Eco-Management and Audit Scheme, commonly referred to as EMAS (Reg. 1836/93 from 29 June 1993). EMAS establishes the legal basis throughout the European Union for business participation in a system of environmental management, environmental audits, and dissemination of environmental information to the public. The directive on environmental impact analysis, generally known as EIA, seeks to promote transparency and public participation in environmentally informed decision making. EIA has been adopted in other regional arrangements, including the NAAEC, the U.N. Economic Commission for Europe (Aarhus Convention), and the Espo Convention.

The great seas of the world have been an environmentally critical regional focus. In 1973 UNEP's governing council declared the regional seas to be an area of special priority. Since then it has sponsored 23 treaties through the Regional Seas Program. The Barcelona Convention of 1976 on the Protection of the Mediterranean Sea Against Pollution was the first and set a pattern. A framework instrument allows member states to adopt jointly or all together appropriate measures to prevent, reduce, and control pollution in general and from various specified sources. Members also agree to cooperate in monitoring and addressing critical problems.

The Mediterranean program was followed with more specific protocols: on cooperation for combating pollution by oil and other harmful substances in cases of emergency (Barcelona, 16 February 1976), on the protection of the sea against pollution from land-based sources (Athens, 17 May 1980), and on specially protected areas (Geneva, 3 April 1982).

Within the Regional Seas Program, countries have concluded the South Pacific Resource and Environmental Protection Agreement with two protocols (dumping and emergency assistance); the Black Sea Environmental Programme evolving from the Bucharest Convention (1992) and the Odessa Protocol 1993 among Bulgaria, Georgia, Romania, the Russian Federation, Ukraine, and Turkey (another case study in Chapter 4); the Caribbean Regional Seas Convention (protected areas and considerations for a protocol on land-based sources of marine pollution); the Kuwait Regional Convention; and those for West and Central Africa (1981), the Southeast Pacific (1981), the Red Sea and the Gulf of Aden (1982), the Wider Caribbean Region (1983), East Africa (1985), and others. Additional regional efforts outside UNEP's regional program address pollution prevention, abatement, and rational management of resources of the marine environment. For example, the Convention on the Conservation and Management of Pollock Resources in the Central Bering Sea (known as the Donut Hole Convention), in force in December 1995 among the United States, Japan, the Republic of Korea, Poland, and China, addressed the problem of declining catches of

Aleutian Basin pollock stock. The Agreement on the Conservation of Small Cetaceans of the Baltic and North Seas (the Ascobans Agreement) entered into force in 1994, and another agreement on cetaceans, this one for the Black Sea, the Mediterranean, and the contiguous Atlantic Ocean, was signed in 1996.

Less ambitiously, but in some cases more effectively, countries have entered into numerous bilateral agreements: the United States and Canada and the United States and Mexico on the transport of hazardous wastes; the United States and Canada on the Great Lakes (also on the Niagara River and on the Arctic); the United States and Mexico on urban air pollution, on the environment at the border (the La Paz Agreement), and on border environment cooperation and its financing (BECC-NADBANK); Brazil and Argentina on nuclear accident consultation; Canada and Chile on trade and environment. There are more than 200 large watercourses that two (or more) nations share, providing a strong motivation for bilateral and multilateral agreements (Upadhye 2000). These exist worldwide with varying degrees of impact, from the treaty involving the Amazon Basin among Bolivia, Brazil, Colombia, Ecuador, Guyana, Peru, Suriname, and Venezuela to those of the Zambezi Basin.

Customary Law

The boundaries of the other sources of international environmental law are less defined than the written, signed, and ratified treaties. Nonetheless, they are recognized by the legal community. The two most important are customary law and soft law. Informal tacit customs are also recognized by some scholars as a distinct category (Chayes and Chayes 1995).

Those norms and rules that are customarily followed by civilized nations and binding on the states make up customary international law. Customary international environmental law includes the duty of a state to warn other states promptly about emergencies of an environmental nature and environmental damages to which other states may be exposed. The duty to warn was called an elementary consideration of humanity in the 1949 Corfu Channel case involving damage caused to warships of the United Kingdom by the placing of mines in Albanian waters.

The point at which a principle achieves the status of customary law is not always clear. Several principles have widespread but not universal recognition: the Stockholm Declaration's principle 21 and principle 2 of the Rio Declaration regarding state sovereignty over all of a nation's natural resources and the responsibility not to cause environmental degradation, the precautionary principle, the principle of prevention, the principle of good neighborliness and international cooperation, the principle of sustainable development, the polluter-pays principle, and the principle of common but differentiated responsibility. Certain global and regional treaties have adopted some of these principles, but only principle 21, principle 2, and the good neighborliness and international cooperation principle are sufficiently recognized and substantive at this time to create a legal obligation, the violation of which would give rise to a legal remedy. A few of these and others are considered by some to be soft law (addressed in the next section) until they are incorporated into an instrument, most likely a framework convention, or in practice become followed by the international community.

Some scholars see custom as "the main source of general international law" (Pauwelyn 2001, 537); however, there is in fact very little customary environmental law. Scholars debate how little or how much in part because the boundaries of the entity are not precise. Those who see a greater incidence have made a couple of generalizations, themselves controversial. Some conclude that customary rules can also apply to countries that are not parties to treaties. For instance, the behavior of a state that permits its ships to discharge substances at sea can be evaluated according to the rules of customary international law even if that state does not belong to the conventions against maritime pollution. Others assert that treaties create "instant customary international law" (D'Amato 1994). The International Court of Justice, discussed below, suggests that treaty provisions can become custom if the number of states that have accepted the treaty is large enough, if among those states are nations important to the treaty's goals, and if the treaty does not allow reservations (Scott and Carr 1996). These conditions strictly limit the proliferation of custom through treaty making.

In certain cases, as in the early fur seals arbitration and the yellow-fin tuna case under the General Agreement on Tariffs and Trade (involving an effort to ban the import of the fish from countries that used purse seine nets), attempts to articulate customary law have been rebuffed on the ground that they were seeking to "apply *national* laws extraterritorially." The attempts might have been more successful if the complainants could have proven the existence of a rule of customary international law (Sands 1995b, 153).

Some theorists are adamant about the limitations of customary law. J. Patrick Kelly (2000) has argued that much customary law is not empirically customary and should be abolished. Critics maintain that such principles are not procedurally sound. They are said to be aspirational or recommendary and not based on an international commitment necessary to create a natural legal conviction. Such law is often based only on normative statements of academics and advocates and is biased toward Western ideology. It is anchored in fundamentally non-specific, indeed subjective, notions such as implied consent of nations. It allows powerful actors to avoid customary objectives simply by their objections: "A theory that applies asserted universal norms to the majority of humankind without consent, while permitting others to escape from consensus norms under the persistent objector principle premised on individual consent, cannot serve as a source of legitimate norms" (536).

Wirth (1999) notes the irrelevance of the body of theory on the obligation not to engage in transboundary pollution and of state-responsibility theory in the case of the 1986 Chernobyl nuclear accident in the Ukraine, about which the USSR did not inform the world for 72 hours. "Genuine proof of a pattern of actual state practice amounting [to] custom is painstaking and often unrewarding work performed surprisingly infrequently by international lawyers despite its central doctrinal role in the field. . . . the mere repetition of words unsupported by action does not give rise to custom" (436). Upadhye (2000, 61), challenging a specific tenant of customary law, asserts flatly that "despite lofty commentary otherwise," international law does not forbid a developing country from exploiting an international watercourse: "Taming a watercourse is a catalyst for evolutionary societal progress; and it behooves a developing nation to act consistently with development, not necessarily with respect for the international environment. The only constraint is that the development of the watercourse cannot significantly damage other nations." Boyle and Freestone (1999) describe how attempts to make the defense of "a state of ecological necessity" a part of customary law have not prevailed.

Customary law plays a limited role in state practice on environmental issues. As norms of environmental protection continue to make their way into international relations, however, custom will play a somewhat more significant role. Civilized nations will behave in a manner consistent with principles that are not yet customary law but that are compelling in their logic and the benefits of their application.

Judicial Contributions

International Courts

International environmental law includes the opinions of international courts, few in number and with limited authority, but of considerable interest to those who promote an international legal presence on environmental matters. These tribunals include the International Court of Justice (ICJ), also called the World Court. It is the principal judicial body of the United Nations, created by the U.N. charter in 1945 and located at The Hague. Its fifteen members are elected by the General Assembly from candidates nominated by national groups (i.e., groups of jurists in the Permanent Court of Arbitration). Since 1993 it has had the Chamber for Environmental Matters, which has seven members. In recent years the ICJ has averaged about 10 cases (rising to 25 in 1999). Many of its opinions have addressed maritime disputes and the Law of the Sea.

Cases can be brought before the International Court of Justice by consensual jurisdiction, by agreement between the disputing parties, or by agreement to a compromissory clause in a multilateral or bilateral agreement [Statute of the International Court of Justice, article 36(1)]. Under this provision it is also possible for parties to an environmental treaty to accept compulsory arbitration or recourse to the ICJ. Under article 36(2) parties to the Statute of the Court can recognize compulsory jurisdiction on several different types of legal matters including treaty interpretation. The court also can give advisory opinions to the United Nations General Assembly and the Security Council. These are not binding, but as with such opinions by courts of other legal systems, in certain circumstances they can be as influential as a legally binding opinion. Under article 41, the court also can indicate interim measures to preserve the rights of parties to a dispute.

Other international courts with some environmental caseload are the Law of the Sea Court, the European Court of Justice, and a few regional treaties tribunals. Their opinions can contribute to customary law, but they may have separate and distinct objectives, such as settling individual idiosyncratic conflicts.

The European Court of Justice (ECJ), also called the Court of Justice of the European Communities, is composed of judges and advocates-general who are appointed by member states for terms of six years. A president of the court is elected from among them. The court sits in a plenary session, if requested, in actions brought by member states or

European institutions. Otherwise, it sits in chambers and deliberates privately. Decisions are by majority vote.

The ECJ may clarify the rights and obligations of the European institutions in relationship to each other and do the same for the member states in relationship to the European Union. It verifies the compatibility of secondary legislation with the treaty and with general legal principles. It may also behave as an administrative court, a civil court, and an arbitration court; and it can provide opinions on the compatibility with the European Community (EC) treaty of planned EU agreements with other entities. Thus, it takes responsibility in monitoring the validity of international laws.

In 1988 the Court of First Instance was added to the ECJ. It now has jurisdiction in actions against measures taken by the European institutions; these may be brought by individuals or entities granted a legal personality. A large percentage of the court's caseload involves economic issues and competition, but it also has addressed human rights and environmental disputes.

The ECJ's judgments are published and are binding, and since 1993 the ECJ has had the power to impose penalties on member states that have failed to comply with a court judgment. Those are enforceable judgments that require payments to be made and can be implemented by the member state.[11]

One of the steps in the development of what is in effect an international common law of the environment is opening judicial forums to parties other than nation-states. Both the EU and the NAFTA countries allow such access for environmental and other complaints. The EU is also considering the creation of a public prosecutor, an individual at the regional level who will be able to bring actions in national courts. The idea is attractive to some because it avoids problems associated with the creation of a supranational authority. At the same time it is responsive to difficulties that can arise when individual states are allowed to process complaints within their own sovereign territories using rules that govern standing and other obstacles to effective enforcement. The idea is to cast a scrutinizing light on the environmental law performance of a party without greatly sacrificing that party's sovereignty.

Domestic Courts

Nation-state courts play an important role in the development of international environmental law in what international lawyers call either monist or dualist legal systems (Cho 2000-2001). In a monist unified legal order, no separate implementing measures are needed to bring the international environmental convention into domestic force. If there is a conflict between the convention and domestic constitutional or statutory obligations, legal norms of hierarchy determine the outcome. In a dualist system, international law is distinct from domestic law; the former regulates only conduct among states. Dualist states are legally bound to a treaty on ratification as a matter of international law. The treaty is not a part of domestic law, however, and has no internal effect until passage of domestic legislation incorporates it.

Incorporation can come in one of three ways: (1) domestic legislation can be amended or extended to take account of a treaty's obligations, (2) the treaty can be rewritten and its text formally incorporated into domestic legislation, or (3) the treaty can be formally incorporated, unchanged, into domestic legislation. International law and national law operate in parallel. In dualist states, therefore, national legislatures faced with a conflict will be required to take steps to harmonize differences. The position of a treaty in relation to domestic legal norms is a matter of national law. Nowhere does an international treaty supersede constitutional provisions. In most nations, treaties occupy a status between constitutional provisions and statutes or are coequal to statutes. In a few countries, treaties are inferior to domestic statutes and judge-made law.

The evolution of the meaning of treaties may come from domestic court interpretation of the international law. The *Japan Whaling* case is illustrative. That dispute involved an attempt by conservation groups to force the United States under the Packwood-Magnuson Amendment to the 1976 Fishery Conservation and Management Act to certify that Japan was acting to diminish the effectiveness of the International Convention for the Regulation of Whaling. Environmentalists took this action despite what the administration considered to be discretionary authority not to certify under that amendment and an earlier law, the Pelly Amendment to the Fishermen's Protective Act of 1967. Beginning in 1981, Japan had exceeded quotas set in accordance with the Whaling Convention, and both Japan and the United States understood that the United States could impose economic sanctions under the amendments if Japan continued to exceed the quotas. The two countries, however, entered an executive agreement in 1984 under which Japan accepted specified harvest limits and pledged to cease commercial whaling by 1988. The Secretary of Commerce for the United States determined that the short-term continuance of limited whaling by Japan, coupled with the 1988 discontinuance, would not diminish the effectiveness of the convention.

In the *Japan Whaling* opinion the U.S. Supreme Court held that a doctrine of United States constitutional law, the political question doctrine, does not bar judicial resolution of a controversy. A political question is one that a court will not decide because of possible encroachment on powers of other branches of government. The Supreme Court further concluded that the courts have the authority to construe international treaties and executive agreements and to interpret congressional legislation. The challenge to the Secretary's decision not to certify Japan presented "a purely legal question of statutory interpretation." [12]

The Concept of Soft Law

The law evolves through international meetings and conferences and other fora that articulate principles aimed at structuring later actions of members of the international community. The principles are often called soft law. They can evolve (and often do, as in the case of the U.N. Declaration on Human Rights) into the hard law of binding agreements or treaties. Some scholars consider soft law with sufficient nation-state recognition to be customary law. Van der Mensbrugghe (1990, 16) points out a hierarchy of nontreaty international law: "those [matters] which are to be situated in the realm of law although they are but weakly compulsory and largely discretionary (so-called soft law) and those that have a purely moral or rather political character and do not entail legal commitments even if they too have to be respected bona fide." Others use the term "soft law" to describe international attempts to "not simply ratify existing practice, but to elevate it" (Koh 1997, 2631).

Among principles of international environmental soft law is the prohibition against causing damage to the environment, principle 21 of the Stockholm Declaration: "States have, in accordance with the Charter of the United Nations and the principles of international law, the sovereign right to exploit their own resources pursuant to their own environmental policies, and the responsibility to ensure that activities within their jurisdiction or control do not cause damage to the environment of other States or of areas beyond the limits of national jurisdiction." This is similar to the provision of the World Charter for Nature of the United Nations General Assembly (1982, resolution 37/7): "Activities which are likely to impose a significant risk to nature shall be preceded by an exhaustive examination; their proponents shall demonstrate that expected benefits outweigh potential damage to nature, and where potential adverse effects are not fully understood, the activities should not proceed."

More generally, actions likely to cause irreversible damage to the environment shall be avoided. This precautionary principle is variously articulated. Slightly different versions are found in the World Charter, the ozone protection regime, the Treaty on European Union, the Biodiversity Convention, the Climate Change Convention, and elsewhere. The Rio Declaration states in article 15: "Where there are threats of serious or irreversible damage, lack of full scientific certainty shall not be used as a reason for postponing cost-effective measures to prevent environmental degradation."

Soft law is not necessarily lesser law, or less law, or less useful law. Sohn (1973) has said of the Stockholm Declaration that despite the lack of specificity, the overall tone of the document counsels dedication to the international norm of protection. Nonetheless, the evaluation of the effectiveness of international environmental law is complicated if one includes soft law principles. Van der Mensbrugghe (1990, 21), describing declarations that need to be carried out in good faith and that "certainly have a legal significance in so far as they announce an action which will (it is hoped) be cast in legal terms, later and elsewhere, at the appropriate levels," comes to an important conclusion: "Undoubtedly, the proliferation of instruments of this kind creates a rather confused situation that impairs the normativity of rules." I include soft law in Chapter 4's assessments but treat it as a separate category where that is possible (i.e., where soft law principles are not integrated with hard law requirements in multilateral environment treaties).

INSTITUTIONAL DEVELOPMENT AS INTERNATIONAL LAW: ORGANIZATIONS AND REGIMES

The adoption of formal instruments is a major source of international environmental law. To appreciate international law, however, it is important to understand the context in which the law evolves and is implemented. Some institutions advocate lawmaking and others implement law. The law interacts with other institutions and organizations, or fails to do so.

Political scientists speak of regimes to promote environmental protection, where "regime" is variously and sometimes imprecisely defined but usually includes "principles, norms, rules, and decision-making procedures, around which actor expectations converge in a given issue-area" (Krusner 1983, as described in D'Anieri 1995). Some scholars add that the resulting injunctions must be effective and durable (Underdal 1995). However defined, the notion is that international law comes about from ideas generated in national and international organizations and is variously effective, depending on the extent to which it is compatible with the procedures, norms, and rules of other institutions. Strategic planning frameworks, for example, such as the United Nations Plan of Action to Combat Desertification (1977), the World Conference on Agrarian Reform and Rural Development (1979), and the World Conservation Strategy (1980), lay groundwork for future treaty consideration. Other entities then make operational international law and attempt to implement it.

Mainly from the development of multilateral environmental agreements (MEAs) has come an innovation in international law, the "autonomous institutional arrangement." These arrangements develop the content of regulatory regimes created by international agreements, and they supervise compliance and implementation. They typically include a conference of the parties (COP) or meeting of the parties, both with decision-making powers. Often they have a secretariat and some subsidiary bodies that are expert in the agreement's functions or goals. These arrangements, "because of their ad hoc nature, are not intergovernmental organizations (IGOs) in the traditional sense . . . [but] as the creatures of treaties . . . [they] add up to more than just diplomatic conferences" (Churchill and Ulfstein 2000, 623). The powers of these entities can include the adoption of amendments without unanimity, as is the case with the Convention on the International Trade in Endangered Species (CITES) and a small number of other conventions. Furthermore, an interpretation of a COP can be legally binding. It could be subsequent practice by the parties, which, according to the Vienna Convention on the Law of Treaties, article 31(3)(b), "is an element that may be taken into account in interpreting the treaty" (641). In a small number of cases these bodies can also suspend voting rights and suspend or expel members. As is the case for the Climate Change Convention, some are international entities with a legal personality (647).

Numerous other organizations make rules that impact the environment and interact with the formal lawmaking institutions. Their performance affects law's influence in the environmental sphere. They include management organizations such as the International Boundary and Water Commission between Mexico and the United States and the Great Lakes Basin Commission between the United States and Canada.

Regional organizations, although not explicitly lawmaking institutions, can greatly influence the evolution of ideas that may be put into law and the implementation of existing international law, and they can affect behaviors that are the target of law. Among the most notable are the Organization of Economic Cooperation and Development and the Organization for Security and Cooperation in Europe.

Since 1948, the International Union for Conservation of Nature, a group of governments and NGOs, has promoted wise use of the environment and assumed a major role in promoting adoption of treaties, CITES among them. The World Bank (or International Bank for Reconstruction and Development), the Inter-American Development Bank, the European Development Fund, the African Development Bank, the Asia Development Bank, the Arab Bank for Economic Development in Africa, and other regional development banks all make loans on projects that can have extraordinary effects on the environment.

The Global Environment Facility, established as a World Bank pilot project in 1991, provides funding for implementation of treaties that target global warming, biodiversity, international waters, and ozone depletion. It is jointly implemented by the World Bank, United Nations Development Programme, and UNEP. Views of its record determine not only approaches to implementing law but also the choice of substantive provisions for future treaties (as in the Global Climate Change debate, addressed in Chapters 4 and 5). The World Trade Organization (WTO) has an immense influence on the environment, as do specialized United Nations agencies that implement policies. These latter include the Food and Agriculture Organization, the United Nations Education, Scientific, and Cultural Organization, the World Health Organization, and the World Meterological Organization. These organizations are intervening actors in the implementation of international environmental law (Young 1993; D'Anieri 1995). In certain situations, such as with regard to the ozone regime, some have played aggressive roles, in part because in the environmental sphere they are not as closely monitored by nation-states as they are in regard to national security issues. In some situations, they are more active than an enabling mandate would suggest (D'Anieri 1995, 160).

COMPLIANCE, IMPLEMENTATION, ENFORCEMENT: PRINCIPLES AND INSTRUMENTS OF CONTROL AND INFLUENCE

The imprecise boundaries of much of international environmental law and the lack of consensus on what makes up a regime create challenges in assessing the effectiveness of this body of law.[13] The student of international law, to appreciate its potential contribution to global environmental protection, needs to understand the meanings of jurisdiction and of norms and the extent to which they are shared and enforceable in the international community. Appreciation of alternative ways of promoting compliance with the law is also essential. Historically each of these subjects has received critical attention but with interpretations that vary, often considerably.

Jurisdiction

"Jurisdiction" can have many meanings and denote varying degrees of strength and reach of legal institutions. In environmental affairs there are numerous examples of initiatives to establish international jurisdiction. At one level the United Nations has jurisdiction on matters of the environment. For example, Agenda 21 recognizes the General Assembly as "the supreme policy-making forum that would provide overall guidance to Governments, the United Nations system and relevant treaty bodies." As Werksman (1996, xiv) observes, however: "The General Assembly's universal membership and extremely broad mandate has allowed it to take up many issues of global concern. Yet it is constrained by powers which are limited to making recommendations that are not binding on its Member States. . . . [It] has had to rely upon subtler stuff, primarily the sensitivity of Member States to the hortatory character of its pronouncements, and the publicity that can attend its debates." Although "subtler stuff" has limitations, persuasion through sound analysis can "make a contribution to the shaping of state behavior and the advancement of sustainable environmental development objectives at least as valuable as the design and enforcement of new standards and regulation" (Werksman 1996, xv).

Some treaties create jurisdiction by common agreement, while others go beyond, providing that the parties need to submit their dispute to some form of arbitration. Referral of the dispute to the International Court of Justice or some other court may be mandated. Under the Convention on the Conservation of Antarctic Marine Living Resources article 25, a not atypical range of options exists:

1. If any dispute arises between two or more of the Contracting Parties concerning the interpretation or application of this Convention, those Contracting Parties shall consult among themselves with a view to having the dispute resolved by negotiation, inquiry, mediation,

conciliation, arbitration, judicial settlement or other peaceful means of their own choice.

2. Any dispute of this character not so resolved shall, with the consent in each case of all Parties to the dispute, be referred for settlement to the International Court of Justice or to arbitration; but failure to reach agreement on reference to the International Court or to arbitration shall not absolve Parties to the dispute from the responsibility of continuing to seek to resolve it by any of the various peaceful means referred to in paragraph 1 above.

Under article 287 of the 1982 United Nations Convention on the Law of the Sea, parties need to confer jurisdiction, by declaration, to one or more of these four fora: (1) the International Tribunal for the Law of the Sea in Hamburg, Germany, (2) the International Court of Justice, (3) an arbitral tribunal, and (4) a special arbitral tribunal. Under the Law of the Sea system, some disputes require compulsory judicial settlement when informal and noncompulsory techniques do not achieve a settlement. Protection and preservation of the marine environment within the exclusive economic zone, freedom of navigation and overflight, and laying of cables and pipelines are among the controlled subject matter. Other treaties, such as the Vienna Convention for the Protection of the Ozone Layer, require submittal to a neutral third party, rather than merely suggesting its possible utility. Finally, parties under certain treaties "may lodge a complaint with the Security Council of the United Nations," as is the case under the Convention on the Prohibition of Military or Any Other Hostile Use of Environmental Modification Techniques.

Jurisdictional issues also arise across treaty regimes. For example, in a case involving Australia and New Zealand against Japan regarding southern bluefin tuna fishing, the arbitral tribunal, in rejecting Japan's position that the dispute arose exclusively under one convention, explained the doctrine of parallelism in international law:

> the Tribunal recognizes . . . that it is a commonplace of international law and State practice for more than one treaty to bear upon a particular dispute. There is no reason why a given act of a State may not violate its obligations under more than one treaty. There is frequently a parallelism of treaties, both in their substantive content and in their provisions for settlement of disputes arising thereunder. The current range of international legal obligations benefits from a process of accretion and cumulation; in the practice of States, the conclusion of an

implementing convention does not necessarily vacate the obligations imposed by the framework convention upon the parties to the implementing convention.[14]

In the European Union, a member state has standing to bring another member state that it alleges has failed to fulfill a treaty obligation before the European Court of Justice. This power was used, for example, when France brought proceedings against the United Kingdom for the latter nation's enforcement of domestic legislation setting a minimum size for prawn fisheries. Under the European system, violation, not demonstrated injury, is sufficient to allow standing.

Under article 169 of the Treaty of Rome (the EEC treaty), the European Commission can bring to the court, as it often has done, a matter of state noncompliance with a reasoned commission opinion that responded to a failure to meet a treaty obligation. Article 230 (ex article 173) also establishes jurisdiction. Under it, the ECJ may review the legality of acts adopted jointly by the European Community Council and the Parliament or by the commission "on the grounds of lack of competence, infringement of an essential procedural requirement, infringement of [the] Treaty or of any rule relating to its application, or misuse of powers." Actions may be brought by a member state, the council, or the commission, or "by any natural or legal person" if the specified act is a "decision addressed to that person or against a decision which, although . . . addressed to another person, is of direct and individual concern to" the former.

Article 177 is another basis for the ECJ to address environmental issues; under it EU national courts may refer to the ECJ interpretative questions regarding the EC Treaty and the validity and interpretation of acts of the EC institutions. This jurisdiction is available if a decision on the question is necessary to enable the national court to give a ruling. As Sands (1993, 58) explains, "Preliminary references from national courts to the ECJ are used when a dispute before the national courts raises a complex question of EEC law or where the dispute turns on the EEC point and no appeal lies against the decision of the national court."

The Court of First Instance of the EU may hear environmental cases brought to it under certain provisions of the treaty, including articles 173 and 175. The court is one of limited jurisdiction, however, extending only to institutions of the community and to certain competition cases. Review on appeal is to the ECJ.

Article 3 of the 1972 Nordic Environmental Protection Convention allows any person who is affected or may be affected by a nuisance caused by "environmentally harmful" activities in another member state to have the appropriate court or administrative authority of that state review the permissibility of the challenged activities. This review extends to questions of compensation and measures to prevent damage.

Although it is unclear to what extent it is being utilized, the 1971 Oil Pollution Fund Convention, article (2)(2), establishes and endows the fund with legal personality. This applies to the laws of each party and gives the fund rights and obligations; it can be a party in proceedings, both legal and enforcement, before national courts (Sands 1993, 155).

Werksman points to the "absolute centrality of a compulsory adjudicatory system to any highly developed body of law" (1996, xvi). Yet he also recognizes the evolution of newer approaches to enforcement, such as noncompliance regimes. More subtly, he points out that the existence of judicial or adjudicatory fora is not necessarily tied to predictability of the promotion of any one set of norms, such as environmental norms: "The absence of a single overarching court of appeal in the international system may allow the institution with the more rigorous dispute settlement procedures to determine the outcome of a particular dispute" (xvii). Particularly the WTO may pose a significant challenge to realization of environmental goals through its dispute settlement procedure for resolution of conflict between environmental protection and free trade objectives, a concern returned to in Chapter 5.

The 1968 Brussels Convention on Jurisdiction and Enforcement of Judgments established rules of jurisdiction for member states (which include European Union nations), including matters "relating to tort, delict or quasi-delict." It conferred jurisdiction on the courts of the nation where the harmful event occurred. In a case involving massive discharges of chloride into the Rhine River in France that caused damage in the Netherlands, the ECJ interpreted the treaty to mean that an action can be brought either at the place where the damage occurred or the place of the event "giving rise to it." [15]

Norms

Whether potential parties to new instruments share understandings of their commitments on acceptable performance, behavior, and comportment is the issue of norm existence. There is now a massive and growing attention in the legal community to norms (Downs et al. 2000; Etzioni 2000; Farkas 1998; McAdams 1997; Mueller 1989; Posner 2000; Rawls

2001; Siegal 1998; Szasz 1992). One's understanding of the effectiveness of international environmental law turns in part on a grounding on the relationship between norms and compliance. Here I consider norms as precursors to rules of law. "Law seeks to realize that which begins conceptually" (Cameron, Werksman, and Roderick 1996, 29). Others differ. Some count rules as norms. McAdams (1997, 340) sees norms as "informal social regularities that individuals feel obligated to follow because of an internal sense of duty, because of fear of external nonlegal sanctions, or both." Law can create, weaken, or strengthen a norm. Jurgielewicz (1995) argues that regime norms and rules may share the same "legally significant expectations" as formal rules. Beyond these distinctions lies the question of whether norms have been expressed with sufficient clarity to be part of a shared communication. The constituent questions about attempts to articulate norms are: Did the parties come to agreement on what they are pursuing? Were they successful in communicating that agreement?

Some cases are clearer than others. The behaviors expected of members to both the Montreal Protocol and the Basel Convention discussed in Chapter 4, for example, are matters of general agreement (if not compliance). The expectations of other regimes, however, are much less matters of consensus. Chapter 38 of Agenda 21 stipulates that "implementation of Agenda 21 and other conclusions of UNCED shall be . . . consistent with the principles of universality, democracy, transparency, cost-effectiveness and accountability." A U.N. General Assembly resolution following up on UNCED specifically endorsed the mandate. Soft law principles such as this and the precautionary principle generate many different understandings of what governments and their peoples must do.

In some contexts the prerequisite conditions are not easily reached. Regarding the protection of the global commons after principle 21 of the Stockholm Declaration, there is no widely shared norm on liability of states for causing harm to the global commons, who represents the international community, which tribunal can receive claims of this nature and how, what are compensable injuries, who is the beneficiary of compensation, how to enforce a decision, and the remedies that are available (Adede 1993, 180).

Enforceable Norms?

Many terms in international law lack precision, often intentionally. If making domestic law is like making sausage, making international law is like making a sausage stew. Shabecoff (1996, 142) colorfully described how "virtually every chapter of Agenda 21 became a combat zone as countries and blocs of countries sought to insert their own favored issues and delete any sentence, phrase, or comma deemed contrary to their perceived interests. . . . Nation after nation wanted to insert its own pet hobbyhorses into the document [Earth Charter] and by the end of the prepcomm more than one hundred countries, from Australia to Zaire, had submitted language."

A binding treaty is elusive when norms are not shared. This has been the case with attempts to protect the forests of the world. Only a vague compromise was reachable: an agreement to negotiate "Principles on World Forests," which might or might not become the basis for a future convention on forest preservation. The Conservation of Biological Diversity in chapter 15 of Agenda 21 offers another illustration. It reads in part, "Biological resources constitute a capital asset with great potential for yielding sustainable benefits." The language allows for a vast range of positions on what is acceptable exploitation of these resources.

Enforceability is the more difficult because legally trained people trying to protect the interests of their own nations write the instrument's terms. More precisely, lawyers may be acting to protect what they perceive to be the interests of what they consider the most important clients among their domestic agencies. In the United States, the State Department and the Department of Commerce weigh more heavily in international negotiations than the Environmental Protection Agency. Legally trained negotiators may wish to avoid implementation of law or they may have little experience in implementation.

Many of the phrases cobbled together by lawyers and policy analysts cannot offset behaviors on the ground. Indeed, in some cases it is not at all clear whose behavior is targeted by the vague, flowery, unfocused language of the instruments assembled by hundreds of negotiators over dozens of months in numerous sites. The very use of the phrase "and other *conclusions* of the UNCED," referred to above in chapter 38 of Agenda 21, raises the issue of implementation. Whatever this refers to, "transparency" and the string of other policy attributes are necessary. Implementation of the agenda and of *concerns* "shall" be consistent with criteria that are themselves imprecise in a legal document that is formally nonbinding.

As Koskenniemi (1996, 237) notes: "The parties may not agree on a procedure for determining what constitutes a 'refusal to fulfill a treaty obligation,' i.e., a formal breach . . . or the alleged violation may concern a collective interest (environmental or human rights treaties are obvious examples) but there is no state or body which could claim to represent that interest," and treaties contain "aspirational and open-textured language" that makes it difficult to determine compliance or breach.

For example, the Convention on the Protection and Use of Transboundary Watercourses and International Lakes states: "To prevent, control and reduce transboundary impact, the Parties shall develop, adopt, implement and, as far as possible, render compatible relevant legal, administrative, economic, financial and technical measures, in order to ensure" several important objectives of the treaty. "As far as possible" is a vague term in any domestic system. In a world law system room for interpretation is almost infinite. Similarly, article 266 of the 1982 UNCLOS states that members "shall endeavor to foster favorable economic and legal conditions for the transfer of marine technology for the benefit of all parties concerned on an equitable basis." Article 13 of the Association of Southeast Asian Nations Agreement on the Conservation of Nature and Natural Resources requires that the contracting parties "shall . . . take all measures possible in their power to preserve those areas which are of an exceptional character and are peculiar to their country or the Region as well as those which constitute the critical habitats of endangered or rare species." There are at least two referents here that can generate vastly different conclusions about what is required.

Flexible norms do have some advantages. International law aimed at protecting fresh water, for example, might more suitably endorse a vague standard of equitable use over a clearer rule (such as no significant harm). The former choice increases the likelihood of cooperation among nations by encouraging negotiation, rather than litigation, and allowing for changing circumstances (Benvenisti 1996).

International environmental law can involve such complex analyses that there is no clear predictor of whether an action violates a norm. The concept of equitable utilization of international rivers offers an example. A "non-exhaustive" catalogue of the criteria to be employed is part of article 6.2 of the Draft Articles of the International Law Commission. It is composed of seven elements, from "(a) geographic, hydrographic, hydrological, ecological and other factors of a natural character" to "(g) the availability of alternatives, of corresponding value, to a particular planned or existing use." The International Law Association, on the other hand, in adopting the Helsinki Rules on the Uses of Waters of International Rivers in 1966 listed eleven relevant factors and concluded that assessment should not be limited to these. Enumerating them makes graphic the gap between existing rhetoric and language that would encourage involvement and realization of a workable international norm:

(a) the geography of the basin, including in particular the extent of the drainage area in the territory of each basin State;

(b) the hydrology of the basin, including in particular the contribution of water by each basin State;

(c) the climate affecting the basin;

(d) the past utilization of the waters of the basin, including in particular existing utilization;

(e) the economic and social needs of each basin State;

(f) the population dependent on the waters of the basin in each basin State;

(g) the comparative costs of alternative means of satisfying the economic and social needs of each basin State;

(h) the availability of other resources;

(i) the avoidance of unnecessary waste in the utilization of waters of the basin;

(j) the practicability of compensation to one or more of the co-basin States as a means of adjusting conflicts among users;

(k) the degree to which the needs of a basin State may be satisfied, without causing substantial injury to co-basin State. (Fuentes 1997, 338)

Fuentes adds the environmental impact of the use of the river on other basin states as a relevant factor in establishing equitable utilization (340).

Do all of these factors need to be assessed in each determination of what is equitable? If a few are not, might that make for a defense by a nation-state that has, for example, engaged in unnecessary waste (i) and has sufficient other water resources (h)? How are the factors to be weighted when they are internally inconsistent? The rules in fact have been used only once and even then not for a specific allocation of water (Beach et al. 2000).

Conversely, absolutist terms are used in international law without generating confidence that a norm has actually been identified and is shared. The World Charter for Nature demands that "Nature shall be respected and its essential processes shall not be impaired." What is the value of this phrase in the context of the innumerable meanings within and across cultures of "respect," "essential processes," and "impair"? To be fair, the charter is viewed as soft law by many, but it has a section on implementation that requires, among other mandates, that the charter principles "shall be reflected in the law and practice of each State" (section 14) and that "Military activities damaging to nature shall be avoided" (section 20). Section 21 states:

> States and, to the extent they are able, other public authorities, international organizations, individuals, groups and corporations shall:

(a) Co-operate in the task of conserving nature through common activities and other relevant actions, including information exchange and consultations;

(b) Establish standards for products and manufacturing processes that may have adverse effects on nature, as well as agreed methodologies for assessing these effects;

(c) Implement the applicable international legal provisions for the conservation of nature and the protection of the environment;

(d) Ensure that activities within their jurisdiction or control do not cause damage to the natural systems located within other States or in the areas beyond the limits of national jurisdiction;

(e) Safeguard and conserve nature in areas beyond national jurisdiction.

In arguing for an ecosystem-oriented norm for international environmental law that is based on sustainability, intergenerational equity, and related principles, Brunnee and Toope (1997, 59) criticize international lawyers for seeking precise definitions before there are shared understandings of fundamental values that an instrument should promote: "Premature attempts to generate binding legal norms are unlikely to solicit adherence.

It is true that unanimity is not required in some newer environmental law instruments, making the need to seek a universally accepted norm less relevant to rule formation and enforcement. Some recent global environmental treaties have included the use of "streamlined international rule making" instead of traditional principles of unanimity

(Dunoff 1995). These approaches are, however, experiments and do not negate the importance of articulating shared norms in international environmental law, especially when the concern is with the effectiveness of resulting rules.

Impacts on Sovereignty

It is generally understood that for law to be effective, compliance with its provisions cannot be voluntary and selective. Yet selective acceptance is common in international law, found mainly through the process of reservation. "Reservation" as defined in the Vienna Convention, article 2 (1)(d), means "a unilateral statement, however phrased or named, made by a state when signing, ratifying, accepting, approving or acceding to a treaty, whereby it purports to exclude or to modify the legal effect of certain provisions of the treaty in their application to that state." A reservation, according to article 21 of the convention, "modifies for the reserving state in its relations with that other party the provisions of the treaty to which the reservation relates to the extent of the reservation; and . . . modifies those provisions to the same extent for that other party in its relations with the reserving state." [16]

Poland, as an example, made a reservation to the 1967 Convention on Conduct of Fishing Operations in the North Atlantic:

> The Government of the Polish People's Republic does not consider itself bound by the provisions of Article 13, which states that any dispute between two or more Contracting Governments in respect of the interpretation or application of the Convention may, at the request of any of the parties to the dispute, be submitted to arbitration or placed before the International Court of Justice for settlement. The Government of the Polish People's Republic states that submitting the dispute to arbitration as well as placing it before the International Court of Justice requires the consent of all parties concerned in the dispute in each individual case.

One blatant attempt to use a reservation involved the 1990 amendments to the CITES. Just before the period for entering reservations was to expire, the United Kingdom and other nations entered a reservation that excluded application of an endangered species ban to Hong Kong. Only through the organized efforts of NGOs was sufficient pressure brought so that the United Kingdom backed away and allowed the reservation to expire. Interestingly, it was through other elements of international law that the reservation was derailed: the NGOs had petitioned for an independent and formal legal opinion about the matter (Sands 1995b, 162).

Sovereignty is clearly compromised under some instruments of international environmental protection. Nation-states, for instance, may be empowered to act outside the boundaries of their sovereign territory. The Brussels Convention on Intervention on the High Seas in Case of Oil Pollution Casualties, as an example, codifies the right of the coastal state to act beyond the limits of the territorial seas in cases of major pollution or threat of pollution caused by maritime casualties.[17] The Law of the Sea Convention has sufficient characteristics of a hard law created, implemented, and enforced by suprasovereign entities that its consideration involved an extraordinarily long period of discussion and controversy. It is "the only example of a global instrument which envisions the protection of the marine environment from the broadest perspective, and which at the same time, clarifies the question of the extent of the coastal states' authority in the various maritime areas" (Scovazzi and Treves 1992, 150). The Montreal Protocol also notably limited sovereignty; it adopted simplified majority decision making and precluded reservations.

Perversely from the point of view of international environmental protection, the worldwide movement toward free trade can compromise national sovereignty exercised to achieve environmental goals. It does so by allowing challenges to environmental laws that aim to have impacts outside the individual nation-state. This applies to both the extraterritorial reach of domestic law and the laws of regions, such as the European community. In world organizations, the WTO, formerly the General Agreement on Tariffs and Trade (GATT), allows members to challenge domestic environmental laws of other nations using the argument that they create artificial barriers to trade.

Theoretically, free trade challenges are not an insurmountable problem for environmental law, and some of the newer-generation regimes have even built environmental protection into trade agreements. To a modest degree this is true under NAFTA and some other trade institutions described in Chapter 4, but the threat of international trade agreements to environmental law persists. Although worldwide concern with environmental protection is high, interest in free trade historically is more powerful globally. Policymakers, politicians, and business people generally accept the assumption that free trade promotes environmental protection. Pro-trade commentators assert that liberalized trade creates wealth, which engenders a greater social interest in environmental quality and a greater capacity to realize environmental goals. Some argue that with greater income, developing nations will be able to collect more taxes and use the increased revenue to fund pollution control measures. Others state that trade agreements affirmatively promote environmental policies. The following chapters return to this issue.

The alleged weakness of international courts is one indication that sovereignty is rarely sacrificed in the international regime. ICJ members, for example, can withdraw from acceptance of compulsory jurisdiction. Furthermore, the ICJ is a very slow-moving institution; long periods pass before cases are heard and judgments reached. When the court does rule, its opinions may be disappointing to environmentalists, as in its decision over diversion of the Danube River for a hydroelectric dam. There the court ruled that both Slovakia and Hungary had broken a treaty and both were "ordered" to negotiate in good faith. The case involved Slovakia's diversion of 80 percent of the river's flow to build the dam. The project threatened extinction of 90 percent of the flora and fauna over an area of 32,000 acres (Perlez 1999).

Sanctions and Enforcement

In international environmental law examples of enforcement capacity exist, although generally they are limited. For example, they do not mirror the U.N. Security Council capacity under chapter 7 of the Charter of Member States to take military action for the maintenance or restoration of international peace and security or the suspension of a party's rights or concessions for violation of GATT (now WTO) obligations. Nonetheless, accretion of enforcement authority has been a quiet but persistent element in the evolution of global environmental law.

The Law of the Sea treaty has a number of sanctioning options, and some scholars hold that the powers set forth in article 220 of the convention are now part of customary law (Scovazzi and Treves 1992, 152). The Straddling Fish Stocks and Highly Migratory Fish Stock Agreement has innovative compliance and enforcement provisions. It authorizes officials of parties to board and inspect vessels on high-seas areas covered by the agreement. It also provides that where there is evidence that the boarded vessel has violated a fishing organization's conservation and management measures, the vessel's flag state shall investigate and enforce or authorize the boarding state to take action. In cases of possible serious violations, the inspectors may remain on board to secure evidence and may even bring the vessel to port.

The Convention on the Conservation and Management of Pollock Reserves in the Central Bering Sea has several important compliance provisions. The Donut Hole Convention requires that (1) parties exchange information on a real-time basis using real-time satellite-fixing transmitters while fishing in the Bering Sea, (2) vessels of the parties carry an observer, preferably from a party other than the flag state, and (3) parties utilize enforcement provisions embodied in the Fish Stocks Agreement.

Regional organizations such as the European Union have stronger sanctioning powers, although they too are limited. As we have seen, the European Commission can enter into infraction proceedings against member states, and a state can be taken before the Court of Justice if it does not conform to a reasoned opinion. If the court recognizes that a member state has failed in its obligations, that state must take the necessary measures to respect the decision of the court. In a typical year the commission cites a majority of the member states for at least some violations. They may range from a challenge to the scope of monitoring required under a directive to a general failure to cooperate. The European Union also allows NGOs to play an active role in enforcement. In one year alone (1991) the commission received more than four hundred complaints concerning noncompliance with environmental obligations, and on the basis of these NGO efforts it initiated several formal investigations (Sands 1995b, 157).

The European Convention on Human Rights and Fundamental Freedoms also works under a system of judicial review in which the decisions of the Strasbourg Court are formally binding. The committee of ministers supervises implementation.

Some international organizations can expel a noncomplying member. This power has seldom been used. As Koskenniemi (1996, 238) notes: "Such a dramatic measure . . . may make settlement of the underlying dispute more difficult." More common is suspension of a violating state's rights or privileges, such as to vote.

There is a small but vigorous movement to create a regime of criminal sanctions for violation of international environmental law. Some enforcement officials have advocated greater United Nations promotion of criminal justice type interventions, using the World Customs Organization and Interpol, the International Criminal Police Organization (*International Environment Reporter*, 4 August 1999, 648). The wisdom of adopting a criminal sanction strategy in selected contexts is addressed in Chapter 5.

Identification of who is authorized to act in the interest of pursuing sanctions is another important issue in assessing the law's effectiveness. Internationally, authorization to pursue environmental enforcement actions is quite circumscribed. Trees do not have standing, rocks do not have rights, and porpoises lack an international legal personality. Who will represent the interests of such environmental resources?

Answers vary with regimes, but overall standing is limited internationally. Koskenniemi (1996, 238) has noted that "reciprocal nonperformance cannot be invoked meaningfully in the context of humanitarian or human rights treaties, treaties that establish rights in favor of third states or that are intended for the protection of collective interests (e.g., environmental treaties)." The Rio Declaration states that effective access "to judicial and administrative proceedings, including redress and remedy, shall be provided" (principle 10), but that principle generally has not been followed. Examples of NGO and private party standing do exist, such as in the European Union and in the NAAEC. Article 18 of the 1993 Lugano Convention was the first international convention to lay out rules addressing access to nation-state courts to allow enforcement of environmental obligations.

Self-help actions are also available in international environmental law, as they are in international law generally. These include retorsion, which involves cutting off economic aid, aimed at injuring the violator of the international law, and reprisals, such as property expropriation, normally illegal but acceptable under international norms if in response to a prior illegal act by another state (Akehurst 1993, 6). Akehurst adds, however:

> The importance of sanctions must not be exaggerated. They are not the main reason why the law is obeyed in any legal system. People do not refrain from committing murder because they are afraid of being punished, but because they have been brought up to regard murder as unthinkable; habit, conscience, morality, affection and tolerance play a far more important part than sanctions. Sanctions are effective only if the law-breaker is in a small minority; if he is not, sanctions are powerless to secure compliance with the law, as is shown by widespread violation of speed limits. . . . It is unsound to study any legal system in terms of sanctions. It is better to study law as a body of rules which are usually obeyed, not to concentrate exclusively on

what happens when the rules are broken. We must not confuse the pathology of law with law itself. (78)

Young (1979) has gone so far as to argue that arrangements featuring enforcement as a means of eliciting compliance are not useful in international society, and that retaliation risks the breakdown of cooperation.

Compliance

Fundamentally, the goal of any legal institution is to achieve compliance with a set of norms.[18] When the objective of law is so stated, a wide range of ideas on means of influencing behaviors or achieving social control comes forward. Enforcement is joined, and in the views of some theorists even supplanted, by management notions.

Many international negotiations conclude that there are more effective means of achieving compliance than through the use of strict sanctions and enforcement. Agenda 21 encourages nation-states to create systems aimed at full implementation. Similarly, the 1993 Lucerne ECE (Economic Commission for Europe) Ministerial Declaration urges contracting parties to environmental conventions to adopt

> noncompliance procedures (NCPs) which (1) aim to avoid complexity; (2) are nonconfrontational and transparent; (3) leave the competence for making decisions to the determination of the contracting parties; (4) allow contracting parties to consider what technical and financial assistance may be required within the context of the specific agreement; and (5) include a transparent and revealing reporting system and procedures as agreed to by the parties. (Handl 1994, 327)[19]

Under the Montreal Protocol's NCP, one or more parties may initiate a complaint about another party's compliance; or the noncomplying party or the protocol's secretariat may begin the procedure.[20] The Implementation Committee then reviews the matter and reports its finding, including recommendations, if any, to the Meeting of the Parties. The review by the Implementation Committee seeks to achieve an amicable settlement respecting the provisions of the protocol. The committee can recommend the provision of appropriate assistance to the noncomplying party, the issuance of cautions, or the suspension of rights and privileges under the protocol. Where a party's inability to comply suggests a general problem, the committee may also recommend "an adjustment of normative parameters" (Handl 1994, 328).

The primary purpose of the NCP is to help a party come into compliance, rather than to label a state as in default (Handl 1994). This is part of an effort at continued consensus building that may reflect the normative weakness of obligations or different levels of normativity within the regime. NCPs "straddle traditional law-making and law-enforcement functions." They are attractive to some international law scholars because they permit the parties "to take a 'boutique' approach to enforcing normative expectations."

> Conversely, as normative expectations among the parties may extend beyond and vary from the formally accepted normative structure or substance of the regime, formal dispute settlement "in accordance with international law" might entail a denial of the "legal quality" of these nonformally established normative expectations. In these situations, NCPs represent a necessary alternative, an internal dispute settlement process that is more attuned to prevailing normative perceptions. In short, NCPs, or equivalent international reporting and review mechanisms, are ideally suited to nudge states towards compliance with the very type of "soft" obligations that make up the bulk of the commitments that were established at Rio. (329)

Both explicitly as parts of NCPs and independent of them, economic strategies may promote compliance. International environmental law already includes considerable use of subsidies and trading schemes. Some environmental policymakers call for more aggressive use of these mechanisms. In Chapter 5 I address the potential contribution of taxes, subsidies, civil liability regimes, joint development approaches, direct payments, and reinterpretation of international property rights.

A loose confederation of experts sometimes grouped as "The Managerial School" asserts that the level of state compliance with international agreements is high, with enforcement playing little or no role in that result. In the words of Chayes and Chayes, what ensures compliance is not the threat of punishment but "a plastic process of interaction among the parties concerned in which the effort is to reestablish, in the microcontext of the particular dispute, the balance of advantage that brought the agreement into existence" (Downs, Rocke, and Barsoom 1996, 380). Downs and his colleagues elaborate that "the causes of noncompliance are to be found in (1) the ambiguity and indeterminacy of treaties, (2) the capacity limitations of states, and (3) uncontrollable social or economic changes."

Several others scholars have elaborated on the pioneering understandings of Chayes and Chayes; they address the dynamics of an effective interaction among states. Many emphasize the important role that evolution of international norms plays in the choice of instruments to promote compliance. I return to those contributions in Chapter 5 and describe the conditions under which "management for compliance" is effective and suggest limitations on achieving law's goals based mainly on participation and interaction.

As important as it is, the managerial approach does not tell nearly the whole story. Some cases exist where intentional, deviant, highly focused behavior causes environmental damage. As Downs and his colleagues (1996, 395) note: "Even in the case of environmental regimes, the source of many of the managerialist examples, enforcement plays a greater role in successes than one is led to believe and its absence is conspicuous in some notable failures." They mention international fisheries commissions and the Mediterranean plan, "an embarrassing failure" (396), and the early failures of international efforts to regulate intentional oil pollution by tankers—prior to the addition of relatively strong enforcement mechanisms. In the latter case the enforcement approach was a detention provision, a single day of which can mean $20,000 in opportunity cost to the noncomplying ship operator. Management may work much better for "shallow" treaties than for "deeper" treaties that require specific responses. Handl (1994, 329) recognizes a serious weakness of the NCP approach: "the procedure might become an avenue for parties to 'hide the real difficulties they have in performing their obligations while avoiding judicial or arbitral scrutiny, or more subtle forms of diplomatic persuasion'" (quoting Koskenniemi 1992).

Some international environmental law also emphasizes compliance as the ultimate objective by focusing on mediation and other processes of alternative dispute resolution where punishment and sanctioning are not relevant. Numerous examples exist in international environmental law and related trade law: the International Joint Commission of the Boundary Waters Treaty, the European Commission, the Dispute Settlement Panels of the GATT, the processes to foster conciliation under the 1985 Vienna Convention and the 1982 Biodiversity Convention, the processes involving complaints by the parties in the NAFTA regime under NAFTA itself and under the NAAEC and the Implementation Committee of the Montreal Protocol. These are only the better known of numerous instruments that adopt mediation or some form of arbitration to promote the ultimate ends of the international law.

CONCLUSION

For more than a century, nation-states have adopted international environmental instruments that aim to have the force of law. They are of various types: global, multilateral, regional, and bilateral within the treaty regime; court-made and customary law; and soft law. They vary in the extent to which they affect national sovereignty and establish jurisdiction. Some law reflects fairly consensual international norms. Other instruments are vague about norms to be enforced. Some are weak on ways to enforce such norms. Certain provisions—strong in articulation of compliance-promoting requirements—are not fully implemented. Meaningful sanctions exist in some regimes; for other treaties the sanctions described are quite different from those actually imposed.

The short history of global environmental law hints that its evolution may be more aggressive than in other areas. "International environmental policy is at the forefront of many progressive developments that prefigure more general trends in public international law, a relatively primitive legal system whose limitations in responding to the pressing demands of globalization are apparent" (Wirth 1999, 927). Several of those developments explain the extent to which the law has been effective, a subject to which I return explicitly in Chapter 4.

3. LAW'S TARGETS: WHOSE BEHAVIOR NEEDS TO BE INFLUENCED?

This chapter describes the sources of environmental degradation world-wide. It classifies them according to how they manifest themselves (global, transboundary, within a nation) and how they affect the environment. The analysis differentiates behaviors as innocent, misfeasant, or malfeasant. It addresses the extent to which they are amenable to change through various interventions, including the law. The chapter focuses on business and commerce, but it also treats the public as a source of environmental impact.

Basic changes in the natural systems that define environmental degradation arise from many sources. Major contributors to worldwide environmental deterioration are mismanaged economic expansion and high levels of consumption. Economic growth has taken an ominous toll on the air, water, soil, plants, animals, and life-supporting microorganisms, "altering the very chemistry of the planet—significantly shifting, for example, the natural carbon, sulfur, and nitrogen cycles." The result has been alterations in the fundamental flows of planetary chemicals and energy (Shabecoff 1996, 16). As we shall see, however, wealth in certain circumstances also promotes environmental protection.

A focus on development and consumption patterns is essential, but it is not the whole story. The etiology of degradation also lies in massive and rapid population growth. The decades-old discussion of the relative contribution to environmental degradation of population and consumption cannot be resolved here, but I will address implications of that debate for international environmental law's approaches and potential.

Other elements of the challenge facing international environmental law involve behavior that is more discreet: hazardous waste abuses including illegal trade and disposal or, in more homely examples, the dumping of waste from cruise ships or the smuggling of ozone-depleting refrigerants; failure to manage resources in ways that would make them sufficiently sustainable to avoid global systems changes, such as the burning of the rain forest to create agricultural land; failure to abide by ordinary rules of commerce, resulting in nuclear and chemical disasters such as Chernobyl, Seveso, Vajont, Bhopal, and Union Carbide.

The law aims to right many other wrongs: hunting of the last individuals of an endangered species (bear, whales, monkeys) to sell their parts or simply as an end in itself; refusal to label the dangers of pesticides destined for foreign markets; refusal to inform downstream parties of the imminent arrival of toxic effluents; refusal to announce in factories of multinational companies the risks of working with certain chemicals; also clear-cutting of regional forests, fishing with banned devices such as long drift nets, refusal to desist from activities (such as tests of nuclear devices) that create considerable environmental risks across a land or water boundary.

The challenges that environmental law faces at the international level fall into several categories that are useful for understanding how environmental difficulties arise and devising strategies to confront them. We can distinguish regional problems from global problems, and we can differentiate among problems that derive from business behavior and from the acts of desperate people and from the behavior of the successful and affluent.

Environmental problems manifest themselves in the global commons, across boundaries, and within regions. Commons problems at the international level are those that result from overuse of resources that have no national status as property. Outcomes include ozone depletion, climate change, destruction of endangered species, and overfishing in global waters. Transboundary environmental pollution problems cross nation-state frontiers. These include acid precipitation in one region of Europe triggered by activities in another (or likewise between the United States and Canada); despoliation of water systems in the Black Sea basin, in the Mediterranean, in the Dead Sea, and in the Gulf of Aqaba; and downstream waterway pollution from human wastes, agricultural production, and industrial flows. Sometimes regional problems manifest themselves in a number of nation-states across several different jurisdictional boundaries. Examples are air pollution throughout Europe, hazardous waste dumping in Africa, and pollution of watersheds that serve several countries. Some problems are hybrids, such as deforestation, where the initial activity is destruction of a resource in one or a small number of countries but ultimately the results are regional or global.

The behaviors that law confronts encompass an entire range of social actors, from the very biggest enterprise to the lone individual. People may pollute and degrade as they try to sustain their very existence. They destroy resources and disrupt environmental systems as they consume well beyond sustenance levels. They do so also through the way they govern and serve themselves. Of course, people motivated to behave with a focus on the environment as a priority are also the source of environmental stewardship.

MULTINATIONAL CORPORATIONS

There were as of the early nineties approximately 37,000 transnational corporations worth, collectively, $2 trillion (Fowler 1995). Surely in the following decade these numbers increased. Large enterprises that do commerce in many nations (loosely clustered under the term "multinational corporation," or MNC) lead many lists of the targets of international environmental law. Many people associate these giant, concentrated, wealthy entities that engage in business transnationally with deforestation, oil spills, destruction of species, degradation of the air and water, and especially with ozone- and oxygen-depleting substances and greenhouse gas emissions. MNCs often engage on a massive scale in exploitation of raw materials, resource cultivation, or extraction; manufacturing with nonrenewable resources or the nonsustainable use of renewable resources; environmentally unsound waste disposal, packaging, and distribution; marketing aimed at creating demand for nonrenewable or inefficiently renewable resources; and wasteful production.

Modern views about the impact of corporate enterprise on the international environment vary. There is no question that MNCs have been responsible for major environmental catastrophes, their new language of green management and enlightened business practice notwithstanding. They export risk, such as when a transnational or multinational corporation decides in its production strategy to site dangerous industrial activities in distant locations, for example, to locate chemical production involving tetrachlorodibenzoparadioxine in Seveso or methyl isocyanate in Bhopal (Scovazzi and Treves 1992, 25).

The Corporation as Villain

Indeed, the list of companies associated with the most sensational environmental disasters of the last quarter-century reads like an international Fortune 500 roster, with names such as DuPont, Exxon, Union Carbide, and Montedison. In addition to the export of the dirtiest, most dangerous processes across borders to less environmentally vigilant countries, MNCs have used river systems as sinks for waste products, denuded giant areas of forest land, threatened the very existence of an ocean resource by overfishing, and exploited mineral resources with little concern for restoration.

The case against MNCs from an environmental perspective has been made eloquently, if not always convincingly, by several activists. Korten (1995, 269) concluded:

> Standardization and uniformity seem to be almost inevitable outcomes of a globalized economy dominated by massive globe-spanning corporations geared to mass production and marketing in a culturally homogenized world. It is difficult to imagine a civilization moving more totally toward standardization and uniformity than one unified by Coca-Cola and MTV. The processes of economic globalization are not only spreading mass poverty, environmental devastation, and social disintegration, they are also weakening our capacity for constructive social and cultural innovation at a time when such innovation is needed as never before. As a consequence, we are rapidly approaching an evolutionary dead end.

Ralph Nader is no less critical. He cites numerous examples of the negative effects of MNC-driven trade liberalization. It will "undo vital health, safety, and environmental protections won by citizen groups across the globe in recent decades" (Nader 1993, 1). Under global and regional free-trade systems, corporations will achieve autocratic governance and further pollute air and water, harmonize environmental standards downward, and exacerbate health problems at borders. These free-trade entities worsen a situation in which "large corporations are already forcing U.S. workers and communities to compete against Dickensian industrialization" (8).

Pearce and Tombs (1998, 49–50) focus on one sector, the chemical industry, and in a measured and analytical manner, they identify serious problems with MNCs:

> Given many of the characteristic features of the industry—the sheer size and scale of many chemicals companies, their dominance in home markets and the role of many chemicals companies as national champions, the restricted nature of entry to oligopolistic, science-technological markets, particular forms of state-industry relationships, the interrelationships between key actors within the largest

companies on an international scale, the vulnerability of companies to recessions and in particular to oil prices—it is hardly surprising that the chemicals industries have a long history of activity bordering upon the illegal.

They mention specifically "death, injury and ill-health caused to workers and populations through occupational and environmental health and safety practices and offences," and they generalize to industries that interact with the chemical group, concluding that these oil and pharmaceutical enterprises are "amongst the most criminogenic."

Because of the immense power and wealth of the modern multinational business enterprise, some question their very ability to behave responsibly from the point of view of environmental protection. The argument is that to compete internationally the MNC must locate where the costs are the lowest, must cut expenditures on health and safety, and must transport in a manner that emphasizes only internal costs. Furthermore, to influence governments in places where MNCs operate, standard operating procedures must emphasize trade over the environment when those two objectives conflict, profit over protection, wait-and-see over the precautionary principle, voluntary measures over required and proven pollution control strategies.

When Ford Motor Company's CEO conceded that sport utility vehicles cause serious environmental problems by contributing more to local smog problems and global warming, he also said that the company would continue to produce them because of their profit margins (*New York Times*, 12 May 2000). At the same time, commenting on Ford's commitment to seek technological improvements, a market analyst concluded that Wall Street "would tolerate the Company's emphasis on social responsibility provided that it did not prove enormously expensive."

MNCs also have "options space" that provides considerable autonomy from national public policy, and that space is created by global production, logistics, and marketing systems (Pearson 1987; Nordquist 1995). A transnational entity may perform in an environmentally sensitive way in one country and much less so in another where enforcement may be weak, infrastructure may be lacking, the workforce may be inadequate, or monitoring may be lax or nonexistent (Fowler 1995).

Still others conclude that it is not their opposition to compliance that impels MNCs to act irresponsibly. Rather, transboundary pollution and other international environmental damage result from "the disparity of the rules of different legal orders, each asserting authority to prescribe, each applying its own laws or its own choice-of-law rules" (Rubin 1994, 12). In this understanding, MNCs may actually desire international environmental standards, codified in law, both to lessen their liability and to communicate information as to what is socially acceptable.

MNC decisions about support of or opposition to proposed environmental regulation (and later the manner corporations choose to promote or to resist even relatively impotent implementation mechanisms) can have mammoth effects on the environment. Consider, for example, the histories of packaging law (Golub 1996b), recycling law in general, and detergent production regulation. Different nation-states have controlled disposal practices of major companies very differently, and the effects on bodies of water through, for example, eutrophication and on land through landfill contamination are dramatic.

Positive Behaviors

These assessments differ radically from descriptions of the new environmental or green management that has become the strategy of choice at some multinationals. They also differ greatly from what many giant corporations say about themselves, sometimes accurately and relatively objectively, sometimes, as an American judge chided, using "flowery corporate happy-talk" to portray (inaccurately) its environmental record to shareholders.[1] There are numerous examples of innovative multinational environmental protection actions. Transnational corporations generally have better records in regard to environment, health, and safety concerns than do local or state-owned companies in developing countries (Fowler 1995). They tend to favor standardization of environmental regulations across nation-states, even if it is at a higher level of harmonization than some of the rules enforced in individual markets. UNEP describes environmental advances by several MNCs and notes they are not "reflected widely in the practices of small and medium-sized companies that form the backbone of economies in many countries" (*Global Environment Outlook* 1997, 3).

UNEP, in collaboration with the International Chamber of Commerce, has recognized some companies as leaders in environmental management. In 2000, they were Aluminium Bahrain, Brazil's Cellulose S.A., the Canadian-based International Forest Products Ltd., HiPP of Germany, BSES in India, Israel's Nesher-Israel Cement Enterprises, the Japanese firm Tokyo Electric Power, Altos Hornos de Mexico S.A.,

Peru's Cervesur, the Swiss-based Rohner Textile Company, Siam Compressor Industry in Thailand, and the U.K.'s Beacon Press. Although not all the firms met each of the criteria used to measure environmental performance, they had all introduced cleaner production and more efficient operating procedures (UNEP 2000a).

In Germany the multinational auto companies have taken a leadership position in pollution control, and green and gold ecolabeling for efficient energy producers has begun (*International Environment Reporter*, 2 February 2000, 79). Swedish industry's early leadership in compressors, based on stringent standards for noise abatement, is well known, as are Japan's strict norms for automobile energy usage. The CEO at Ford was labeled green on his appointment and promised to have his company at the forefront of environmental protection.

Numerous surveys suggest that multinationals seek to incorporate environmental concerns as a priority. McKinsey and Company (1994) noted overwhelming support for environmental protection worldwide and described how numerous multinationals have adopted environmental policies and internal audit systems. Senior executives of these companies also have come out in favor of international harmonization of governmental policies of environmental protection.

MNCs may disseminate environmental ideology. Garcia-Johnson (2000) points to the U.S.-based chemical industry and its export of a form of corporate environmental volunteerism called Responsible Care to Mexico and Brazil. Importing countries may adopt the new approach in order to be accepted within the world of international trade. There remains the question of whether the program is actually implemented; nonetheless, at some level a commitment has been made to certain goals of international environmental policy: sharing of information; adopting comprehensive health, safety, and environmental management programs; risk communication; and public monitoring and reporting of emissions.

MNCs may take these initiatives to gain competitive advantages, to counter competitive disadvantages, to promote an image that is favorable, or to preempt strict environmental controls.

There are cases where private vice is public virtue in the classical political theory recognition, or as Oye and Maxwell (1995) note, when the green and the greedy come together. In addition to the ozone-depletion case developed in the next chapter, they cite several other instances when profit from a product substitution has led MNCs to accept, if not hail and promote, environmental controls. A market for unleaded gas was created by the ban on leaded gas. The manufacture and sale of higher priced pesticides followed restrictions on DDT use.

Then there are headline-grabbing individual decisions and programs. Ford Motor Company finances Conservation International's research in the Pantanal on the conversion of cattle ranches into private reserves and on other wildlife management activities (Friedman 1998). Chevron has joined a partnership with the World Wildlife Fund to protect flora and fauna around the Kikari oil fields of Papua, New Guinea. Home Depot announces that it will stop selling products made from wood from areas that are environmentally sensitive. Unilever, a major purchaser of frozen fish, helps fund the Marine Stewardship Council. British Petroleum limits its emissions of greenhouse gases, expressing a concern over global warming not articulated by its major competitors. It later commits to a voluntary reduction of emissions of these gases to 10 percent below 1990 levels by 2010. Daimler Chrysler drops out of an industry consortium that opposes regulatory restrictions to achieve climate stabilization. The Chemical Manufacturers Association in the United States and the Canadian Chemical Producers Association push Responsible Care, pledging to make environmental health and safety a priority for all products and processes (Farha 1990, 394). Toyota, General Motors, and Honda begin development of a hybrid vehicle to curb emissions of greenhouse gases (*International Environment Reporter,* 27 October 1999, 886). Shell International, Suncor Energy Inc., Ontario Power Generation, Alcan (a Canadian aluminum company), and Pechiney Ca Frena create a partnership with environmental groups to reduce emissions of greenhouse gases 15 percent below 1990 levels by 2010 (*International Environment Reporter,* 25 October 2000, 831).

Collections of businesses and industry groups can also wield considerable influence on markets that affect environmental quality. Dow Jones in September 1999 created a new set of indices, the Dow Jones Sustainability Group Indexes, with a market capital value of $4.3 trillion. The indices allow tracking of industrial and financial performance. Indices are both global and regional (*International Environment Reporter,* 15 September 1999, 757). Japan may list products linked to global climate change and greenhouse gas reductions on its commodities exchange (Aritake 2000). Also, while controversial among environmentalists, some market theorists suggest that the type of environmental performance reporting that major companies have undertaken can translate into stockholder and company attention to environmental improvement. Germany leads the world in percentage of major companies that report annually on their environmental performance (*International Environment Reporter,* 15 September 1999, 774).

The potential environmental contribution of the multinational corporation is staggering. A world where hydrogen fuel cells break consumer dependence on fossil fuels or where biodegradable plastics are produced from organic matter would need fewer environmental legal controls (Berle, Plant, and Wirth 1999). If the private sector would lead the way in finding alternatives not only to the internal combustion engine but also to the appeal of the individually owned vehicle, the effects could be revolutionary. Should a major maquilladora company decide to dedicate itself to the environmental repair of a border city in Mexico, its results could easily outpace the underfunded activities of governmental enforcers. There are countless environmentally constructive activities the company could choose to do (or be legally required to do): help fund a treatment plant, promote environmental education, create foundations with environmental protection goals, and fund local cleanup projects, all at costs well below those required to meet environmental standards in affected regions from which they must move, such as Los Angeles. There, even some of the most cooperative manufacturing industries cannot meet air quality requirements. Should MNCs choose to invest in new clean technologies rather than to continue their reliance on end-of-pipe strategies, as is their preference in some regions,[2] the industrial impact could be substantial, both in a direct manner and through multiplier effects.

As few as ten international companies could meet the world's needs for industrial wood and wood fibers while halting logging of old-growth forests (Environment News Service, 15 March 2001). McDonald's commitment to purchase recycled materials for renovation and construction of new restaurants and to buy millions of dollars of recycled paper products is an example of forward-looking approaches. So too is its effort to push its suppliers to provide environmentally friendly products without charging a premium. The company spends $350 million a year on dining trays, construction materials, paper, and other products (*International Environment Reporter,* 2 February 2000, 84). Starbucks has one fifth of the $10 billion annual coffee sales market and is expanding throughout the world. Its decision to serve shade-grown coffee has significant environmental implications. Many other sources of coffee beans involve forest clearing, done to produce coffee in the open sun, which has major negative environmental effects. A tiny innovator, Green Martin Coffee of Vermont, has seen its market share grow rapidly because of consumer preferences for organic blends.

GREEN MANAGEMENT AND INTERNATIONAL ENVIRONMENTAL REGULATION

These examples, cases, and anecdotes do not aggregate to a world of ever-improving environmental quality with no need for law; however, multinational corporations are among the major foci of a worldwide interest in environmental management. Sometimes colloquially called "green management," the strategy (which can both respond to and influence environmental law) involves a profusion of activities undertaken by firms that have effects on the natural environment. Green management has several constituent parts. They include a commitment to research and development to create innovative technologies and processes for use in a company's own production or as a product for sale, innovations aimed at improving environmental quality in the firm's relationships with its dependents and subsidiaries, and development of products that do less environmental harm than others in the same market. Green management is the set of activities that moves firms to act independently of existing domestic and international standards for environmental protection so as to decrease environmental costs or increase benefits from the company's actions.

If one believes the rhetoric of green management, the need for international environmental law is understood quite differently from the view that the MNC has to be cajoled and coerced to behave in an environmentally acceptable manner. Thus it is important to understand how green management is promoted and to assess its potential critically within international environmental law. The relationships are not linear and direct. Incentives to manage with regard to environmental considerations may be internal, may come from the outside, and often are a combination of both.

Internal incentives derive from conclusions that it is in the firm's self-interest to adopt a green strategy. This view was made famous by Michael Porter's analyses of the competitive advantages of being a leading firm in terms of environmental indicators (Porter 1990). Modern economic theorists predict that market niches will be found, market shares will be increased or a market will be truly dominated, and costs associated with the economic waste of actual waste will be minimized.

Green management also has the potential to improve the firm's relationships with government regulators. It can increase both customer and employee satisfaction. Insurance may be less expensive, especially liability coverage, and related business world advantages may be reaped.

Externally, among the best-known international initiatives to promote green management are those of the International Standards Organization and those of the European Community (the first nongovernmental, the second involving international environmental law). The International Standards Organization or International Organization for Standardization (ISO) is a Geneva-based body, composed of about 120 entities. It is the official standard-setting and labeling body recognized by the World Trade Organization and other international agencies. Members are governmental institutions or organizations that have been incorporated through the public law. ISO's budget is provided by corporate members and by governments. Given its makeup, ISO is sometimes referred to as a quasigovernmental entity, but that is not a precise term and the organization is not a government, although its procedures, which include voting by all member countries, resemble governmental processes. For example, a draft international standard becomes an international standard if 75 percent of the voting members support it.

The ISO 14000 series is its environmental management element. The aim of the standards, recommended by a technical committee composed of industry, government representatives, and some NGOs, is to encourage environmental management and to rely on market forces to effect environmental performance improvement, aided by environmental impact analysis and auditing. Other elements of the 14000 series are product life cycle assessment and environmental product labeling. ISO 14000 standards are action-forcing in that they require a firm to do several things to be certified: articulate an environmental policy, create senior management commitment and an organizational structure and training and implementation systems, and monitor whether the firm is actually making progress as measured by environmental performance.

Among the requirements under EMAS (the European Union environmental management regulation that became effective in 1995) are: an inventory of environmental impacts of production processes, a written corporate environmental policy, a program to track performance that uses environmental measures, and the audits and other activities of a full management system. In the European law, a company must meet these requirements to be certified, and to maintain certification it must be periodically assessed for compliance by a third party recognized under established criteria.

The Organization for Economic Cooperation and Development has also considered recommendations for establishing environmental management programs for its members (*International Environment Reporter*, 2 February 2000). Bilaterally, the United States and Mexican governments have recruited companies on both sides of the border to a "Seven Principles of Environmental Stewardship" program. Cosponsored by business, it promotes company strategies to surpass environmental compliance, to invest in pollution prevention systems, to practice efficient energy use, and to support sustainable development. Adopting ISO 14000 or another environmental management system is encouraged.

When a country defines environmental standards for products sold domestically and its standards are more restrictive than those of other countries, it may be able to limit importation of the regulated items. Examples include the German Packaging Law, which requires that almost three fourths of beverages must be sold in a specified type of bottle, and the Danish ban on marketing liquids in certain types of glass and plastic. After a challenge by competitors, the European Court of Justice upheld the Danish law, concluding that environmental protection requirements can limit the rules of a free market. On the other hand, the introduction of rigorous standards from an international perspective can also favor foreign competitors if the domestic industry is not prepared to meet such standards. In response to United States EPA regulations, the U.S. multinational Cummins Engines developed a low emissions diesel engine that allowed it to gain international market position.

In some cases external pressures combine with industry strategy to create coalitions for international environmental controls. DeSombre (2000, 10–11) explains that although industry and environmentalists rarely have identical goals, nevertheless they both have on their priority list an interest in subjecting other nations to similar regulations, or to use her term, "internationalizing environmental regulation." MNCs and environmental activists may be more likely to attain their shared goals by working together. DeSombre points to cases (endangered species) where environmentalists were most important for internationalizing environmental regulations and cases (fisheries) where industry led the coalition. Thus tuna fisheries joined environmental organizations to promote worldwide dolphin protection. Environmentalists have also partnered with MNCs to promote environmental goals in developing countries. Sometimes they link with government regulators to assert a philosophy of "going beyond compliance" with existing law (Garcia-Johnson 2000, 193). In fact, governments, both domestic and international, may refrain from rule making when industry and the environmental community are dramatically at odds.

The predicted markets for green products are staggering in size. The United States Agency for International Development (USAID) reported that the market for technology and services to mitigate greenhouse gas emissions could grow into an amount counted in the trillions.

DuPont is an interesting case of MNCs and international law. In the eighties, DuPont controlled about 50 percent of the U.S. domestic market of CFCs. Globally, DuPont also was a major player, representing 25 percent of the world's total CFC production. In September 1987 the Montreal Protocol was signed. The treaty (the subject of a case study in Chapter 4) might have been seen as a menace for the CFC industry and for DuPont especially. Instead, in March 1988 DuPont announced that it would cease production of CFCs. In 1990, while the Montreal Protocol was being renegotiated to include a ban on CFCs, DuPont was making large investments, twice those of the entire rest of the industry, to develop alternative products. Its strategy as industry leader was to push regulators to force consumers toward substitute products and thereby to achieve a competitive advantage.

Another DuPont example is its voluntary emissions inventory for greenhouse gases. DuPont's goal is to reduce its emissions by 65 percent by the year 2010 from the 1990 levels. Fewer than 200 other companies began climate change measuring and tracking activities early on. DuPont officials concluded that eventually there would be regulations (perhaps national, perhaps international) to control the pollutants. Again the effect on its reputation was a plus, and by taking the lead it may be able to influence the way government eventually forms its regulatory standards (*International Environment Reporter*, 15 September 1999, 766).

MNCs may also choose to be an early innovator in environmental management for defensive purposes, to preempt national and international efforts to set standards that they oppose or believe they cannot meet. Concerns of regulators nationally, regionally, and internationally are lessened if they conclude that companies truly are pursuing environmental protection on their own and are self-regulating. Signing environmental codes of conduct is one action that a firm can take to communicate its commitment to environmental quality. Examples are the CERES (Coalition for Environmentally Responsive Economies) principles in the United States and the Valdez Society principles in Japan. They include a commitment to waste reduction, use of renewable resources if possible, wise use of energy, the appointment of environmental managers and directors, and protection of company whistleblowers against retaliation. As of 1997, only 50 companies had adopted the CERES principles (Stenzel 2000).

There are criticisms of reliance on green management strategies for international environmental protection. Corporate cultural shifts, despite rhetoric, are difficult to achieve, and there is no reliable evidence that executive management can develop and sustain a green orientation (Crane 1997). Some environmentalists complain that environmental management strategies seek to make the firm's decisions even less transparent and the relationship between industry and government less open to NGOs and other groups. Lipschutz (2000–2001) and Hauselmann (1996) note that for ISO 14000, ISO's procedures on consensus and participation have not been well followed—"civil society groups" have not been allowed to attend standards-setting meetings. Some fault the ISO series for focusing on environmental conformance rather than performance (Gleckman and Krut 1998) and procedural standards rather than emissions limits and process changes (Roht-Arriaza 1995). The series is also criticized for failing to embrace the spirit of democratic international decision making and for countering the evolving norm of right-to-know by viewing environmental information gathered by the firm as confidential (Gleckman and Krut 1998). ISO standards may also become harmonized at a low level. Most serious, according to critics, is the legal significance given to ISO standards when higher standards are challenged under world rules banning technical barriers to trade (discussed in Chapter 5). Here, again, the result may be harmonization downward.

The immense range of opinion about what are necessary elements of modern life leads to dramatic differences in assessments of actions to improve and maintain environmental quality. These differences translate to conclusions about whether a corporate act is a significant environmental protection measure or just green-marketing camouflage of a process or product that is fundamentally inconsistent with global environmental improvements. For some critics the environmental problem associated with multinational fast-food companies is not only packaging. The consumptive patterns that McDonald's meets, indeed fosters, are at the heart of the concern. The environmental disruptions created by the production of an ever-increasing amount of meat demanded by fast-food companies may be much more serious than whether the product is delivered in a package that will biodegrade in a year or in ten years.

Similarly, although some environmental groups have hailed Dow Chemical Company's development of light materials that make cars less consumptive of fossil fuels or automobile manufacturers' efforts to produce vehicles that use alternative fuels or are relatively fuel efficient, others take a more skeptical position. It is the very dependence on the automobile that produces environmental degradation. It creates a need for more roads and for more open space for greater suburban development. The products themselves create significant waste streams as vehicles become accessible to millions, if not billions, more consumers. Other discreet contributions to environmental initiatives often are viewed differently by environmentalists and business. When the government of Gabon and a French logging company completed agonizing negotiations over land transfers in Gabon's rich tropical forest, some saw the result as saving sections of the Lopé Reserve; others concluded that it was a giveaway of valuable land to the foreign company. The government could instead have simply enforced its other environmental laws to protect its remarkable herds of mammals.

Independent of their record to date, multinational corporations can be viewed as amenable to major environmental contributions. After all, they are another way in which parts of society organize themselves. If society becomes concerned or afraid enough, those who are influential in the global firms can organize to produce products that recycle, that do not emit toxins, that do not overheat the atmosphere, that are compatible with environmental protection worldwide.

DOT COM AND THE INTERNATIONAL ENVIRONMENT

The massive increase in the use of the computer and other high technologies raises another question about the international environmental law challenge. What worldwide environmental impacts will the cyber revolution and its related phenomena have?

Proponents of greater use of electronic and related means for commerce point to several promising dynamics. Computer-based business can lessen energy consumption by limiting the need for physical movement of the buyer. Networks driven by computers can increase the efficiency in use of transportation entities. Now, for example, almost half of all trips taken by truck are return trips when the vehicle is empty.

Computers can lessen the need for virgin products, and rapidly available information about inventories can decrease demand for storage space and decrease spoilage. Ease of modeling can promote control of harmful emissions. Computers can dramatically increase the flow of ideas on environmental protection strategies, on new laws and their potential effectiveness, and on appropriate sustainable technologies. E-based networks can make for the rapid dissemination and effective use of environmental management systems. Telecommuting, evaluated one way, consumes much less energy than working at the office or factory. A person at home reportedly uses about a third as much energy as an office worker (Hemminger 2000). In recent years, the proliferation of e-commerce overall has been accompanied by a slowing of growth in energy consumption.

To be sure, there is another possible scenario. The work-at-home figure does not account for the impacts the at-home worker may have in nonwork ways. The rapidity with which e-commerce allows consumption can accelerate the use of natural resources. Per capita shopping may increase online. High-technology industries themselves have challenging environmental problems, including the risks of contamination from the use of solvents in the production process. Considerable waste accrues with the rapid obsolescence of computer devices. It is becoming common now for families to have half a dozen old machines sitting unused and awaiting disposal. Will the equipment enter landfills and compete with other waste, will it be dumped in the Third World, or will it be used in the production of a new generation of machines? The paperless society seems far away as word-processing equipment allows for numerous printed drafts. "Our ignorance about this is deep and profound and our knowledge superficial and consists mainly of ideology," concluded Braden Allenby, an AT&T executive at a symposium on e-commerce and the environment (Hemminger 2000, 21).

NATIONAL ENTERPRISES

It is not only with the multinational enterprise that international law concerns itself. Companies doing business exclusively within a nation-state also affect the global environment. Large multinational companies may have the potential to do massive environmental harm or good, but individual companies, even those with small numbers of employees and with charters in only one country, can also have a considerable effect on environmental quality. The *Harvard Business Review* reported that while 70 percent of the large companies in Mexico have implemented some type of environmental management, only one fifth of smaller companies have done so (Champion 1998). For many developing countries, small companies generate up to 95 percent of economic activity; often they lack, or claim to lack, resources to behave in an environmentally responsible manner.

The leading environmental criminal cases of the last several years often have involved relatively small national companies. Toxic wastes illegally disposed of across borders can create serious localized, but binational, environmental problems. Microenterprises such as tanneries often are macropolluters (Blackman 2000), and small companies may engage in midnight dumping that creates environmental hot spots across boundaries. Dumping from vessels flying one national flag can pollute large regional seas, and independent fishing companies can have significant effects because of the technologies they use for their catch. A small whaling business can disrupt a species in the global commons. Yet an environmentally sensitive production process adopted in a single border town (such as a brick maker in Mexico who substitutes a less polluting fuel like propane for commonly used car tires) can dramatically improve air quality both at home and in border cities. An innovative company can create technologies that combat pollution in one district and improve the quality of the air or water across frontiers.

Similarly, the large company without multinational presence, an increasingly rare entity in the global economy, can be motivated to mine, manufacture, sell, and dispose in ways that are either environmentally sensitive or profoundly harmful internationally. In some ways, large national companies are simply another version of the smaller polluters. The distinction is made here, however, for two reasons. Large companies have greater potential for creating specialized environmental units within their corporate structures, which can act as the environmental control centers of the firm. Second, large companies are potentially more difficult to influence if such systems are not created. The absence of divisions responsible for environmental compliance can make it difficult to attribute responsibility for performance and to punish and reward the firm's various segments.

Classic research found that size may not be a good predictor of environmental performance. Larger firms tend to commit more violations of all types; however, they commit "no more violations per unit size than do smaller corporations" (Clinard and Yeager 1980, 130). The research is not definitive, but environmental performance appears to be a function of factors (economic health, corporate culture) that are independent of the size of the company.

ROGUES, POOR PEOPLE, THE DESPERATE

One complicating and sensitive consideration for those who seek to improve the environment, or to slow down its destruction, is that significant environmental degradation results from actions of the poorest and least organized human beings. Recognizing that environmental damage can be correlated with improvement in standard of living creates challenges in designing legal tools to promote environmental quality. Many examples of environmentally destructive behavior by the poor are well known. Settlers, whose labor options are miserably limited, burn ecologically important jungles, including rain forests in Indonesia and Brazil, to clear land for cultivation. Mexican brick makers rely on highly polluting energy sources to fire their kilns. Tribes people in some African nations sacrifice giant mammals to sell them or their parts in illegal markets for rare and exotic goods. Unemployed people in South America rob from the world's cultural heritage and archeological resources to pay for a day's worth of food. Rural fishermen use techniques that destroy the living resources of a body of water in order to be competitive in fish markets. American villagers cut precious and rare hardwood trees and smuggle their lumber to luxury furniture producers.

Like the multinational corporations, however, the poor can be models of environmentally sensitive behavior. They offer appropriate technology, ecotourism, and sustainable practices to the larger world audience. They model how to fish and log. They use clothing materials that biodegrade. They create habitats based on local conditions rather than importing life styles that disrupt ecological niches. They recognize what is a sustainable hunt. They know how to make use of much of what they gather and catch.

CONSUMPTION AND THE KUZNETS CURVE

Attempts to improve international environmental quality must also address the economically well off and the middle class. Consumption patterns create and contribute to major environmental challenges.

The *Global Environment Outlook* (1997) concluded that if the Chinese population had the same number of cars per person as Americans, a fifth of China's arable land would be covered by roads and parking spaces. It also calculated that if all the billions of people on Earth emulated the consuming patterns of the advanced industrial nations, "rapid ecological collapse would be the inescapable sequence." Almost 80 percent of all marine pollution can be traced back to terrestrial sources. Agriculture, car traffic, industrial emissions, domestic wastes, and erosion all are major contributors (Biermann 1998, 39). Canada and the United States rank number one and number two internationally in consumption of energy, with annual use around 220 Btu per person. Within those countries, however, there are dramatic differences that are related to life styles, land use patterns, and consumption choices. Alaskans use 1,139,000 Btu annually, but New Yorkers use only 215 Btu per year (*New York Times* 1 November 1998).

Both population and per capita consumption are increasing in most regions. The *Global Environment Outlook* (1997, 224) reported that "the growth in the number of motor vehicles world-wide is among the factors responsible for continuing high levels of nitrogen oxides emissions despite technological advances in the design of car engines." The Asian economic miracle and the sometimes predicted African boom indicate further growth in use of the automobile, primarily vehicles with an internal combustion engine.

Industrial countries still account for almost two thirds of the total global emissions of the principal greenhouse gas, carbon dioxide, and the United States alone is responsible for almost a quarter of those emissions, though developing countries pose a major potential problem. Within two decades, carbon dioxide emissions in developing countries are predicted to exceed those of industrialized countries. China could emit within the century more greenhouse gases than the entire world does today (Bodansky 1997a). Thus population size and shifts in regional resource use can negate many of the regulatory victories that come from environmental law control.

The worldwide duplication of the consumer patterns of the upper-income suburban American could have dramatic environmental impacts: a utility vehicle that averages 12 miles of travel per gallon of fuel, another one to two automobiles, two refrigerators, a tenth acre of land with a heavily irrigated and treated lawn, a garbage disposal, central heating and air conditioning for a 2,400-square foot wood and stucco home, perhaps a power boat, a golf cart, a dishwasher, a trash compactor, two to three computers with printers, washers and dryers, a Jacuzzi or swimming pool, furniture built from hardwoods like mahogany, overhead fans to blow rising heat back down in rooms built with mansion-style high ceilings.

In addressing the role of law when both the poor and the better off are sources of global environmental degradation, it is interesting to consider theorized relationships between economic growth and environmental quality. Some studies have shown that although pollution increases in the early stages of industrialization, once income reaches a certain level pollution levels fall. Put another way, as incomes rise, so too does the quality of the environment. Graphing pollution against income produces an inverted U, in this context known as an environmental Kuznets curve, or EKC (Spengler 2001).[3] The conclusion for some, including strong free trade advocates, is that environmental problems are self-correcting with economic growth.

If the curve is an accurate description of a dynamic that applies worldwide, the implications are significant for the types of international law promoted. Perhaps, for example, this relationship would favor trade liberalization over the negotiation of multilateral environmental agreements, or perhaps those multilateral agreements should emphasize economic incentives and subsidies over other compliance-promoting mechanisms. Interpretation of Kuznets curves, however, is a matter of considerable disagreement (Arrow et al. 1995). Some analysts conclude that the turning of the curve is not automatic but rather results from political and social will, which exerts pressure on institutions, usually democratic institutions, to undertake environmental policy improvements.

According to a 1999 report by the World Trade Organization, the EKC hypothesis "may be valid for some types of environmental indicators, but equally untrue for other important indicators" (WTO Secretariat 1999, 6). The inverted U patterns are seen for some air pollutants such as sulfur dioxide and some types of freshwater pollutants such as arsenic but not for pollutants of a more global nature, including carbon dioxide (Charnovitz 2000). Thus, the "existence of an eventual turning point depends almost entirely on the type of emission reviewed" (WTO Secretariat 1999, 53). There may be more than one turning point and very differently shaped curves, and some changes come at very high incomes. For certain emissions such as heavy metals and inert toxic compounds, the turn may come too late because "the cumulative harm inflicted during the transition up to the peak of the EKC may exceed the ecosystem's carrying capacity and may even be irreparable" (58), suggesting the need to apply the precautionary principle.

The WTO reached other important conclusions. Overall economic growth does not necessarily bring down pollution. Rather, active intervention by governments is needed to promote environmental quality, and democratic decision making tends to favor such intervention. Pollution reduction requires increased income to be followed by tighter environmental standards. In one interpretation, less hydraulic than earlier economically driven views, "governments promulgate regulations not because countries are richer but because citizens demand that regulators act" (Charnovitz 2000, 534).

Beyond the overall aggregate effects of increasingly large numbers of consumers are the environmental effects of certain discrete actions. Some are linked to cultural and religious practices. In India, believers put human corpses into the Ganges because it is thought to be a holy place. Some cultures use gall bladders of protected bears as aphrodisiacs. Pills made from tiger parts are treasured by some, because the penis bone is believed to promote virility and relieve rheumatism. Elsewhere, turtle eggs are coveted as a delicacy and also for supposed aphrodisiac powers. In 1997 in the Mexican state of Oaxaca, government officials seized a truckload of 300,000 turtle eggs. The poignancy of the legal struggle for environmental protection was captured in a report describing Mexican officials' attempts to stop illegal poaching of eggs of an endangered turtle. "Before finding the intact nest that moonlit night, Valdarez [an enforcement officer] had come across two others that poachers had visited first. They had scooped up the eggs as the mother had laid them, two by two, before she carefully covered up the empty nest and lumbered back into the ocean" (Kraul 1997). In some nations, whale meat is a gourmet item and whaling represents a historically significant tradition. For certain tribes, whaling is a spiritual act and defines members as a people (Philbrick 2000). Others covet feathers, serpents, tusks, and rare birds.

Industrialized Western food consumption patterns also create major resource problems. The environmental strains caused by daily meat-based diets are well documented, but tastes for specialty foods also can cause serious damage. Caviar consumption, 44 tons annually in Germany, for example, may lead to the disappearance of sturgeon from the Caspian Sea. Tragically, fish that do not produce the delicacy eggs are sacrificed in the caviar search. To obtain females, fishermen kill males in equal numbers because it is difficult to distinguish the sex of the fish (Tagliabue 2000).

Some of these habits can be tolerated, judging from one indicator of environmental health, the absence of systems breakdown. Some are more serious, based on many indicators, including species loss.

Debates on the issue of consumption were central at the Rio Conference. The United States (almost alone) opposed language about global consumption patterns. In finally deciding to attend the summit, then-president George Bush warned that the American life style was not negotiable.

Should consumption patterns that have major negative environmental effects be against the law, including international law? Forms of global environmental agreements that focus on attempts to alter standards of living face formidable political opposition, yet many activists maintain that international law of the environment must address pollution and natural resource depletion aggressively. Others conclude reluctantly that the challenge is one best put aside: reductions in consumption patterns are the least likely phenomena to be successfully targeted by law. Still others say that focusing on some forms of consumption is legal colonialism. The whale, for example, is said to be "the poster child of our politically correct age" (Philbrick 2000, 6).

If consumption patterns that allegedly despoil the environment are to be an international legal focus, nations need to agree on the criteria for choosing subjects. Whether actions are targeted because of the nature of their environmental impact, as opposed to, for example, their ease of regulation, is a question of equity. Major elements of the air pollution in Los Angeles come from the private automobile. Many commuters drive alone 10 to 15 miles to work and back each day. That threatens the lung capacity of children of the area and, according to the regional Air Quality Management District, prematurely kills 1,600 people annually. It also affects environmental conditions across boundaries. The driving occurs side by side with now closed factories, the stationary sources that once were more concentrated and targetable sources of pollution whose activities were made illegal. Many of those sources provided employment to lower-income residents in the region. Along the same lines, consider attempts to regulate pleasure boats in the Mediterranean and the other great seas. Should rules against their disposal of wastes be more strictly enforced, as opposed to focusing legal resources on stationary sources that provide employment?

GOVERNMENTS

Ironically, nations that make policy and law to promote global environmental quality also often are a major source of international environmental challenges. National governments destroy the international environment in many ways. They undertake regionally or globally destructive military tests. They engage in environmentally devastating wars. They fail to warn of incidents that have serious transboundary environmental and environmental health effects. They aggressively pursue policies that favor nonsustainable energy use, exploiting resources for short-term economic gain. Through their export credit agencies, they promote investments in developing countries that increase air polluting emissions (World Resources Institute 2000).[4] They support commercial activities at home that have insidious long-term effects on resources and people across national lines, destroying seas or countrysides.

Governments fail to act in situations in which the linkages to environmental degradation are less direct, such as in setting transportation fees for recycling, establishing energy taxes on various fuel sources, and removing subsidies for forms of nonsustainable development. They refuse to enforce their own environmental law. They ignore assessments of environmental impacts of major public works and private development actions. They place ill-informed cultural clichés over rational analysis of consumer behaviors that destroy species. They allow transboundary movements of dangerous and risky materials to places that cannot process the received hazards and toxics. They allow their flags to fly on commercial vessels that disgorge polluting emissions into the land and water. They permit uses on fragile lands that cannot be sustained. Finally, they take positions in international fora that favor destructive activity in natural resource or wildlife sectors over more environmentally protective positions.

It must be noted, however, that governments also can be the major source of environmental protection. They pass domestic environmental laws, of course, and that is fundamental. They have almost limitless potential for environmentally protective programs. Take some examples: Germany contemplates an electronics recycling ordinance for the collection of old appliances and the dismantling and reuse of components. That country alone has 2 million tons of discarded electronic products a year (*International Environment Reporter*, 4 March 1998). It also proposes proliferation of environmentally acceptable technology in its annual (more than $40 billion) investment program (Schmitt-Roschmann 2000). European cities, this time led by Italy, develop an approach to car-sharing to stem the high use of second vehicles among households (*International Environment Reporter*, 27 October 1999, 889). National governments create certification programs, such as Switzerland's for wood products from sustainable forests, that encourage use of environmentally sensitive commercial and consumer products (*International Environment Reporter*, 15 September, 761). In the United States, New Jersey leads a group of state and local governments in an effort to coordinate climate change policies with programs that include buying properties in sensitive floodplains (Johnson 2000). The European Union regulates label criteria for products ranging from footware to refrigerators and washing machines (*International Environment Reporter*, 2 February 2000, 79). The Scandinavian countries fund environmental mitigation activities well outside their borders. Nations establish substantial prizes for environmental leadership. States and regions put high priorities on cultural and world heritage preservation.

Governments can promote ecotourism. Travel to natural areas can be part of the environmental education of foreigners and at the same time generate revenues for national environmental protection projects. Ecotourism can include trips to areas of special ecological significance that increase appreciation of sustainable practices of the area and its local peoples. The Annapurna mountain range in Nepal (part of the King Mahendra Trust for Nature Conservation), the Masai Mara Reserve in Kenya, and Costa Rica's Monteverde Cloud Forest Reserve are all ecotourist attractions. To be sure, ecotourism can also open up significant resources to degradation as the numbers of the environmentally curious surpass a nation's ability to protect a site or ecological systems or subsystems are damaged by overzealous tourists. Breeding patterns can be disrupted, coral reefs overwhelmed, river systems polluted.

Governments, alone or with other governments and trade organizations, can establish certification programs that characterize products or processes as less damaging to the environment or even environmentally friendly. These programs are created for individual foodstuffs, such as organically grown coffee, or for whole industry sectors, where regulation through conventional international laws and regimes has been limited.

Government is involved in new forms of global regulation of forestry practices, including public agreements and conventions (Lipschutz 2000–2001). These are primarily interstate and intergovernmental and seek harmonization of standards. An example is the Kyoto Protocol; its signatory countries may establish terms and conditions to meet its provisions regarding management of forests and their role as carbon sinks. The U.N. International Tropical Timber Organization has committed to have all tropical timber that enters international markets come from sources that promote sustainable management (*International Environment Reporter*, 22 November 2000, 910).

Sustainable forestry regulation has moved toward certification of national as well as private practices through ecolabeling. For example, the

Forest Stewardship Council (FSC) does third-party independent labeling and auditing. It also has adopted global "Principles and Criteria" for forest management, and it accredits organizations that agree to abide by them. FSC aims to monitor the operations and portfolios of certifying groups. Fourteen countries have created regional or national processes to provide more detailed standards for these principles. Though actual ecological and social outcomes of the FSC system are not yet clear (Lipschutz 2000–2001), the potential for real improvement is very high. FSC certification requires a company to undertake comprehensive inventories of trees to be cut; to employ technologies that move lumber with minimal damage to soil, water, and biodiversity; and to prove that a forest, once cut, can recover. The World Wildlife Fund has estimated that the amount of acreage certified will increase dramatically in the next several years (Kopp 2000).

CONCLUSION

An effective international environmental law recognizes the myriad sources of environmental degradation, from the poor rural villager to the multinational corporate entity. It reflects an understanding of the relative seriousness of impacts. It understands how behaviors manifest themselves, across borders, multinationally, regionally, and globally. It also creates incentives for beneficial environmental behavior of people and groups, exploiting the models they have created. It does so while prioritizing environmental harm within other public policy concerns, including recognition of cultural diversity, deep poverty, and social welfare.

4. AN ACCOUNTING: SUCCESSES AND FAILURES IN INTERNATIONAL ENVIRONMENTAL LAW

This chapter presents several overall assessments of the contribution of international environmental law. It first lays out the complexities of undertaking global evaluations. After summarizing the negative and positive evaluations, the chapter then takes a closer look at five case studies. It closes with a description of a set of characteristics linked to effective law.

International environmental law contains a broad range of instruments. Assessing it is complex not only because of its scope but also because of distinctions among the instruments. Some instruments aim at most to be policy prescriptions without the same referents as hard law provisions, which generally are clear and substantive about what is required. Some are frameworks, articulating broad principles that will guide future international legal considerations. Many are hybrids with characteristics of framework development, policy promotion, and hard law.

Assessment is also complicated by the varying criteria used to define success and the seriously inadequate data and institutions for generating better data. The *Global Environment Outlook 2000* (xvii) found

> The monitoring and data collection infrastructure of most developing countries is severely handicapped or non-existent due to limitations in resources, personnel and equipment. Constraints are also faced by international organizations. Keeping well-trained personnel in publicly funded institutions is difficult. In some cases, there is no organization mandated to collect and report time-series data internationally on specific issues on a regular basis. . . . Data are reported for different geographical areas by different agencies and organizations. As a result, it may be impossible to use and compare otherwise valuable aggregated datasets in global and regional assessments [and] . . . the data management infrastructure of many countries is weak and data reporting is fragmented.

Nonetheless, evaluations can be made. At the millennium, many observers, including several leading international law experts, concluded that the great inventory of treaties, conventions, international tribunal decisions, custom, agreements, soft law principles, and other instruments aggregate in substance to less than the sum of the parts, and the sum itself is disturbingly inadequate. As we shall see, however, this general conclusion masks several elements of a history of success in some areas.

NEGATIVE ASSESSMENTS

It is common to reach conclusions about this body of law that point to its weaknesses, its lacunae, its failures. Koskenniemi (1996, 236) illustrated the tendency:

the massive increase in international legislation during the last quarter of a century, particularly in the environmental field has not created a new world order. In fact, the gap between law in books and how states act may now appear wider than at any other time in history—the more rules there are, the more occasion there is to break them. After years of active standard-setting, global and regional organizations stand somewhat baffled in front of a reality that has sometimes little in common with the objectives expressed in the inflated language of their major conventions and declarations.

Koskenniemi's view has been characterized as approaching the "nihilistic." He believes that most international environmental law bears a "minimal relationship with general international law." Furthermore, dispute settlement clauses are more a reflection "of ritual than any realistic belief that compliance problems should, or could, be dealt with through the doctrines of fault and attributability which characterize the legal doctrine of state responsibility" (1996, 247). Worse yet, even if compliance was achieved, the compliance is with law that cannot solve the problem that it putatively addresses. The Italian international scholar Gaja agrees (1998).

Pallemaerts (in Sands 1993, 18–19) is also highly critical, claiming that international environmental law has been regressive. He attempts to show how the concept and ideology of "sustainable development" undermines the autonomy of environmental law as a body of rules and standards created to prevent environmentally destructive activity. There may even be reason to fear that the Rio meeting was the beginning of the decline of international environmental law as a separate branch of international law. Pallemaerts worries that international environmental law could become a mere appendage of international development law. It would then be subordinated to economic considerations.

Nespor (2001) argues that international law has wrongly responded to the desires of Western environmentalists. In doing so, it has sacrificed work on solvable pressing and real environmental problems in the Third World, the poor and developing countries, to focus on speculative global disasters that could affect future generations. Meyer and his colleagues (1997, 647) conclude that the "environmental sector," which includes law, "is clearly ineffective in comparison to the rapidly expanding claims on it."

Susskind (1994a, 16), in a treatise seeking a new approach to negotiating environmental agreements, maintains that knowledgeable observers agree that the most notable global treaties have failed to reverse environmental deterioration. Those who look to reform international environmental law will "see glaring weaknesses: the rules are very sketchy; no one is really in charge; much of the negotiation process is ad hoc and unregulated; there is no central authority to manage the process or compel compliance; and the dispute resolution mechanisms available through the International Court of Justice are not definitive" (29). Hurrell and Kingsbury (1992) similarly conclude that the majority of international environmental agreements they studied had not substantially improved environmental conditions.

The Environmental Law Network International (1999, 2) is pessimistic: the law often is worded in "vague and cautious" terms, raising the question of the extent to which the international enterprise is only "symbolic legislation . . . without . . . creating binding rules with teeth capable of setting concrete and precise standards of environmental behaviour and conduct." Biermann (1998, 46) characterizes the legal and policy framework for the management of global marine pollution as insufficient, "a patch work approach" that lacks significant coordination and sufficient cooperation between the northern and southern hemispheres.

Handl (1994, 305–306) first acknowledges that the U.N. Conference on Environment and Development (UNCED):

> has had a tremendous impact in terms of raising global environmental consciousness, setting in motion or accelerating the search for solutions to global environmental problems, and refocusing attention on the necessity for a more equitable distribution of resources among nations. It has helped narrow . . . the gap between the concepts of en-

vironment and development and has made a major contribution to . . . empowerment of nonstate actors.

But he concludes that "a careful analysis provides a much less reassuring picture," pointing to weaknesses in the Climate Change Convention, polarization over issues at sessions of the U.N. Conference on Straddling Stocks and Highly Migratory Fish, and problems in movement toward a global forest convention.

Sands (1995a, 143–148) concludes that mechanisms for improving compliance are underutilized and questions whether law can address the growing range of challenging environmental issues. Not optimistic about UNCED, he argues that it will likely not significantly improve existing arrangements. Further, he suggests that domestic compliance with environmental obligations is inadequate and compliance with international obligations is largely absent. Many states fail to meet the most basic requirements of the law, such as reporting, and substantive obligations remain unimplemented. The data he presents are discouraging: only 19 of the 64 parties to the 1972 London Convention reported on the number and types of dumping permits they issued in 1987; only 13 of the 57 parties to MARPOL 73/78 reported violations and penalties they had imposed in 1989; only 25 of the more than 100 parties to the 1973 CITES submitted reports on 1989 import and export certificates for listed endangered species.

Others similarly conclude that effective enforcement of the treaties has been lacking (M. J. Kelly 1997, 448) and that there simply are too many treaties, engendering a kind of "treaty congestion" (Kelly 1997; Weiss 1993). An analysis by the U.S. General Accounting Office (1992b, 3–4) of implementation also is quite negative: "many reports are submitted late or incomplete, or are not submitted at all." Almost half of the reports to the Montreal Protocol Secretariat had information gaps. Equally if not more discouraging responses were reported for MARPOL, CITES, and the International Tropical Timber Agreement. The GAO further noted that those nations that carry out agreements may be put at a competitive disadvantage compared with countries that do not because of the high costs involved in coming into compliance. After citing some success in the number of international environmental instruments being concluded, Freestone warns that if they are not implemented, they "may not simply be worthless: they may be worse than worthless if they give the impression that all is well when the opposite is in fact true" (Boyle and Freestone 1999, 360).

At the regional level, assessments are more varied but still critical. Johnson and Corcelle (1992, 340) conclude about the European Union:

> Generally speaking, numerous weaknesses and gaps in the implementation of environmental directives have been noted by the Commission: often inclusion of these directives in national law is delayed; they are often only partially incorporated; in practice, the directives have been considered as recommendations, rather than provisions having a restrictive legal power; in some cases even the decisions of the Court of Justice recognizing an infraction on the part of a Member State, have not been followed.

Enforcement procedures within the European Community, both at national and at community levels, are ineffective (Sands 1995a); definitions within European law remain elusive; and it is characterized by "messiness in certain areas and absurdities in others," although the case with European waste law may ultimately make for a more balanced assessment (Tromans 2001, 156).

In a criticism that she generalizes to the UNEP, Kutting (1994, 238) notes the potential weakness of focusing on compliance rather than the effectiveness of international environmental law. About the Mediterranean Action Plan (MAP) she observes, "If cooperation rather than implementation is seen as the aim of MAP, it can be described as a successful agreement. Unfortunately, cooperation without implementation does not improve the state of the marine environment. Thus, MAP lacks effectiveness." Explicitly addressing progress in environmental terms, John Carroll (1988, 276) concluded of the International Joint Commission that "in broader societal concerns of water and air pollution, it has achieved little of significance *when measured against getting the problem solved,* and that should be the only real measure."

Some observers attend to the weakest parts of treaties and generalize therefrom. They see vague definitions such as the undeveloped "ecosystem approach" in the Convention on the Conservation of Antarctic Marine Living Resources (Redgwell 1999); loopholes, such as through bilateral agreements in the Basel Convention; incentives to defect from the Montreal Protocol and absence of effective compliance-promoting mechanisms; failure to address air pollution emissions from vessels under MARPOL and related regimes; creation of polarization rather than consensus with the Straddling Stocks and Highly Migratory Fish Treaty and its failure to address protection of the 90 percent of the world's fisheries within the 200-mile exclusive economic zones of coastal nations; the possibility of trade between members and nonmembers of CITES, its provision allowing downgrading of species from extremely endangered to threatened, and failure to provide adequate financing to meet obligations; ineffective monitoring and management under certain fish protection conventions; and vote buying, expensive use of scientific research, and aboriginal catch exemptions under the international whaling regime.

In addition, the Commission on Sustainable Development has made only modest progress in implementing Agenda 21, and its activities have been decried as "depressingly slow" (Handl 1994, 307) and remaining in a very preliminary stage (Bergesen and Botnen 1996). The Bamako Convention has a noble objective and contains a precautionary principle, but it lacks an effective monitoring and enforcement mechanism, commitment from some African states, and sufficient funding (Schneider 1996, 265). The International Convention for the Conservation of Atlantic Tuna has been ineffective in reversing the trend of declining tuna stocks in part because some fishing nations did not sign the treaty. Among those that did are countries, such as the United States, that have not been sufficiently influenced by the regime's compliance rules. Quotas set by participating parties have been unlawful. For example, the U.S. quota was set at three times its allocation (Nickler 1999). True, a trade measure element exists in the regime, but it is focused on nonmembers.

Dauvergne (1998, i) is anticipatorily pessimistic on forestry: "Even if current efforts to develop a global forest convention are successful, even as governments embrace new environmental institutions and laws, and even as international activist groups and local nongovernmental groups gain influence, genuine reforms will still occur slowly, perhaps too slowly to save the remaining old-growth tropical forests of the Asia-Pacific." By 2000, internationally traded tropical timber was to come entirely from sustainable sources (Humphreys 1996b). That goal has not been met.

Anecdotes fuel these negative assessments. The standoff between the United States and Canada on overfishing in the Pacific Northwest has been embarrassing. Canadian fishermen were a graphic reminder of the fragile nature of international environmental law, as they encircled American ships with their small vessels to block them from leaving the bay.

Other examples are regressive: Germany's plan to phase out a water pollution tax established in 1976, an action incompatible with principle 16 of the Rio Declaration and chapters 4 and 18 of Agenda 21 (Handl

1994, 308); the European Union's failure to adopt an EU-wide carbon tax, despite the EC's political commitment to stabilize carbon dioxide emissions at 1990 levels by the year 2000 (308); the American reliance on voluntary cooperation by business and industry for reducing greenhouse gas emissions (308); the failure at the U.N. Conference on Environment and Development to produce a global forests convention (Humphreys 1996b).

The 1991 Air Quality Agreement between the United States and Canada lacks external control over environmental impact assessment. Neither it nor the ECE Convention on environmental impact assessment has substantive value if the procedural obligations (consultations or conciliation) are unsuccessful. Indeed, in a survey the Secretariat of the United Nations "was unable to uncover any instance where an activity was enjoined on account of the environmental risks it entailed, even though such requests had at times been made" (Okowa 1997, 288).

The 1986 Convention on Early Notification of a Nuclear Accident allows a state to evade its duties by concluding that the accident is not "radiologically significant" (Okowa 1997, 297). With regard to a procedural obligation provided by treaty, pertaining to the exchange of information, Okowa (301) summarized:

> The determination of breach of obligations of this character is bound to be problematic in so far as their performance cannot be tested objectively. There are no uniform principles or rules regulating the collection or dissemination of information. A State may decide to supply minimal information, or install inadequate monitoring equipment, but in the absence of institutional or third party mechanisms or criteria for determining the level of compliance it would be very difficult to make out a case of breach.

The provisions regarding land-based sources of marine pollution in the controversial Law of the Sea Treaty (UNCLOS) are strikingly weak, "certainly the weakest formulations to be found in international legal documents" (Biermann 1998, 39). UNCLOS articles 207 and 212 may be understood only as a general rule of state conduct whose content is still determined by the individual will of states (Biermann 1998, 39) and collective scientific interests of the community of nations as a whole are not protected (Burke 1996). UNCLOS had devoted little attention to the conservation and management of high-seas fish stocks. From 1982, fishing outside the 200-mile zone increased as nations sought new areas to exploit. Concomitantly, there was mismanagement and overexploitation of resources within the 200-mile limit, renewing pressures on those fish stocks that straddle the 200-mile boundaries (Davies and Redgwell 1997, 200), although the protection of these stocks has been addressed in an agreement that came into force almost two decades after UNCLOS. The continued hegemony of the flag state in respect to prosecution of violations of fisheries conservation measures on the high seas is another defect (273). Furthermore, the UNCLOS mechanisms for dispute settlement have contributed to the proliferation of international tribunals, whose uncoordinated actions can fragment both substantive law and procedures for settling disputes (Boyle 1997).

With the exception of the European treaty regimes, the 40 regional seas environmental treaties have not been effective. The regimes are characterized by a vagueness similar to UNCLOS articles 207 and 212. The Antarctic Treaty System has prohibited mining under a comprehensive environmental protection regime, but a long-run solution for stopping the evolution of mineral exploitation is not in sight. The protocol's 50-year ban rule has temporarily resolved some discrepancies, but this issue can be reopened at any time and certainly will be in the future (Schram and Vidas 1997, 293).

POSITIVE OVERALL ASSESSMENTS

Other assessments are more positive. Sands (1993, 147) counters his own dismal statistics on compliance in general with much more encouraging data for the International Whaling Commission and the Montreal Protocol. Susskind (1994a, 17–18) points to countries previously uncaring about natural resource management that now make explicit commitments to be responsible. He also cites the increased number of whales, the recognition of wetlands preservation and the rescue of 30 million hectares of wetlands (an area the size of Italy), control of mineral development in the Antarctic, protection of 80 "natural world heritage" sites, and clear delineation of migratory flyways. Also, many provisions of the Law of the Sea have come into practice. Susskind's list goes on and includes reference to the ozone treaties and those on hazardous waste transport.[1] De Yturriaga (1997) also locates strengths in his assessment of the Law of the Sea.

Scovazzi concludes that "There is hardly any doubt that treaties are considered to be the best tools in improving the protection of the environment at the international level" (Scovazzi and Treves 1992, 28). The *Global Environment Outlook* (1997, 2) concluded: "World-wide, the greatest progress has been in the realm of institutional developments, international co-operation, public participation, and the emergence of private-sector action. Legal frameworks, economic instruments, environmentally sound technologies, and cleaner production processes have been developed and applied. Environmental impact assessments have become standard tools." The policy grandfather of domestic environmental impact assessment law, Lynton Caldwell (1999), has in his later analyses praised the contribution of international global law. He recognizes a body of precedent-setting law and practice as having the character of an international constitution for the world environment.

Juxtaposing his assessment with Henry Kissinger's view of diplomacy as the exercise of competitive power politics among nations, Shabecoff (1996, 116) states that "the rise of green diplomacy in the latter part of the 1980s seemed to reflect something different: a growing awareness of a new *realpolitik* that must be addressed not by competition but by co-operation and not by unilateral exercise of sovereign power but by pooling that power to confront the complex array of environmental and economic problems that threaten all nations." He enumerated the targets of international environmental law to demonstrate its importance: nothing is more real than poverty and hunger, disease caused by polluted water, massive relocations of people to avoid scarcity, and global climate change and ozone depletion.

The Environmental Law Network International (1999) balances some of its negative analysis, noting that environmental law principles "are by no means devoid of legal force and effect." The International Court of Justice has given weight to certain of those principles, as have individual nation-state courts, including the German Federal Constitutional Court. Although the ICJ's pronouncements are more recommendatory than prescriptive, such as in the Gabcikovo-Nagymaros case between Hungary and Czechoslovakia-Slovakia over damming of the Danube and interpretation of a treaty on locks and other facilities, the U.N. judicial organ is helpful in promoting "a process of ongoing negotiations geared toward achieving a political result that is mutually acceptable" (Oxman 1998, 278).

French (1992), attributing a long list of achievements at least in part to international agreements, noted that sulfur dioxide emissions fell substantially in Europe from 1980 to 1990, the health threat of radiation from atmospheric testing decreased dramatically since the 1963 test ban, and the percentage of "clean and safe" beaches in the Mediterranean grew impressively since the adoption of the 1975 Mediterranean Action Plan. Also, whale harvests have fallen from tens of thousands to tens since the International Whaling Commission tightened its regulations; poaching of elephants dropped precipitously in Africa since 1989; Antarctica has been protected from mining, military activities, and other environmentally degrading actions; and hazardous waste imports have fallen. Nonetheless, for each success, French names a rather daunting "remaining challenge."[2]

Stone (1993, 119–120), in a comprehensive treatment of law and other institutions as means of protecting the global environment, identifies several significant weaknesses in environmental treaties, most notably vagueness in language, and then concludes:

the notion of more ambitious multilateral conventions will and should go forward. . . . Nonetheless . . . no one should doubt that even without "hard" sanctions backing them up, treaties, and even vague, aspirational declarations of principle, have significant effects on patterns of behavior in the international community. Indeed, no one should doubt the salutary effects in the mere process of bringing diplomats together to discuss global problems.

Other analysts focus on the strengths of particular treaties, such as: the effective use of trade-related environmental measures (TREMs) to promote compliance in the Basel Convention, numerous innovations including the funding mechanism for TREMs in the Montreal Protocol, and effective regulation of the international trade in pesticides. Hough (1996) concluded that (unlike other pesticide-related issues such as industrial safety and environmental pollution) "the rules established by UNEP and the FAO [Food and Agriculture Organization] have been observed by both the chemical industry and government and have had an impact on political behavior." Hough's assessment is important because the most powerful affected actors—the agrochemical industry and the United States and Great Britain—did not support the establishment of the FAO and UNEP rules, which appeared, they proclaimed, "not to be in their interests."[3]

In their thorough review of fourteen case studies, Victor, Raustiala, and Skolnikoff (1998, 2) concluded that for most of the eight areas of regulation they identify, "regulated behavior has changed markedly in the past two decades." They cite virtual elimination of ozone-depleting substances, dramatic decreases in emissions of sulfur dioxide, stabilization of emissions of nitrogen oxides, the banning of hazardous chemicals and pesticides, protection of whales, and elimination of dumping at sea of high-level radioactive wastes—all at least in part related to implementation of international environmental law. Weiss and Jacobson (1998) at about the same time concluded that compliance with the World Heritage Convention has been quite respectable; that notwithstanding some weaknesses, CITES has been linked to an end of trade in some species; that despite major problems with compliance, the London Dumping Convention has been relatively successful, with decreases measured in the millions of tons of dumped wastes; and that the Montreal Protocol has been unusually effective. Van Heijnsbergen (1997, 217) also concluded that CITES "functions well," despite noting that a third of the parties do not have adequate implementing legislation and that the convention does not have a binding dispute resolution mechanism.

A quarter-century after the UNEP Regional Seas Program was initiated, Boyle and Freestone (1999) found a mixed record that included some positive results. The Mediterranean Action Plan has established, with "a measure of success," the legal and institutional basis for coordination of national programs and measures. Potentially devisive issues, such as interregime control of land-based pollutants, have been addressed through the MAP process. The Kuwait Action Area agreement has successfully introduced environmental impact assessment into its region and has fostered an innovative approach to control of land-based pollution. Similar successes with regional control of land-based and other emissions have been achieved in the North Atlantic and the Baltic Sea. Nonetheless, again, there are "major short-comings" in all the regional arrangements, including poor implementation capability, insufficient attention to dispute resolution, and neglect of civil-liability strategies.

As to oil pollution of the seas, Mitchell (1994), contrasting the MARPOL regime to that of an earlier convention, found that MARPOL has achieved nearly universal compliance. He gave several explanations for its success: transparency of actions, provision of potent and credible sanctions, and reduced implementation costs for states because MARPOL builds on established infrastructures. Duruigbo (2000) also recognizes the value of MARPOL's compliance-promoting devices (with near universal installation of ballast tanks and oil washing), although he notes challenges to enforcement related to limitations on jurisdiction, part of a "predicament" that hangs "like an albatross around the neck of international law generally."

Okowa's assessment of the procedural requirements of consultation is fairly positive, and her overall conclusion (1997, 334–335) regarding this type of treaty obligation ("procedural environmental") is at least mixed:

In many contexts the obligations are not defined with precision, and much uncertainty persists as to their essential components. . . . As found in treaty regimes, [however,] there is little doubt that these obligations have legal force for the parties to them. To that extent the obligations they impose are strictly speaking justiciable, notwithstanding their general imprecision. . . . As independent legal duties, procedural obligations are likely to influence the behaviour of even the most reluctant of States.

Assessments of soft law, customary law, and framework law also vary. The campaign to control high-seas pelagic driftnet fishing through nonbinding legal means "seems to have succeeded" (Rothwell 2000, 145). U.N. resolutions are being reevaluated with increasing respect for their effectiveness (Shelton 2000). The International Law Commission concluded that "there is overwhelming support for the doctrine of equitable utilization as a general guiding principle of law for the determination of the rights of States in respect of the non-navigational uses of international watercourses" (Nollkaemper 1996, 44). But Nollkaemper characterized the doctrine as "highly indeterminate," based on an unwieldy weighting of seventeen factors. It is "an open-ended framework for political compromise without an independent legal identity. . . . The flexibility of the principle means that it easily dwindles into a 'might-is-right' paradigm" (46). Bergesen and Botnen (1996) conclude that the activities of the Commission on Sustainable Development have remained in a very preliminary stage. Kaplan (1991) concludes that customary law has not been able to address adequately the challenge of subseabed nuclear waste disposal.

A CLOSER LOOK: FIVE CASE STUDIES

These very different assessments reflect the variable success of individual efforts, but they also underscore the different criteria for evaluating success, different understandings of the goal of an international law of the environment, and different accounting schemes. Another way of looking at the record is offered by detailed case studies that examine evaluative criteria and give a more textured picture of success and failure and the methods used to reach those conclusions. The following cases cover international attempts to protect the air (Montreal Protocol and its amendments), water (Black Sea Environmental Programme), and land (Basel Convention) and, more generally, environmental protection and enforcement (the NAFTA-related North American Agreement on Environmental Cooperation). Global climate change is the focus of the last study, which addresses earth systems more generally.

AIR: THE MONTREAL PROTOCOL AND ITS AMENDMENTS

No consensus has emerged on which international environmental law has been the most successful. Among the most broadly acclaimed treaties, however, is the Montreal Protocol and its amendments. The protocol, which aims to reduce the release of gaseous chemicals that damage stratospheric ozone, is hailed as a model for north-south cooperation on global environmental problems.

Certain chemicals used in industrial and industrializing societies have caused an increase in the amount of ultraviolet radiation that reaches the earth's surface. Refrigerants (CFCs) used in private homes and automobiles, flame retardants (halons) found in fire extinguishers, and other gases react with ultraviolet radiation when they reach the stratosphere. Chlorine free radicals are released by the ultraviolet radiation, and a series of chemical reactions is catalyzed. "The natural stratospheric removal processes for ozone are then supplemented by chlorine-based sequences. . . . The average ozone molecule survives for a short time and less ozone is present than before" (Rowland 2001, 1269). The reactions upset the natural processes of ozone creation, destruction, and re-creation. (A single chlorine atom can destroy thousands of ozone molecules in the stratosphere.) As a result, the protective layer of ozone that surrounds the earth is weakened and the earth's surface is exposed to elevated levels of ultraviolet radiation. Increased exposure to ultraviolet radiation induces cataracts, suppresses or destroys the human immune system, and causes some forms of skin cancer. It endangers many species of phytoplankton, essential to the survival of nearly all fish populations. Man-made materials also suffer damage.

None of this was known when chlorofluorocarbons were first produced in 1928. According to the standards used at the time to test new chemicals, chlorofluorocarbons were thought to be safe. They were not toxic. They were not flammable, and they are chemically stable in the lower atmosphere. The inventor of the first CFC compound sought to illustrate its safety by inhaling its vapors and using his CFC-loaded breath to blow out the flame of a candle (Litfin 1994, 58).

By the eighties, use of CFCs and other ozone-depleting substances was well established in industrialized countries. Their production and use in developing countries had been small by comparison, but absent the presence of accessible and affordable alternatives, these nations would be likely to increase use greatly. Scientific understanding of the nature, magnitude, and consequences of the CFC problem was growing, but the issue was still controversial in the seventies. In 1974 Mario Molina and F. Sherwood Rowland published a paper showing the chemical process by which CFCs, which remain in the atmosphere for decades, could cause continued damage to stratospheric ozone. The paper launched a heated scientific debate, and industrial acceptance of the existence of risk was slow. As of 1980, leaders at DuPont, the world's largest CFC producer, maintained that the environmental threat posed by CFCs was not established well enough to warrant continuing research on replacement compounds (Litfin 1994, 70).

Later, when the dangers were recognized, it was clear that the possible effects of reduced levels of stratospheric ozone could not be controlled by any nation in isolation. Without international cooperation, efforts to cut back on production in one country would likely be offset by activities elsewhere. Some effects of ozone depletion are concentrated in particular nations, but others are more diffuse. Many political leaders were begininng to conclude that an international agreement was essential to reduce the likelihood and magnitude of potentially devastating damage to life around the globe.

International Environmental Law Response

In 1976 the Governing Council of UNEP organized a meeting of IGOs and NGOs to review information about the ozone layer, and one year later UNEP began working on ways to address the ozone issue. It created a Coordination Committee on the ozone layer in collaboration with the World Meteorological Organization. This group of IGO, NGO, and national and scientific organization representatives was to produce a semiannual assessment of the depletion of the ozone layer and its effects. There followed several important events. In 1985 the Vienna Convention on the Protection of the Ozone Layer was adopted. It called for cooperation on many matters: on research and information exchange on human effects on the ozone layer and human health effects of modification of the layer; on formulation of protocols and annexes; on basic scientific research; and on exchange of relevant scientific, technical, socioeconomic, commercial, and legal information (article 4). It established a conference of the parties to adopt protocols. It described how amendments to the convention would be made by consensus, except, "as a last resort," by a three-fourths majority of parties present and voting; how amendments to any protocol were to be made; and how annexes were to be adopted and amended. Settlement of disputes would be by negotiation, good offices, or mediation by a third party, and arbitration or submission to the ICJ.

The convention solidified the commitment to find ways to protect the ozone layer and improve understanding of stratospheric ozone reduction, but it contained no specific CFC standards or regulations. As late as December 1986 only half a dozen nations had ratified it. The next two years witnessed greater public interest in the ozone problem, further scientific publications reporting on its severity, the recognition by industry (most notably DuPont) that CFC substitutes could be developed within a small number of years, and continued expert workshop activity under the auspices of UNEP.

In 1987 governments of developed and developing countries agreed to the Montreal Protocol on Substances that Deplete the Ozone Layer, despite continuing uncertainty about the existence of damage to the ozone layer and conflicting political interests over possible courses of action. Under article 8 of the Montreal Protocol, parties must establish means of determining noncompliance with the protocol and they must also determine how to treat noncompliance. The Copenhagen Amendments (1992) met this requirement by creating an implementation committee constituted of ten parties and giving that committee the authority to receive submissions by a party regarding reservations about another party's implementation of protocol obligations. The committee makes recommendations to the Meeting of the Parties. In Copenhagen hydrochlorofluorocarbons (HCFCs) and other substances were added to the list of controlled substances. The 1997 Montreal Amendments determined several measures that the Meeting of the Parties would be able to take in cases of noncompliance, namely: suspend protocol privileges, issue warnings, and provide financial and technical assistance. This is done through the Montreal Protocol Multilateral Fund, the institutional characteristics of which are were laid out in article 10 of the 1990 London Amendments.

There are several fundamental requirements of the protocol regime. Specific timetables for restrictions have been created, and a phaseout or ban of most of the ozone-depleting substances (ODSs) has been adopted; for some substances the requirement is a freeze on production. Cooperation in scientific research and exchange of information are promoted. Abatement measures for ODSs have been adopted. those substances now include CFCs, halons, carbon tetrachloride, methyl chloroform, fully halogenated CFC, HCFC, hydrobromide fluorocarbons, and methyl bromide. A permanent funding entity is in place and trade restrictions can be imposed for noncompliance. Member countries commit to establish licensing systems for trade, and a mechanism for avoiding disputes and settling them when they are not avoidable, the noncompliance procedure has been initiated. The regime adopted the revolutionary concept in international law of simplified majority decision making, and no reservation is allowed. The ozone regime, in addition to the state parties, includes the Meeting of the Parties, the Implementation Committee, and the UNEP Ozone Secretariat, which is empowered, among other matters, to initiate a formal dispute resolution procedure, a first in international law (Yoshida 1999).

Ambassador Richard Benedick, who led the United States participation in the negotiations for the Vienna Convention and the Montreal Protocol, said that negotiations were characterized by "a sense of history making." At the conclusion of the negotiation of the Montreal Protocol, Mostafa Tolba, the UNEP executive director whose strong personality had helped build support for substantive commitments in the protocol, stated that "the environment can be a bridge between the worlds of East and West, and of North and South. . . . This Protocol is a point of departure . . . the beginning of the real work to come" (Benedick 1991, as cited in Hunter, Salzman, and Zaelke 1998, 214). This agreement was achieved despite the lack of measurable evidence of damage to the ozone layer at the time (545).

Assessment: Physical Parameters

The Montreal Protocol and its amendments will lead to a reduction in the magnitude of loss of stratospheric ozone in the twenty-first century provided that signatory nations comply with their commitments. Because the ozone-depleting substances that are currently in the stratosphere will continue to affect stratospheric ozone for a number of decades, the problem has not been eliminated.[4] Assuming that all commitments made in the Montreal Protocol and its amendments are met, the ozone layer is predicted to stabilize near the year 2050 (Hunter, Salzman, Zaelke 1998, 576), although some analysts conclude that it will be the middle of the century before an adequate comprehensive assessment of the regime's impact can be undertaken (Sims 1996).

In the United States, many organizations that have used large amounts of substances regulated by the Montreal Protocol are now exemplary in their compliance, especially McDonald's (no more CFCs in packaging), Whirlpool (CFC-free refrigerants), and the U.S. military (phaseout of halons in fire-fighting equipment)(World Resources Institute 1996). There have been some problems associated with the incentive-based mechanisms for industrial compliance, most notably the black market in chlorofluorocarbons. DeSombre (2000–2001) argues that changing economic, technological, and regulatory conditions will reduce the magnitude of the problems over time.[5] Other challenges, however, are not based on bad faith but are simply reflections of capacity to implement. The United Kingdom, for example, faced with destroying CFCs in the foam of millions of refrigerators, lacks adequate facilities to perform the task (Tracey 2001).

Meanwhile, measurements of CFCs in the atmosphere indicate continued growth in absolute terms but a decrease in the rate at which CFCs are added to existing levels.[6] Evidence from the U.S. National Aeronautics and Space Administration and the National Oceanic and Atmosphere Administration shows that the loss of stratospheric ozone continues to affect all latitudes outside the tropics, with areas near the South Pole experiencing the greatest losses.[7]

The worst year to that point for the size of the ozone hole was 1998 (Environmental News Network, 7 October 1998). Because temperatures in the stratosphere over the South Pole were warmer in 1999, the ozone hole did not grow as large as it did in 1998 (Associated Press, 7 October 1999). Global climate change is expected to contribute to the size of the ozone hole. Although global climate change is anticipated to increase average temperatures near the earth's surface, it is expected to decrease temperatures in the stratosphere. Colder temperatures in the stratosphere create conditions conducive to larger losses in stratospheric ozone due to CFCs and other ozone-depleting substances (Environmental News Network, 7 October 1998).

Assessment: The Contribution of International Environmental Law

Expert assessments of the effectiveness of the ozone regime are predominantly positive. The Vienna Convention and the Montreal Protocol and subsequent amendments are structured so that efforts to address stratospheric ozone reduction can evolve with improvements in scientific understanding of the situation and political willingness to act. Flexibility of the regime has enabled international cooperation to reduce the use of ozone-depleting substances. The flexibility is made possible by three characteristics of the agreement: the convention-protocol structure, the adjustment system, and the role of the administrative bodies created to implement the protocol (DeSombre 2001). Success of the regime derives in part from UNEP's decision to involve both environmental NGOs and industry groups, in this case a concentrated class (Petsonk 1990).

The convention-protocol structure involves progressive levels of political commitment and technical specificity. Through the convention, signatory parties agree to support a general idea and to participate in periodic negotiations over details. The details are noted in the protocols and their amendments subsequently negotiated. Parties are obliged to comply with the convention, protocols, and amendments agreed to prior to their ratification, but they can choose among subsequent protocols and amendments.

The adjustment system, in contrast, allows substantial scientific but limited political flexibility. To adjust the specific commitments of the Montreal Protocol (e.g., the time frame for ending the use of a chemical), a majority of developed and a majority of developing countries (provided that their numbers combine to equal at least two thirds of the parties to the agreement) must vote in favor. If they do, then all of the signatory parties are obliged to comply, whether they voted in favor of the change or not.

The organizations created by the Montreal Protocol to oversee implementation and the expenditure of funds have been very effective in insisting on coordination among work programs and in reporting efforts and concerns at each meeting of the parties. In addition, the parties have established a number of subsidiary bodies, which facilitate ongoing working-level communication on new issues.

Another feature of the Montreal Protocol's flexibility is its noncompliance procedure. It enables a fast and conciliatory approach to noncompliance (Yoshida 1999). Under the procedure, parties that do not comply with their commitments are subjected to informal persuasion and a "politics of shame." This strategy relies on public reporting, economic incentives, and multilateral pressure from other signatory parties. The NCP regime is a dispute avoidance and settlement mechanism internal to the regime, based on a collective reaction rather than confrontational bilateralism common to formal dispute settlement mechanisms. Yoshida (1999) considers it more flexible, simple, and rapid than traditional judicial settlements and claims that it demonstrates great respect for the sovereignty of member states. Flexibility is also evident in the protocol's use of economic incentives to promote industrial development of technologically derived alternatives and the participation of developing countries in the phaseout of ozone-depleting substances.

Perhaps the most important means by which the protocol solicits a poorer country's participation is its willingness to hold industrialized and developing countries to different standards. For instance, less developed countries consuming ozone-depleting substances below a specified level (0.3 kilograms per capita) can delay compliance with their commitments under the protocol for ten years beyond their scheduled implementation dates (article 5). In addition, the protocol fund helps developing countries meet the costs incurred by eschewing the use of ODSs. The protocol also contains technology transfer mechanisms to facilitate the diffusion of replacement technologies to developing countries. Nonetheless, there are varying degrees of responsiveness among developing nations, linked in part to differing assessments about north-south relations encompassed in the regime. China, for example, was more accepting than India of the Montreal Protocol (Sims 1996).

The Montreal Protocol, as the first "precautionary treaty," provides a precedent that diplomats can draw on in future negotiations on global environmental problems fraught with scientific uncertainty (Hunter, Salzman, and Zaelke 1998). In particular, it employs technology-forcing mechanisms to enable implementation as future hazards and circumstances require (545). The protocol regime entities have been active and effective. By the end of 1997, for example, the Meeting of the Parties, in accordance with the Rules of Procedure, had already made more than 200 decisions, many of them related to noncompliance and ODS regulation (Yoshida 1999, 118).

Even Lipschutz, who is skeptical about traditional top-down treaty-based regimes, concedes that the Montreal Protocol "seems to have worked" (1996, 27). "The ozone agreements have been ratified by most of the countries of the world and include provision for the transfer of technology and resources to Third World countries that might otherwise find themselves put at an economic and technical disadvantage by the ban on ozone-depleting substances." Miller and McFarland (1996) are sufficiently positive to advise that the climate-change regime might do well to explore characteristics of Montreal: (1) the power of scientific consensus, even when under conditions of some uncertainty, (2) the value of affected industries working with government and environmentalists, (3) the economic benefits of early action, and (4) the need for recognition of the impacts on developing countries.

There have been criticisms of the regime. There is a risk of noncompliance with its rules because it is not everywhere clear what compliance means (Yoshida 1999). Norms are not well defined. Furthermore, choice of the World Bank as the main implementing agency of the fund has been strongly attacked because, allegedly, the bank continues to fund projects that use technologies that rely on ozone-depleting substances. The bank also reportedly established markets in the south for destructive, obsolete technologies (Greenpeace 1994). The financial assistance mechanism sets a precedent and creates expectations for similar subsidies in other environmental agreements. A demand by developing countries for financial and technical help may be construed as a failure to take responsibility for a share of the costs of protecting the global environment. In a political atmosphere in some nations of waning support for overseas development assistance, these demands can weaken diplomatic support for international environmental agreements. Furthermore, if the assistance decreases the amount of profit obtainable from research investment in replacement substances, it will reduce the incentive for industrialized countries to develop new technologies and undermine research efforts in developing nations as well. Provision of subsidies may also result in perverse rewards for developing countries to increase production of ODSs in the short run. China exploited such an opportunity for short-term gains from ODS production (DeSombre 2000–2001). Finally, although experts differ, some observers feel that illegal CFC trade is inevitable and will continue because of problems inherent in the regime, such as exemptions for recycled CFCs (Clapp 1997) and a grace period for developing countries (Papasavva and Moomaw 1997).

Conclusions

The Montreal Protocol with its amendments is a historic precedent. In the face of a severe global environmental problem steeped in scientific uncertainty, industrialized and developing nations agreed to an innovative arrangement. One of the new principles set forth by the protocol is the idea that nations should take precautions against plausible environmental threats even if irrefutable evidence of their existence is not yet forthcoming. Another principle applies to the distribution of costs and benefits across nations that bear common but differentiated responsibilities for past and future threats to the global environment. This approach is characterized by differentiated commitments among signatory nations and technology transfer to assist developing nations to reduce the environmental damage that their industrialization is likely to cause. Because of the development of a black market in ozone-depleting substances, the ozone layer is unlikely to stabilize as soon as scientists had predicted. As subsequent provisions of the agreement come into force, however, black-market demand is expected to subside. Also of central concern to policymakers in the international arena are the possible countervailing effects of controls on certain climate-change gases.

In addition to the flexibility that allows the regime to incorporate an evolving scientific consensus and the regime's use of innovative strategies to promote compliance, a few other factors help explain the considerable success of the Montreal Protocol. The goals of the agreement are clear, precise, and straightforward, and their realization is subject to objective evaluation. Entry into the agreement was not a major obstacle to the agreement's creation. Through an innovative multilateral fund, support has been adequate to help meet defined goals. The Secretariat and its subsidiary bodies have been professional and effective. The approach to dispute resolution is clear, recognizing increasing outside assistance if required. The regime builds on ever-developing political acceptability linked to the private sector's recognition of the importance of the ODS problem and industry's role in creating substitutes.

WATER AND THE GREAT SEAS: THE BLACK SEA ENVIRONMENTAL PROGRAMME

The Black Sea efforts represent one of more than forty in the UNEP Regional Seas Programme. The Black Sea Environmental Programme is not the most developed, and it is not representative of the degree of success reached in other seas; however, its history is useful for describing the challenges to a regional water effort and for isolating the factors linked to the success of such a regime (DiMento 2001).

The Black Sea region denotes the six riparian states, a presently unrecognized former Soviet republic (also riparian), and the neighboring states that are part of the mammoth watershed of the Black Sea. The riparians are Bulgaria, Georgia (Abkhazia), Romania, the Russian Federation, Ukraine, and Turkey. Major rivers that drain into the sea include the Danube, Dnieper, and Don, which rank second, third, and fourth among major European rivers. The sea's surface area is one fifth the size of its catchment area, and its depth in parts exceeds 2 kilometers. The only ocean outlet to this gigantic water resource is the narrow and shallow 19-mile-long Bosporus Channel, established as an international sea lane under a 1936 convention. The environmental problems associated with the Black Sea are immense, and its environmental management is a formidable task.

While scientists analyze and debate just exactly how serious the situation is, pollution and ecological degradation of the Black Sea is on almost every list of major environmental problems in the world.

Under the Soviet system (which in a sense was an international effort, albeit a peculiarly centralized one), a large number of specialists in all areas of relevance to water-body management worked on Black Sea environmental problems; however, connections between their work and official decision making were not strong. As a Georgian retrospective summarized: "National environmental legislation was often based upon objectives and standards which were too strict to be enforced or were not linked to effective economic instruments such as fines or permit charges. As a result of years of isolation, many institutions lacked the modern equipment and know-how necessary to face the challenge of providing reliable information on the state of the environment itself" (Republic of Georgia 1996). The problems were even greater than this summary suggests, involving lack of coordination among the Soviet states and their neighbors, lack of public participation, nontransparency of decision making, and absence of other factors that promote implementation, such as a modern regulatory approach, technical assistance, and adequate funding.

The environmental problem in the Black Sea is multifaceted, ranging from loss of landscape to the extinction of species. The Black Sea's ecosystem has changed "irreversibly" (Global Environment Facility 1997, 139), and by the early nineties, terms such as "dead," "close to collapse," and "unholy mess" were common descriptors of the status of this giant and beautiful natural resource. Widespread pollution discourages or destroys recreation, tourism, biodiversity, fishing, and water quality. The destruction of the fish species alone in the sea is "one of the greatest ecological catastrophes" of our time (Woodard 1997).

The riparians include Turkey and nations whose cleanup technologies, monitoring stations, and environmental laboratories are in considerable disrepair. As the watershed area (the drain) for more than thirty rivers, the sea receives the effluents of 160 million people from seventeen nations, one third of Europe. It is also polluted by oil and the radiation fallout from the accident at Chernobyl and, by some accounts, by heavy metals including chrome, copper, mercury, lead, and zinc (Sampson 1995).[8]

A great quantity of organic matter from rivers feeds the Black Sea. In the Bosporous Strait alone the untreated sewage of 10 million people is regularly dumped, and that represents only about 6 percent of the pollutants received into the Black Sea (Sampson 1996). Dissolved oxygen cannot complete the process of decomposition. Organic material strips oxygen from sulfate ions, creating hydrogen sulfide, a toxic gas. The Black Sea "is the single largest reservoir of hydrogen sulfide and the biggest natural anoxic basin in the world. To a depth of 150–200 meters, the sea is teeming with life, but below that level, the water is 'anoxic' or 'dead.'" With no oxygen there are no fish, shellfish, or bacteria (Global Learn 1996), a condition that in part dates back to the waning of the last ice age as rising waters from the Mediterranean entered the Black Sea basin (Ballard 2001).

The loss of biodiversity is a major problem resulting from eutrophication, "clearly the main ecological concern in the Black Sea" (Global Environment Facility 1997). Eutrophication is the overfertilization of a water body with nitrogen and phosphorous compounds. In the Black Sea, that results from fertilizers and urban and industrial sewage. An overproduction of phytoplankton and reduced sea grass and algae result in a concomitant loss of crustaceans, fish, and mollusks. Besides, *Mnemiopsis leidyi* was introduced into the region by accident from the eastern seaboard of America in the ballast water of a ship. This jellyfish-like species consumes fish larvae and tiny animals that small fish feed on. The species reached a mass of 900 million tons, which is ten times the annual fish harvest worldwide. Many fish species were pushed to extinction, and the fish catch in the sea degenerated to 250,000 tons in 1991 from a total of 850,000 tons less than a decade earlier. One estimate is that the number of fish species in the sea dropped from around 25 to only 3 to 5 in the ten-year period from 1986, when the sea had five times the fish production of the Mediterranean, to 1996.[9] Giant sturgeon are endangered, other sturgeon species are depleted, and many other species are either depleted or in serious decline. In addition to pollution effects, sturgeon and shad cannot run upstream to breed because of damming of the big rivers that drain into the sea.

Tanker and operational accidents have been sources of oil pollution (about 45,000 tons annually), as has the direct dumping of solid waste into the sea or onto wetlands. The pollution from rapid oil industry development (1,500 tankers and tens of thousands of other cargo boats carrying 32 million tons of oil pass through the Bosporous Straits in each direction annually), sedimentation, beach erosion, and the overall absence of coastal zone conservation are also strongly felt. About 82 million tons of hazardous and explosive materials also pass through the strait each year (Moore 2000).

International Environmental Law Response

The Black Sea Environmental Programme (BSEP), developed under the auspices of UNEP and the Global Environmental Facility (GEF), is one response to the sea's degradation. The program was established in the early nineties and modeled on the 1976 Barcelona Convention for the Mediterranean Sea. Bulgaria, Georgia, Romania, the Russian Federation, Ukraine, and Turkey signed the Convention for the Protection of the Black Sea Against Pollution in April 1992 in Bucharest, and it was rapidly ratified. The Ministerial Declaration on the Protection of the Black Sea followed; it was signed in April 1993 in Odessa. Reflecting the thrust of the Agenda for the Twenty-first Century (Agenda 21) adopted at the Rio Summit in 1992, it declared among other goals "protection, preservation and, where necessary, rehabilitation of the marine environment and the sustainable management of the Black Sea." Furthermore, countries were to elaborate and implement national integrated management policies, including legislative measures and economic instruments, in order to ensure sustainable development. The declaration encourages public participation (including by NGOs), the precautionary principle, use of economic incentives to promote environmental protection, environmental impact assessment, environmental accounting, and coordination of regional activities.

The Bucharest Convention entered into force on 15 January 1994. Other affiliate international legal instruments that make up the BSEP regime include the Protocol on Protection of the Black Sea Marine Environment Against Pollution from Land-Based Sources (21 April 1992), the Protocol on Co-operation in Combating Pollution of the Black Sea Marine Environment by Oil and Other Harmful Substances in Emergency Situations (21 April 1992), and the Protocol on the Protection of the Black Sea Marine Environment Against Pollution by Dumping (not yet in force).

Initially GEF, the European Union, Austria, Canada, Japan, the Netherlands, Norway, and Switzerland provided funding. Funding also comes from UNEP and is to be contributed by the member countries.[10] The Program Coordination Unit of the BSEP was located in Istanbul. In spring 1998 it was replaced by the Project Implementation Unit, comanaged by the U.N. Development Programme, with the hope that it becomes a precursor to a secretariat to be financed by the member countries.

The regime that evolved was noteworthy for at least two reasons. First, it came into being very quickly. Nation-states that were on opposite sides in the Cold War developed ways (theoretically, at least) to cooperate a few short years after Turkey and the former Soviet Union states developed formal relations. Second, rather than easing into the world of international environmental law, the parties became the first to adopt a regional seas agreement built on the principles of Rio.

In 1993 three objectives of the BSEP were highlighted: improve the capacity of Black Sea countries to assess and manage the environment, support the development and implementation of new environmental policies and law, and promote sound environmental investments. Activity centers to be hosted by the individual Black Sea countries were created.[11]

In October 1996 the Black Sea border countries signed the Strategic Action Plan (BSEP 1996). Its preamble reaffirms the commitment of the member states to the rehabilitation and protection of the Black Sea and the sustainable development of its resources. One element of the short plan, which the BSEP describes as a flexible document responsive to contingencies, sets out principles seen as the basis for international cooperation. In addition to reaffirming ideas in the 1993 Ministerial Declaration, it emphasizes regional cooperative and coordinated activity and enhanced transparency through rights of access to information and improved public awareness.[12]

Assessment: Physical Parameters

There is some scientific debate about several aspects of the Black Sea's environmental status, including the extent of the human contribution to the hydrogen sulfide cycles and the amenability to midscale interventions. Another area of scientific uncertainty is the discharge of chemical and microbiological contamination in coastal and marine areas. Only in recent years has there been movement toward standardization of the protocols and methodologies for scientific investigation, even within the participating nations (Sampson 1995).

As of 1996, a BSEP report could provide a somewhat more encouraging perspective of the physical status of the sea. The *Black Sea Transboundary Diagnostic Analysis* "clearly demonstrates that the Black Sea environment can still be restored and protected." The Strategic Action Plan of 1996 concluded that "environmental monitoring conducted over the past 4–5 years . . . reflects perceptible and continued improvements in the state of some localized components of the Black Sea ecosystem." Furthermore, there are reports that *Mnemiopsis,* although still a plague, is in decline and that water quality along the Turkish coast is within national limits, not a "desperate situation" (Ozturk and Tanik 1999, 172). Improvements have not been linked explicitly to international environmental law, however, and may be a result of other factors, such as the extraordinary economic downturn in the former Soviet Union after the collapse of communism.

Assessment: The Contribution of International Environmental Law

The program has had serious problems with implementation, including very slow realization of the commitment to modest funding by the member states. At his departure, its first head gave the program an extraordinarily candid evaluation: "The truth . . . is that very little has been done to fulfill the initial commitment made to the people of the Black Sea countries when their six legislative assemblies ratified the convention in 1993. . . . decisions taken through democratic processes have been disregarded and political momentum has been lost. This scenario is a depressing one" (UNDP et al. 1998).

Some factors linked to successful implementation of international environmental law are clearly present in the Black Sea regime, not only in relationship to the specific entity but also in the larger context of institutional initiatives. The analysis of other elements suggests, at least for now, slow movement toward international water cooperation in the sea. "BSEP appears to have contributed little to overall regional awareness about environmental problems or their solutions, except for people who have participated directly in the BSEP education and publicity efforts" (Sampson 1999, 76).

Major barriers to cooperation include the emergence of two types of inward-looking movements in the region, nationalism and religious fundamentalism. Also, the infrastructure for communicating across national boundaries, even when the intention is established, is very limited (Sampson 1995). Furthermore, economic conditions hinder the realization of the full potentials of the scientific and environmental communities in the former Soviet states. A leading example is Romania, where economic problems combined with concerns over sovereignty threaten to make the Black Sea program largely a "dead letter" (Oldson 1997, 519). Finally, as in many other regional treaties, dispute resolution methods are not developed.[13]

There are some other countervailing forces in the region that make prospects for the refinement and implementation of new regimes more promising. Among them are:

1. Scientific findings on the nature and scope of the environmental challenge: The search for better data, more precise models, better equipment to test models, and basic science to underpin the models is an opportunity for cooperation recognized by most actual and potential participants in the Black Sea processes. The region has a rich resource of scientific expertise. Besides, the international community, environmentally progressive nation-states, and U.N. organizations have targeted the Black Sea as an area deserving major contributions of technical expertise and funding.

2. Shared perspectives: The Black Sea has had immense historical importance for each of the riparians. Common understandings on the environmental challenge may be more readily achieved than on other matters of international policy, on which cultural, ethnic, and religious differences make consensus difficult. Also, there is increasing interest, shared by each of the riparians, in economic development. The relative success of the Black Sea Economic Program, a parallel regional effort, demonstrates that trade and commerce may be effective vehicles for promoting cooperation.

3. Further, the Black Sea regime, at least de jure, recognizes new principles of international environmental law. Numerous new NGOs are rapidly appearing in the region. Removing obstacles to their participation in decision making may be an effective means for reaching environmental goals, more so than creating official new government structures (Laurence D. Mee in UNDP et al. 1998) or adopting additional agreements. Under evolving national and transboundary legal systems, this may mean granting legal standing to parties, individuals, and NGOs not formerly recognized in the decision-making structures of some of the member-states.[14]

4. Epistemic communities may further develop. Epistemic communities are communities without borders—of scientists, lawyers, engineers, or other specialists. Their members share core beliefs and understandings and have strong alignments with objectives that transcend

their affiliation with a political jurisdiction or position (Haas 1990). In the Black Sea region, at least for certain goals, they may play somewhat the same function as they did in the early years of the Mediterranean Action Plan. They may demonstrate how to cooperate on international matters. They may create new understandings of appropriate responses to environmental degradation, making policy choices a bit easier for government officials. They may give governments supporting rationales to take difficult, even unpopular, steps to control pollution. They may attract much-needed funding as outside groups become impressed with regional cooperation. They may offer a means for transferring technology.

The fragility or strength of the BSEP depends in significant part on the commitment of leaders in the area. These leaders are involved in a two-level game: one level is international, the other domestic. At home, there are several constraints on a leader's ability to cooperate across national boundaries. The economic and political challenges in the Black Sea region, with problems of currency devaluation, ethnic conflicts, and priority setting, serve as significant obstacles to an official's attention to water issues. So too does the extreme weakness of the environmental sector in each of the Black Sea governments (Mee in UNDP et al. 1998, ii). Significantly, even some MARPOL provisions and those of other agreements related to oil pollution management have not been implemented in the past several years. With the death of President Turgut Ozal of Turkey, there remained little political push for Black Sea environmental cooperation (Sampson 1999); however, support of environmental protection is now attractive in the region, both to please emerging green domestic constituencies and for extraregional motives, such as to gain admission to the European Union and access to the GEF and other international environmental funds.

Conclusions

BSEP incorporates, at least at a rhetorical level, elements of a new understanding of transboundary interaction structured by international environmental law. It institutionalizes procedures that can be the core of productive linkages among Black Sea nations, the type of ongoing iteration essential to international cooperation. International law has made a preliminary modest contribution to improving the region's environmental quality. Sound environmental management of the Black Sea, however, remains an immense challenge. It was so under previous regimes, and there are many reasons to hold only limited expectations about major shifts under the embryonic international environmental law.

The BSEP has not had ongoing strong NGO involvement from the parties themselves, and the dispute resolution process has not been developed. The regime has made environmental impact assessment a centerpiece as a legal goal, but not in practice. Means of promoting compliance are nicely stated, but they have not been sufficiently implemented. Furthermore, although entry into the agreement was made easy in part through the flexibility built into instruments, there is little political commitment to even the limited steps necessary to make a difference on the ground. Additionally, the sometimes embryonic political and legal systems of the parties have made it difficult to monitor actual commitment. Finally, funding has been miserably inadequate, and an effective secretariat has not yet evolved.

On the positive side, BSEP's goal-setting has generally benefited from agreement on the appropriate science to aid in decision making. There is at least a commitment to the generation of relevant scientific information through cooperative means, and a community of Black Sea scientists has at times been useful. Environmental impact assessment and NGO involvement are formally provided for, giving the regime some potential if other factors can be addressed. External interest in the region, both for environmental and sociopolitical reasons, also suggests that funding may become available.

LAND: THE BASEL CONVENTION

The Basel Convention on the Control of Transboundary Movements of Hazardous Wastes and Their Disposal is the major legal response of the international community to the problems caused by the annual worldwide production of 400 million tons of wastes that are toxic, poisonous, explosive, corrosive, flammable, ecotoxic, or infectious. Improper disposal results in soil contamination, underground water degradation from leachate and runoff, and destruction of habitat for fish and animals. It is also linked to increased cancer and birth defects (Abrams 1990). Management problems result in large part from the extraordinary gap in the cost of disposal in developed and developing countries and the serious challenges involved in monitoring movement of dangerous wastes.

Prior to Basel, there were many scandalous stories of developed countries' attempts to get rid of hazardous waste at the expense of developing nations. The Koko case is one such episode. In 1988 a farm in Koko, a small town in Nigeria, was used as the dumping ground for 18,000 drums of waste, including polychlorinated biphenyls (PCBs), asbestos, and perhaps dioxin, from Italy. The waste arrived, as wastes had been arriving in other parts of Africa from the United States, France, and other developed nations, based on an agreement with an unscrupulous businessman. For about $100 per month he would store the materials on one of his commercial properties. The barrels were labeled as substances "relating to the building trade, and as residual and allied chemicals."

An official government response to the illegal dumping followed the publication of an article in a Lagos newspaper based on a tip by Nigerian students. The resulting cleanup led to the hospitalization of many workers, and one report linked the toxicity at the dumpsite to a cluster of premature births (Nigeria-Italy Waste Trade n.d.).

To communicate their outrage and to pressure the Italians to remove the waste, the Nigerians seized control of an Italian ship. The international media also placed pressure on Italy to respond. The Italians then removed the waste from Nigeria. Signifying international censure, one waste-laden ship was denied entry into the United States and a number of European ports. It took over a year for the Italians, facing protests at home over water contamination linked to disposal of the materials, to find resting grounds for all of the materials.

To prevent the human and environmental toll associated with the Koko case and others, Nigeria banned the importation of hazardous waste. Cameroon did the same. In both countries the penalty for violating this ban is death (Wallace 1994; Ovink 1995 as cited in Hunter, Salzman, and Zaelke 1998, 860).

Shortly before the Koko contamination, a shipload of hazardous waste from the United States was caught in a similar international scandal. The *Khian Sea* left port with 15,000 tons of incinerator ash containing low concentrations of heavy metals from Philadelphia. After being denied permission to dump its cargo in the Bahamas, the ship moved on to Haiti. The captain told Haitian authorities that the cargo was fertilizer ash and received permission to unload. One fifth of the cargo had been put ashore before the Haitians learned what the material was. Compelled to leave, the ship tried various other ports over an eighteen-month period but was unable to gain admission. Somewhere along the way, the cargo was illegally dumped, and the ship arrived in Singapore unburdened (*International Environment Reporter,* 14 October 1987, 504; Allen 1995; Gudofsky 1998).

Other cases involve developed nations as victims. In 1983, 41 barrels of topsoil contaminated with dioxin were found in a barn in northern France. They were products of a notorious chemical plant explosion that had occurred in Seveso, Italy, years earlier, materials transported without notice across European national boundaries (Abrams 1990).

The bizarre world of hazardous waste pollution results from a number of factors. Few sites are capable of proper disposal of hazardous waste, as political opposition holds up their construction. Additionally, the nature of the facilities needed makes sanctioned disposal very expensive. Most significant, the opportunities for immense profit are considerable, as the cost of disposal in industrialized nations can be 50 times that in developing nations (Hunter, Salzman, and Zaelke 1998, 858). Disposal cost in Africa in the eighties averaged between $2.50 and $50 per ton; in OECD (Organization for Economic Cooperation and Development) countries it ranged up to $2,000 per ton (Krueger 1998; Tolba and Rummel-Bulska 1998). In 1988 Guinea-Bissau was offered $600 million, an amount five times that nation's gross national product, to accept private companies' toxic wastes from Europe and the United States.

International Environmental Law Response

In 1982 UNEP addressed the international transportation and disposal of toxic wastes after a group of environmental experts met in Montevideo, Paraguay. In 1985 it issued the Cairo Guidelines and Principles for the Environmentally Sound Management of Hazardous Wastes (Basic Document 5.3). Two years later UNEP established a draft Convention on the Transboundary Shipment of Hazardous Waste and created an ad hoc working group composed of legal and technical specialists. The group analyzed several UNEP drafts and ultimately developed a final recommendation for the Basel Convention. It needed to address both the strong preference by developing countries for a ban on hazardous waste transfers from the north to the south and the OECD regulatory orientation favoring notification and consent. After two years of debate, 34 nations signed the Basel Convention on 22 March 1989. It entered into force 5 May 1992. By 2002 the number of parties to the convention had reached 150.

The Basel Convention regulates the transport and disposal of hazardous and other wastes and seeks to make transport a matter of public record. "Hazardous" is defined by the originating, receiving, and transit countries. The goal is to protect human health and the environment from the dangers of such wastes. The principle underlying the convention is that wastes should be disposed of in the state where they were generated. Basel ultimately seeks to have parties take appropriate measures to ensure that the generation of hazardous and other waste is reduced to a minimum. The convention restates the right of every state to ban the entry or disposal of foreign hazardous wastes in its territory [article 4(1)], either by reference to categories set out in an annex (1), unless they do not possess the characteristics listed in another annex (3), or if so classified by national legislation (article 1). Exports to Antarctica are prohibited (article 4.6).

Many obligations also apply to "other wastes," listed in annex 2, which encompasses household wastes or residue from the incineration of such wastes (article 1). Radioactive wastes and wastes discharged from the normal operation of ships so long as they are regulated by other international instruments are not covered by Basel. Subsequent to a period of controversy and confusion, the fourth Conference of the Parties (COP-4), in 1998, clarified somewhat which wastes are covered by the convention so that recyclable materials including scrap paper and scrap metal are not wastes under Basel.

Other annexes (8 and 9) now list waste by classification. Countries exercising their right to prohibit the import of hazardous wastes are to inform the other parties and to provide information on any national legislation pertaining to the definition of hazardous wastes (article 3). Each party must prohibit the export of such wastes to any state that has notified the party of its prohibition (article 4). Under Basel, "disposal" is broadly defined to include not only disposal but also recovery and recycling. Countries may enter regional agreements with nonparty countries. Thus, for example, the United States, although not a party to the treaty, can continue to trade in recyclable wastes with OECD countries.

Any waste transported or disposed of in contravention of the convention is considered an illegal traffic and can be made a criminal offense [articles 4(3), 4(4), and 9], although the convention does not contain enforcement provisions and relies on parties to take domestic measures. Movement of waste is permitted only if the generating state does not have the technical capacity or sites suitable for its disposal or if the importing state needs the waste as raw material for industries engaged in recycling or recovery [article 4(9)]. Legal movements of waste must be tracked by a written document.

A duty to reimport applies when a movement of hazardous waste has been consented to but "cannot be completed in accordance with the terms of the contract" (article 8). Article 11 allows transfer of wastes to parties and nonparties where movements are subject to another appropriate bilateral, multilateral, or regional agreement.

The Conference of the Parties reviews implementation of the agreement and promotes harmonization of waste management policies (article 15). Dispute resolution takes place through any means the parties choose. The convention allows the parties to agree to submit their disputes to the International Court of Justice or to arbitration as provided in annex 6 (article 20).

Article 15 provides for representation: "The United Nations, its specialized agencies, and States not party to the Convention, may be observers at meetings of the Conference of the Parties. Other national, international, governmental, or non-governmental organizations that are qualified in fields relating to hazardous wastes may be admitted as observers after informing the Secretariat, unless at least one-third of the parties present objects."

The convention specifies a preference that amendments be adopted by a consensus at a meeting of the Conference of the parties, but if that should prove elusive, amendments may be adopted by a three-fourths majority of the parties present and voting (article 17). A further exception is that adoption may also be achieved by two thirds of the parties to the protocol to be amended who are present and voting [article 17(4)]. After adoption, amendments must be ratified by a specified proportion (three fourths or two thirds, respectively) of the parties who voted to subject themselves to its provisions.

Decision 3/1 is the most controversial amendment that emerged from the decision at COP-3 to ban hazardous waste exports for final disposal from OECD, the European Community, and Liechtenstein (annex 7 countries) to nonannex 7 countries. That decision would also ban exports intended for recovery and recycling. To enter into force, the 1995 amendment must be ratified by the 62 parties present at the time of its adoption. Initial movement was slow, with only 8 countries ratifying in the first three years. The Protocol on Liability and Compensation for Damage Resulting from Transboundary Movements of Hazardous Waste and Their Disposal was adopted by the parties at COP-5 in Basel in December 1999. At that time, the ministers declared minimizing hazardous wastes a major focus for the decade 2000–2010.

Assessment: Physical Parameters

The actual effects of Basel on the movement of hazardous waste are difficult to ascertain. A main source of information is the UNEP Secretariat of the Basel Convention, which reports on data supplied by the parties. The Secretariat cautions that "due to the differences in national definitions of hazardous wastes, variations in national reporting and the difficulties in comparing the quality and availability of accurate data, figures presented are not directly comparable" (Basel Convention 1998). For the reporting year 1998, the Secretariat noted that of the 74 parties that provided information, 47 supplied data on the export of hazardous and other wastes, 20 reported that no export took place from their countries, and 23 parties gave figures for import of wastes. Total wastes exported were 4,114,722 metric tons; the import figure was 3,816,232 metric tons. The export data indicate that of the wastes that moved worldwide, 10 percent went for disposal and 83 percent were recycled.[15]

Assessment: The Contribution of International Environmental Law

Assessment of Basel has been mixed, although recent activities of the Conference of the parties generally have been supported.

On the negative side, in a thorough and balanced assessment, Gudofsky (1998, 285) concludes that although Basel is "the backbone of the international waste regime. . . . The Parties . . . have been gradually moving away from developing a unified system for controlling wastes and have instead bifurcated the system by creating one group of countries . . . that are entirely inaccessible to another group." Further, insufficient attention has been paid to recycling and recovery. In general, the convention has been widely criticized for being "curiously ambivalent on the question of distinguishing hazardous wastes that were being exported for purposes of final disposal (e.g., landfill or injection) from those that were destined for reclamation, recycling or other methods of resource recovery" (O'Reilly and Cuzze 1997, 515). Some parties recognized potential benefits of recycling, others predicted "sham recycling."

The convention fails to address the principle of liability both with regard to actors (generator, exporter, receiver) and with regard to type (fault-based or strict liability) (Hackett 1990; Schneider 1996; and Hunter, Salzman, and Zaelke 1998). Parties supposedly were to cooperate to develop a protocol to establish rules and procedures for liability and for damages arising from the transboundary movement of hazardous wastes (article 12); however, Basel does not comprehensively answer the question of who should pay for damages (Hackett 1990). Critics question the wisdom of imposing fault on nation-states rather than on multinational corporations that violate the convention. A more effective regime would focus on building capacity to help all countries to manage and dispose of wastes safely rather than on the relatively rare sensational incidence of illegal transboundary transport (Hunter, Salzman, and Zaelke 1998). Furthermore, the Secretariat based in Geneva has limited supervisory functions and is underfunded (Krueger 1998), and the Trust Fund established in 1992 suffers from late and missing payments.

Moreover, aspects of the convention counter the overall objectives of the agreement. For example, the preamble includes vague language: "Convinced that hazardous wastes and other wastes should, as far as is compatible with environmentally sound and efficient management, be disposed of in the State where they are generated" and "Taking into account also the limited capabilities of the developing countries to manage hazardous wastes and other wastes." Similar phrases appear throughout the agreement: "take such steps as are necessary" [4(2)(c)], "to the maximum consistent with the environmentally sound and efficient management of such wastes" [4(2)(d)], "shall take appropriate legal, administrative and other measures" [4(4)], "in accordance with other criteria to be decided by the Parties" [4(9)(c)]. The definition of hazardous waste itself is problematic since the convention allows nation-state variability in definition.

The convention's early versions were laden with such ambiguities and loopholes. The classification scheme for wastes is susceptible to divergent interpretation and engenders confusion (Schneider 1996, 268), although at COP-4 a list drawn up by a technical working group was accepted. There is insufficient involvement of NGOs (Schneider 1996) and no executive body for enforcement (Jaffe 1995). Cusack (1990, 420) has been wide-ranging in criticism: "The Basel Convention has legitimized the international toxic waste game and proclaimed industrial nations the winners. . . . Supporters . . . are not challenging the fundamental bipolar economic inequities that force Third World nations to accept shipment of toxic wastes."

Furthermore, the ban under decision 3/1 does not reflect a true consensus among developing countries. It unreasonably assumes that all non-OECD countries are and will remain incapable of processing recyclable wastes (Grout 1999), leading some countries and analysts to conclude that needy economies will be deprived of the benefits of receiving imported wastes that can be economically and safely recycled (Waugh 2000). These countries are joined here by some environmentalists who bemoan the possible decline in recycling, including forcing the use of virgin materials. Business interests also conclude that revisions are necessary to make clear which are "benign wastes" that can be exported (O'Reilly and Cuzze 1997). Finally, a ban on trade in recyclable wastes may violate important trade principles (Grout 1999) as a nonenvironmentally based barrier.

On the positive side, "It is generally accepted that the Basel Convention has helped to eliminate the most harmful of international hazardous waste transfers destined for final disposal " and some environmentalists characterize the "Basel Ban" as the most significant environmental achievement since the Rio Earth Summit in 1992 (Krueger 1998). There now is international consensus that rich countries should not send hazardous wastes to poorer countries for final disposal.

Other assessments of Basel praise the scope of its objectives. Because its scale includes a large number of countries, world economic forces and political pressures favor compliance. Also, the regime establishes a framework for a common definition for hazardous waste. Compliance with the tracking system for waste meeting the Basel definition is enforceable under domestic law of the party in which the international transportation of hazardous waste was instigated. For example, individuals illegally exporting hazardous waste from the United States to another country are subject to U.S. criminal law. Under this system two men who knowingly exported hazardous waste from the United States to Pakistan without obtaining the required consent from the importing country were convicted by a U.S. federal jury for violations of the U.S. Resource Conservation and Recovery Act (Henry Weinstein 1993). This enforcement system was employed and convictions achieved even though the United States is not a party to the agreement.

Tolba and Rummel-Bulska (1998, 116), active leaders in the Basel negotiations, conclude: "We believe a reasonable goal was achieved: a flexible treaty that can be amended or adjusted in view of new facts or new information."

"Positive," of course, is a relative term. The Secretariat reported in October 1999 on the "growing commitment of the Parties to report on articles 13 and 16 of the Convention." The evidence was the 63 responses received by late 1999 to a 1997 questionnaire seeking information on, among other items, transboundary movements, measures for implementation of Basel, and sources of advice and expertise. The number of responses grew to 74 parties for 1998; thus, just over half of the total number of parties met the modest commitment of reporting.

Conclusions

By regulating the transport of hazardous waste and requiring prior informed consent from importing nations, the Basel Convention facilitates the collection of information on the location of dangerous material. Although it does not reflect a true consensus and it contains a number of ambiguities, Basel provides an increasingly standardized definition of hazardous waste and a clear mechanism for determining enforcement jurisdiction. Its Secretariat has performed its modest obligations relatively effectively. The convention itself is designed to allow ease of entry. More difficult issues are subject to later amendments by parties who find its goals palatable. Nongovernmental organizations have not been uniformly pleased with Basel's progress, but they have de jure been given rights as observers. The Basel Convention does not yet, however, protect developing countries from the risk of becoming colonized by other people's hazardous waste. Nor does it substantially alter the economic incentives that make such a scenario attractive to unscrupulous individuals. It does not fully address the polluter-pays principle. Nor does it utilize the most advanced understandings of the law's compliance-promoting potential.

Despite its initial enthusiasm and its early signing of the Basel Convention, as of December 2001 the United States has not yet enacted domestic implementing legislation. Here as in other areas of international law, the question arises whether a treaty bypassed by the world's leading power can be effective. In the case of Basel, considerations are unique and countervailing. Because the United States is responsible for such a large proportion of the world's hazardous waste [e.g., in 1995 it produced 279 million tons of hazardous waste and exported 226,000 tons of it (U.S. EPA 1998)], its failure to ratify the Basel Convention can undermine the treaty's potential to operate effectively. In any event, refusal to participate weakens the ability of the United States to influence international environmental law on waste transport.

The absence of the United States may also reduce the amount of hazardous waste that can be legally transported across national boundaries. Recall that parties to the Basel Convention are prohibited from transporting hazardous waste to or from nonparties unless a separate agreement with the nonparty has been made. Such agreements must be compatible with the Basel agreement if they predate Basel, or they must require procedures that are more stringent than Basel if they postdate Basel. Parties are required to notify the Basel Secretariat of the existence of agreements between parties and nonparties. Where agreements or arrangements have not been made, the nonparty status of the United States prevents the possibility of legal transport of hazardous waste between the United States and other nations. The United States has entered into a multilateral agreement among OECD countries regarding recyclable wastes and bilateral agreements with Canada, Mexico, Malaysia, and Costa Rica (U.S. EPA 1998).[16]

Incentives for U.S. ratification are limited. Only 1 percent of U.S. hazardous waste is exported, and 95 percent of that 1 percent goes to Canada and Mexico. Ratification may make the United States more susceptible to private legal actions both by domestic parties and foreign plaintiffs under the Alien Tort Statute (Rogus 1996). Changes in domestic law needed prior to ratification (including in the U.S. Resource Conservation and Recovery Act) are complex and cumbersome.

GENERAL ENVIRONMENTAL PROTECTION AND ENFORCEMENT: THE NORTH AMERICAN AGREEMENT ON ENVIRONMENTAL COOPERATION

Pressure groups, including environmental NGOs, linked the international trade of goods and services to environmental degradation, if not disaster, during negotiations for the North American Free Trade Agreement (NAFTA) among Canada, Mexico, and the United States. In response to these concerns, the North American Agreement on Environmental Cooperation, or the Environmental Side Agreement, was entered at the same time as NAFTA (DiMento and Doughman 1998).

NAFTA and the Environmental Side Agreement were developed in the face of growing concern about the effects on the environment of liberalized international trade. One fear was that environmentally insensitive growth would become unstoppable, especially though not exclusively at national borders. A second worry was that green firms would be less competitive than nonconcerned businesses, thereby weakening incentives for compliance. Also, national laws and policies would be compromised by trade liberalization, a fear exacerbated by the 1991 ruling by the GATT dispute-resolution panel on the tuna and dolphin case. The panel declared that the U.S. Marine Mammal Protection Act, intended to protect dolphins from harm from certain kinds of nets used in tuna fishing, constituted an unacceptable barrier against Mexican trade. In addition, trade liberalization raised the possibility that polluting industries would flee jurisdictions with high environmental standards for lax jurisdictions, resulting in a net increase in pollution from a global perspective and greater unemployment in communities intent on protecting air, water, and soil from contamination.

Despite controversy, negotiations for NAFTA were completed in August 1992. Signed four months later, NAFTA created the world's largest free trade zone, containing 370 million people and more than $6.5 trillion in goods and services each year.[17] Reflecting political pressures, NAFTA was the first trade agreement to address the environment directly. It contains provisions governing environment and investment [articles 1114 and 2101(3)], food and safety standards (chapter 7), and other environmental standards (chapter 9). It also lists three international environmental agreements that take precedence over NAFTA, particularly in regard to dispute resolution procedures (article 104). These are the Montreal Protocol, the Convention on International Trade in Endangered Species, and the Basel Convention on Hazardous Wastes.

Many influential environmental groups felt that NAFTA had not adequately addressed environmental issues.[18] In addition, the processes set up under NAFTA were seen as insufficiently transparent and representative and, therefore, undemocratic (Greenpeace 1993). Some environmentalists began shifting focus to negotiations for the side agreement, seeing it as a vehicle to remedy some of NAFTA's omissions.

International Environmental Law Response

William Clinton, as the U.S. president-elect, had promised to negotiate and sign the environmental (and a labor) side agreement before the promulgation of NAFTA (Winham 1994). With divided environmental group support, Canada, the United States, and Mexico signed the NAFTA Environmental Side Agreement on 13 September 1993. Subsequently, NAFTA and the side agreements were ratified and promulgated by the legislatures of the parties.

The objectives of the environmental agreement are general and broad and are carried out through several distinct programs. The goals are to foster protection and improvement of the environment, to promote sustainable development based on cooperation and mutually supportive environmental and economic policies, and to increase cooperation to better conserve, protect, and enhance the environment. To further those objectives, the Environmental Side Agreement establishes the Commission for Environmental Cooperation (CEC), composed of a council, the Joint Public Advisory Committee (JPAC), and the Secretariat. The CEC Council consists of one cabinet-level (or equivalent) representative from each party. The JPAC is responsible for facilitating public participation and communication regarding CEC activities. It consists of fifteen presidential appointees, five from each party. The Secretariat is the administrative arm of the CEC. It is responsible for implementing the agreement, including undertaking studies and assessments and overseeing the consideration of submissions (as specified in articles 14 and 15) asserting that a party "is failing to effectively enforce its environmental law." Such submissions are a form of complaint made by private citizens and NGOs. The most severe penalty under this NAFTA procedure, if such an assertion is substantiated, is release of a factual record to the public. "Factual record" is not defined in the agreement, but in practice it has contained a summary of the submission, a summary of the challenged party's response, a summary "of all other relevant factual information," and annexes that give a chronology of the case and maps of the area involved. Part 5 of the side agreement provides for a party to allege that there has been a persistent pattern of failure by another party to enforce its environmental law effectively. Under it, a party could be fined and ultimately denied NAFTA free trade privileges up to the amount of the unpaid fine.

Assessment: Physical Parameters

"Many environmental indicators in the North American region are worsening, and these alarming trends are particularly evident at the U.S.-Mexico border, an area that figured prominently in the political debate leading to NAFTA's adoption," summarized a leading student of NAFTA institutions. Mumme noted, however, that the chain of causation is not easily tied to NAFTA's Environmental Side Agreement. The situation may be due more to economic and social trends already at work in 1994. NAFTA, he notes, strengthened governmental commitments to environmental protection within the North American region, "commitments that otherwise might not have been attainable" (Mumme and Sprouse 1999).

An analysis of physical effects of an international instrument as general and as complex as the side agreement must rely on approximations and models and relationships that can be described in theory but not empirically by means of convincing statistics. Data can be compiled, but they say very little about the influence of an agreement that is not specific to a particular place or physical resource. Some information, however, is available. The CEC did conclude that pollution releases from industrial sites in Canada and the United States increased 1.2 percent from 1995 to 1997, reversing progress seen in earlier years. Direct releases decreased 9 percent, but transfers of toxic pollutants to offsite facilities for treatment rose 27 percent. (Braninga 2000). Such data, however, are virtually irrelevant to the analysis of the side agreement's effects.

The CEC's own attempt to address the impact of NAFTA on environmental parameters resulted in a highly intricate description of possible relationships in an early report and a set of evaluative papers in 2000. These papers addressed fisheries, the forestry sector (including the export of finished wood products), North American air pollution, transboundary shipment of hazardous wastes, and wastewater treatment. Again, limited access to data and the complexities of the links made for few convincing conclusions. For example, regarding fisheries, one paper (Chomo and Ferrantino 2000) concluded that NAFTA "could have either a positive, negative, or negligible environmental impact." The paper on forests was somewhat more conclusive, reasoning that tariff elimination under NAFTA itself would have a degrading effect on Mexican forests and that the industry likely will oppose national forestry regulations in order to stay competitive. Some commentators concluded that the NAAEC framework was not sufficiently developed to fulfill the side agreement's mandate to protect the North American environment.

The side agreement submission process is likely to have little direct impact on environmental quality. Bugeda (1999) cites as an example the Cozumel case, which involved challenges under article 14 to the construction of a 1,800-foot pier for luxury cruise liners near a coral outcropping off the Yucatan Peninsula. Environmental groups charged that the project was initiated without a declaration of environmental impacts and was located within the limits of a protected coastal zone. The release of the factual record "had very little impact on the environmental community, and none whatsoever on the tourist project in Cozumel."

Assessment: Contribution to International Environmental Law

Assessment of the NAAEC has been mixed, with an initial criticism of its weaknesses evolving into a conclusion that if looked at broadly, its effects on environmental cooperation and ultimately on the North American environment may be positive.

There are several noted weaknesses of the agreement. Its definitions of "environmental law" are problematic; most important, it excludes laws regulating the harvesting of natural resources. The agreement is unclear as to whether strip mining, soil conservation, energy extraction, coastal fishing, and sustainable timber harvesting are included or excluded (Charnovitz 1994b, 267). In general, submissions on timber harvesting have been ruled to be outside CEC purview, but submissions regarding coastal fishing have not been rejected on such grounds.[19] In 1999 a submission against the United States was filed, linking timber harvesting to the death of migratory bird species, and a factual record was ordered.[20]

The term "failure to effectively enforce" has created implementation challenges, and the submission process has generated several citizen initiatives but relatively little action by governments.[21] Applying definitions internationally also raises challenges. A government is the expert on its own law (Charnovitz 1994b). A dispute system based on second-guessing a country's conclusions involves complex matters of judgment. A reasonable exercise of prosecutorial discretion and deference to bona fide resource allocation decisions are allowed under the agreement; however, this deference makes it more difficult to demonstrate noncompliance (280). In practice, the submission process has provoked Mexican, Canadian, and U.S. government opposition in which they deny its applicability to the issues involved.

The general nature of certain duties under the agreement also makes judging implementation difficult. An example is the obligation to "strengthen cooperation on the development and continuing improvement of environmental laws and regulations." Other duties are discretionary: the agreement lists eighteen issues for which the council may consider and develop recommendations (Charnovitz 1994b, 263). Furthermore, the principles laid out in the preamble to the agreement conflict; they "reflect the intrinsic difficulty of integrating environmental concerns into international trade law" (Johnson and Beaulieu 1996, 141). Vague language such as that indicating that the council "may consider and develop recommendations" also is a barrier to tracking successful implementation.

Because of differences in domestic environmental law in the three countries, determinations of harmonization and of the failure to enforce are problematic matters for international organizations. What is "downward movement" in environmental protection, which the agreement is intended to counter, when the law requires environmental assessment or lays out procedural rules for participation?

Support for development of NAFTA side institutions has been limited. Agency positions within the United States about the value of, and means of implementing, the agreement are ambivalent and mixed. There is strong interest in protecting domestic missions, including the State Department, the United States Trade Representative, and the Environmental Protection Agency. The political side, in efforts both to shield ministers from demanding, overly sensitive or overly powerful positions and to protect against unacceptably independent acts of the CEC Council, has constrained the ministers. Many government officials in fact are not bothered by slow institutional development. Some American environmental and labor groups saw in NAFTA "the first hemispheric link between trade and social policy," but governments, Mexican officials in particular, felt that an American social agenda was forced on them. Greater integration such as in the European Community is not a goal (*Economist*, 18 February 1994).

Experts criticize the absence of independence of the Secretariat (Charnovitz 1994b, 265; Hogenboom 1998, 221), failure to make clear whether the council or Secretariat has a legal personality such as exists for other international organizations, and failure of the organizations to act independently of governments. The provision for citizen submissions diminishes the control that the CEC has over the types of issues that it must address, exposing it to more criticism than if regulation were limited to governments (Mumme and Duncan 1998, 11). Finally, the CEC has no explicit role in the important work of the NAFTA committees on sanitary and phytosanitary measures and standards-related measures.

The enforcement strategies incorporated in the agreement are soft teeth, but opinion differs on whether such soft teeth are necessary for the agreement to be successful. A representative of the World Wildlife Fund concluded that "NAFTA's so-called teeth are small, soft, and way in the back of the mouth," and that is how it should be (*International Environment Reporter*, 16 December 1994, d3). Stone (1999), however, finds the sanctioning mechanism possibly "worse than weak; it may actually provide perverse incentives. A Party that toughens its laws increases the risk of being judged a persistent non-enforcer." The enforcement approach is "more like a tunnel hole . . . than a loop hole" (Lavelle 1994). Further, the NAFTA regime offers a strong defense for enforcement laxity. Mexico can argue that its failure to enforce the law results from a commitment of its limited resources to more pressing problems. Imposing trade sanctions against a country that failed to enforce its environmental laws is a protracted and cumbersome process (Charnovitz 1994b, 270); it takes, at a minimum, 755 days from the initiation of a complaint. Even then the agreement lacks any real commitment to action beyond consultation. Nonetheless and somewhat ironically, both private environmentalists and the JPAC expressed grave disapproval to the CEC of "secret negotiations" in 1999 over possible change in the guidelines for submissions under articles 14 and 15 on enforcement matters. Although flawed, the guidelines could only be made weaker by party intervention without involvement by the NGO communities.[22]

Facing the strong and nontransparent dispute resolution processes under NAFTA proper, the side agreement does not achieve a balance between promoting trade and protecting the environment. The NAFTA processes allow companies to challenge imposition of environmental protections that they interpret as disguised barriers to trade. If such barriers are found by an appointed panel, the government enforcing those rules faces significant costs, payments that would not be likely under domestic laws on infringement of property rights.[23]

By other, positive accounts, the side agreement is an initiative that meets critical criteria for effective international environmental law.

The submission process does focus international attention on the environmental records of the parties. Although specific CEC conclusions may not dramatically affect the outcome of any one case, the attention that Mexico, Canada, and the United States receive regarding enforcement positively influences their decisions regarding environmental protection. Submissions can also foster cooperation among challenging entities. Jointly, Canadian, Mexican, and U.S. NGOs have brought several of the CEC complaints. What's more, although individual challenges may lack merit or be considered trivial (one asserted that the construction of a paved, multipurpose bicycle path through the Jamaica Bay Wildlife Refuge, in Queens, New York, will "destroy critical habitat for endangered and threatened species and . . . result in the taking of migratory birds"), the dozens of actions add up to a report card and force governments to review environmental policy implementation. If the parties make even a modest commitment to continuing implementation, the agreement "will directly and durably undermine the idea that environmental enforcement is a reserved domestic jurisdiction solely with the exclusive sovereignty of the parties. . . . That is not very far from saying that environmental policy is no longer a strictly sovereign matter within the NAFTA area" (Johnson and Beaulieu 1996, 257).

Cooperative activity that the agreement has engendered may be more significant than the submission process. The side agreement has potential to make a contribution to environmental protection in North America by focusing on matters other than immediate physical change or number of cases filed. Its organizations facilitate environmental problem-solving by state and local governments and NGOs, providing them with modest amounts of money, expertise, and organizational capacity. Its institutions allow for a degree of influence for the previously unheard, such as Mexican farmers (Wilder 2000). The CEC has promoted several joint efforts among enforcement officials. For example, it has helped enforcers control illegal big game hunting and game farming, understand better the legal framework for hunting in North America, and find ways to counter import and export fraud and smuggling. The CEC has brought together promoters of organic agriculture to promote sustainable crops, such as shade-grown coffee. The agreement also helps development of epistemic communities that have worked on plans for pervasive environmental contaminants and studies of means to protect ecosystems.

Conclusions

The Environmental Side Agreement, one part of the institutional arrangement that evolved from the NAFTA considerations, has achieved some important goals and retains a promise for achieving greater environmental protection. Several factors help explain its relative success. It has benefited from the parties' agreement on appropriate science to aid in decision making and the generation of scientific information through cooperative efforts. It has allowed for considerable NGO involvement. It has taken environmental impact assessment seriously, both in its constituent actions, including review of a party's activities when challenged under submissions, and also as a fundamental element of the regime's architecture: the environmental impacts of NAFTA, difficult to conceptualize let alone measure, are nonetheless a fundamental spotlight of the CEC's concerns.

To the extent that the agreement has been disappointing, certain factors have been at play. NGO involvement in the public advisory committee has been inefficient at times. The means of promoting compliance that NGOs emphasize are not innovative. Rather, they rely on a cumbersome adversary process with almost meaningless sanctions, themselves highly improbable in most cases. Furthermore, the goals of the agreement, while clear, are imprecise. Although entry into the agreement was not a major obstacle to its creation, the provincial legal system of Canada has made that country's participation less than smooth. Finally, while funding has been adequate to help assemble a relatively effective Secretariat, it is insufficient for achieving the comprehensive goals of the agreement.

GLOBAL CLIMATE CHANGE

Sources of greenhouse gases contributing to global climate change are so numerous that they are virtually uncountable. The effects of global climate change are just beginning to be felt. The causal links among emissions, climate destabilization, and environmental damage have only recently become matters of scientific consensus. Impacts, which include some benefits, are relevant to most peoples of and places in the world. Institutions at several levels of government and many nongovernmental organizations have now recognized climate change as an international problem.

Correlates of climate change, including carbon dioxide and other greenhouse gases (methane, nitrous oxide, CFCs, HFCs, PFCs, sulfur hexafluoride), as well as black carbon soot, have increased substantially in the last hundred years. With these higher concentrations have come reductions in the flow of infrared energy to space. Thus, the earth receives somewhat more energy than it radiates. In the long run, the earth must shed energy into space at the same rate that it absorbs it from the sun.

> Climate change can be driven by an imbalance between the energy the earth receives from the sun, largely as visible light, and the energy it radiates back to space as invisible infrared light. The "greenhouse effect" is caused by the presence in the air of gases and clouds that absorb some of the infrared light flowing upward and radiate it back downward. The warming influence of this re-radiated energy is opposed by substances at the surface and in the atmosphere that reflect sunlight directly back into space. These include snow and desert sand, as well as clouds and aerosols. (Jacoby, Prinn, Schmalensee 1998, 56)

Estimating the effects of greenhouse gases on the earth's weather and climate systems is complex, and even now some of the assessment remains controversial. Nonetheless, advances in the science and technology underlying climate models have facilitated consensus building within the scientific community, although more research is needed before regional climatic surprises can be more confidently predicted (IPCC 1995, sec. 2.12). There is still some debate over the extent of change in global temperature that is man-made, but there is no serious doubt that "the balance of evidence suggests a discernible human influence on global climate" (IPCC Working Group I 2001). Knowledge about the dynamics of climate change is converging, although questions about what interventions will be successful over what periods of time generate serious disagreements across scientific disciplines, including in the social sciences, and across parties.

In 1988 the U.N. Environment Programme (UNEP) and the World Meteorological Association (WMO) created the Intergovernmental Panel on Climate Change (IPCC) to assess available information on global climate change.[24] In its Second Assessment Report, released in 1995, the panel concluded that the global average surface temperature had increased 0.3–0.6 degrees Celsius and sea level had risen 10–25 cm in the twentieth century (IPCC 1995, sec. 2.4). The IPCC then predicted that global average temperatures would increase by about 1–3.5 degrees Celsius and sea level would rise by 15–95 cm in the next hundred years. For the next century (from 1990 to 2100) the range of predictions based on recent assessments was: temperature increases of 1.9–2.9 degrees centigrade and sea level rises of 46–58 centimeters. These changes are predicted to increase the number of heat-induced deaths, the spread of disease, threats to food security, water resource problems, and a decline in the viability of important natural ecosystems (IPCC Working Group II 1995). By 2000 in the Third Assessment, the report had changed its prediction to an increase of 1.5–6 degrees centigrade by 2100, almost twice the previous IPCC predictions.

The effects of global climate change may actually be aggravated by progress in the control of other emissions. The *Global Environment Outlook* (1997, 228) reported that if emissions of gases associated with acid rain were reduced while those of greenhouse gases were not, "decreasing sulfur dioxide particle concentrations would 'unmask' the warming caused by greenhouse gases, leading to even greater increases in global temperature affecting both industrial and developing nations." Levels of greenhouse gases in the atmosphere have increased substantially since about A.D. 1750: carbon dioxide from 280 to 360 parts per million by volume, methane from 700 to 1,720 parts per billion by volume, and nitrous oxide from 275 to about 310 parts per billion by volume (IPCC 1995, sec. 2.3).

Developed countries have played the leading role in emissions linked to climate change. A major cause has been the burning of fossil fuels. In 1990 the United States was responsible for roughly a quarter (23 percent) of global carbon emissions each year. The European Union contributed another 13 percent. The total contribution of industrialized nations, which account for one fifth of the world's population, was about two thirds of the total global emissions of carbon dioxide.[25]

U.S. emissions of carbon dioxide per unit of gross national product (GNP) are greater than all other nations, except China if GNP is measured in purchasing power parity exchange rates (World Resources Institute 1996).[26] Many developing countries have rain forests that provide important carbon absorption functions in the global climate system (sometimes called sinks). Nonetheless, developing nations are expected to release a growing proportion of global greenhouse gas emissions in the coming decades. China alone will emit more of these gases by the end of the century than the whole world does today.

The International Environmental Law Response

Over the last few decades scientific and political debate on climate change has influenced and been catalyzed by milestones in the creation of an international legal response. The perception of an emerging scientific consensus on the existence and severity of the problem, the possibility that multinational corporations may profit through the manufacture and sale of innovative clean technology, and the political willingness of some historically egregious emitters of greenhouse gases (e.g., developed countries) to commit to legally binding reductions of emissions have influenced the development of the international response.

In 1979 the concern among scientists regarding global climate change prompted the WMO and other international organizations to sponsor the First World Climate Conference, held in Geneva. Its focus was scientific modeling of the potential effects of global climate change on natural resources (such as agriculture, fishing, forestry), hydrology, and urban life. Conference participants endorsed the "Declaration of the World Climate Conference" (IUCC 1979). The declaration stressed the role of carbon dioxide in global warming and identified the leading causes of its release into the atmosphere (e.g., the use of fossil fuels and deforestation). Furthermore, it asked that governments around the world "prevent potential man-made changes in climate that might be adverse to the well-being of humanity." Conference participants also supported the WMO suggestion to establish a new program for climate research. This suggestion led to the creation of the World Climate Programme.

In 1987 the World Commission on Environment and Development, formed by the United Nations General Assembly, issued *Our Common Future* (the Brundtland Commission Report). In its wake the IPCC built on the World Climate Programme foundation, endorsing sustainable development. Popular concern over global climate change grew from other events, including the success of the Montreal Protocol, the North American heat wave and drought in 1988, press coverage of the concept (*Time* magazine named Earth the "Planet of the Year"), a number of important consensus-building international conferences, the release of the IPCC's First Assessment Report in 1990 (Bodansky 1997a), and, in 1998, the devastation caused by Hurricane Mitch in the Caribbean and Central America (COP-4 1999).

The Second World Climate Conference, held in November 1990 in Geneva, attracted 137 nations and the European Community. It marked the arrival of global climate change on the worldwide political agenda. Participating nations were unable to endorse specific targets for reducing emissions, but they did agree on a number of concepts, including the view that global climate change is a "common concern of humankind" and that equity and the principle of "common but differentiated responsibilities" should figure prominently in future negotiations. They also endorsed the precautionary principle, an evolving notion of preventive policy, and stressed the importance of sustainable development. The "Declaration of the Second World Climate Conference" recorded these and other areas of agreement.

In December 1990 the United Nations General Assembly created the Intergovernmental Negotiating Committee (INC) for the Framework Convention on Climate Change (FCCC). One hundred and fifty nations signed up. The INC was charged with producing a draft consensus document in time for the 1992 Rio Conference. They had less than a year and a half to make their deadline.

Through the five negotiating sessions of the INC, several innovative policy mechanisms were proposed. A carbon tax imposed by each member state, emissions trading, and joint implementation[27] were among the most important and popular, although controversial, ideas. Fairness questions arose over each of these proposals. The negotiations proved too contentious to enable the INC to include firm limits on emissions by the time of the Rio Conference. Most prominently, the United States refused to agree to stabilize emissions at 1990 levels by the year 2000.[28]

Conflicting interpretations of the science underlying global climate change were used to justify changes in the policy stances of the United States and some nation-states.

At Rio the great majority of participating parties adopted the framework. Delegates from 154 nations signed the convention, characterized by a nonbinding aim to reduce greenhouse gases. But the initiative was weakened by the United States position on an abatement target. The framework did include the idea that global climate change was a "common concern of humankind" and that equity, "common but differentiated responsibilities" (article 3.1), sustainable development, and the precautionary principle should characterize any international response.[29]

Common but differentiated responsibilities were assigned according to the leadership principle (article 4.2.a):

Each of these Parties shall adopt national policies and take corresponding measures on the mitigation of climate change, by limiting its anthropogenic emissions of greenhouse gases and protecting and enhancing its greenhouse gas sinks and reservoirs. These policies and measures will demonstrate that developed countries are taking the lead in modifying longer-term trends in anthropogenic emissions consistent with the objective of the Convention.

As international leaders, developed countries (also referred to as annex 1 parties)[30] were expected to provide the "agreed full incremental cost" of developing countries' treaty compliance, including money for the transfer of technology (article 4.3). Furthermore, the signatory nations agreed that annex 1 parties would adopt policies and measures to reduce greenhouse gases "with the aim of returning individually or jointly to their 1990 levels of these anthropogenic emissions of carbon dioxide and other greenhouse gases not controlled by the Montreal Protocol" (article 4.2.b). For developing countries, the FCCC encourages voluntary commitments to reduce greenhouse gas emissions (article 4.2.g).[31]

In addition to the leadership principle, the FCCC holds that response measures "should be cost-effective so as to ensure global benefits at the lowest possible cost" (article 3.3). The framework also recognizes that greenhouse gas emissions can be "addressed" through "the conservation and enhancement, as appropriate, of sinks" (article 4.1.d).[32]

Following the entry into force of the FCCC in May 1994, the Conference of the Parties process organized implementation and negotiation efforts.[33] The first conference (COP-1) was held in Berlin in March 1995. Participants agreed to establish a negotiating process to strengthen the

FCCC commitments to reduce global greenhouse gas emissions for the period following 2000. The document that authorized and defined the purpose of that negotiating process was called the Berlin Mandate. It elaborated policies and measures "to set quantified limitation and reduction objectives within specified time-frames such as 2005, 2010, and 2020." It also required that the negotiations be based on an equitable distribution of burdens and benefits, acknowledge the principle of common but differentiated responsibilities, and refrain from adding any new commitments for parties not included in annex 1. Newly industrializing nations (Brazil, India, and China are among the most significant from the environmental perspective) would continue to be exempt from future, legally binding agreements to reduce emissions.

It was also in 1995 that the IPCC published the Second Assessment Report (SAR). Based on peer review by 2,000 experts, it concluded that the balance of evidence suggests that humans do in fact influence the global climate.

At COP-2 in Geneva, in July 1996, the European Union, as well as a number of its member states, was a strong advocate for the Second Assessment Report and argued that it should be used as the basis for the work of the Berlin Mandate. A number of oil-producing countries (Nigeria, Syria, Kuwait, and the Russian Federation, among others) opposed using the SAR as the basis for policy.

Despite conflicting views, representatives did agree to hold COP-3 in Kyoto, Japan, and to "take note" of a COP-2 summary statement, which they called the Geneva Declaration. Among other things, it encouraged countries to

> recognize and endorse the SAR, . . . noting in particular its findings that the balance of evidence suggests a discernible human influence on climate and that significant reductions in net GHG [greenhouse gas] emissions are possible and feasible; believe that the findings of the SAR indicate dangerous interference with the climate system; . . . recognize the need for continuing IPCC studies to minimize uncertainty; and reaffirm existing commitments to the FCCC, especially of Annex I Parties.

In December 1997 about 10,000 delegates, observers, and media representatives gathered in Kyoto, Japan. The negotiation text prepared under the Berlin Mandate served as the basis for a COP-3 agreement known as the Kyoto Protocol to the Framework Convention on Climate Change. In the 27 articles of the Kyoto Protocol, annex 1 countries agreed to reduce greenhouse gas emissions by "assigned amounts" specific to each country: "The parties included in Annex I shall, individually or jointly, ensure that their aggregate anthropogenic carbon dioxide equivalent emissions . . . do not exceed their assigned amounts . . . with a view to reducing their overall emissions of such gases by at least 5 percent below 1990 levels in the commitment period 2008 to 2012" (article 3.1).

Annex 1 countries are most industrialized and some central European nations. Annex 2 countries do not include the latter. Their "reduction commitments" range from 92 percent (change from the base year) to 108 percent (for Australia). No developing country that signed the FCCC, including China, committed to any assigned amount or quantitative limit on greenhouse gas emissions. The role of developing countries in reducing greenhouse gases is not specified in the Kyoto Protocol other than as potential partners in efforts by annex 1 countries to meet their commitments (articles 4 and 6)[34] and as recipients of technology transfer (article 3.14). Developing countries are mentioned as potentially subject to undesirable side effects that may result from reduction of greenhouse gases. To guard against such outcomes, article 2.3 of the Kyoto Protocol requires annex 1 countries to "strive to implement policies and measures under this Article in such a way as to minimize adverse effects, including the adverse effects of climate change, effects on international trade, and social, environmental and economic impacts on other Parties, especially developing country Parties." Similarly, article 3.14 of the protocol requires annex 1 countries to "strive to implement the commitments mentioned in paragraph 1 above in such a way as to minimize adverse social, environmental and economic impacts on developing country Parties."

After a 1998 meeting in Argentina, the Fifth Conference of the parties took place in Bonn, Germany, in 1999. It addressed details of emissions trading, the clean development mechanism (CDM), joint implementation (the so-called flexibility mechanisms), accounting of greenhouse gas emissions, and development of a "credible" compliance system (FCCC 1999). Emissions trading occurs among industrialized nations. Joint implementation offers emission reduction units for financing projects in other developed countries (such as power plant conversions). The CDM provides credit (certified emissions reductions, or CERs) for financing emission-reducing or emissions-avoiding projects in developing countries.

In November 2000 at COP-6, parties met in The Hague to move the general language of the Kyoto Protocol to specifics on how the goals of the regime would be met. On the one hand, and as characterized by much of the news media, the meetings were a failure (*Corriere della Sera,* 26 November 2000; *International Herald Tribune,* 27 November 2000). The percentage of a nation's goals that could be met by use of the flexibility mechanisms, the extent to which sinks could be counted against emissions limitations, and the nature and application of compliance-promoting mechanisms divided the participants. Blame was assigned variously to the refusal of the Americans to recognize the need for at least some changes in their profligate use of energy, to the inflexibility of the European Union or the failure of their lead nation (France) to comprehend details of the highly technical proposals, to the extreme proposals made by the Saudis for compensating oil-exporting nations that would be economically hurt by decreased reliance on fossil fuels, or to the inertia of less developed nations that continued to insist that they need do little to solve the problem since they do not cause it.

With the inauguration of George W. Bush as president, the United States decided that it was not interested in the Kyoto Protocol because that instrument was "fatally flawed." Nonetheless, when 180 nations met again in Bonn in July 2001 to complete COP-6, 178 of them reached a compromise agreement. Attributed in part to the persistent efforts of the chairman of the conference and the willingness of Europe to make concessions to Japan, the conference agreed to several points. Emission credits will be earned for carbon sinks and can include revegetation and management of grazing lands, forests, and croplands, but sinks can account for only a fraction of a nation's target. Developed parties are to refrain from using nuclear facilities in their CDMs. Rights to emit will be tradable; those nations that do not meet their own targets can purchase rights from those that have exceeded theirs. The flexibility mechanisms all are to be supplemental to domestic actions. The aim of the program to address noncompliance with emission limitations will be to insure "environmental integrity," not "reparation of damage to the environment," a phrase that was deleted from the regime's language. Enforcement was limited to the notion of increasing emission reductions in a later phase for every ton emitted above a party's target. Three new funds were created that will assist developing countries: an adaptation fund, one for assisting with implementing climate-related measures, and a third for the least developed countries. In November 2001 COP-7 met in Marrakech, where steps were taken (based on a compromise between Japan, Russia, Canada, and Australia on one side and the European Union on the other) to develop a compliance-promoting mechanism and to determine credit mechanisms under the flexibility programs.

The climate change regime's fundamental characteristics are summarized in Table 4.1.

TABLE 4.1. Climate Change Regime Summary

- Its ultimate objective is the "stabilization of greenhouse gas concentrations in the atmosphere at a level that would prevent dangerous anthropogenic interference with the climate system. This level should be achieved within a timeframe sufficient to allow ecosystems to adapt naturally to climate change, to ensure that food production is not threatened and to enable economic development to proceed in a sustainable manner."

- The regime is guided by several principles. The *precautionary* principle holds that lack of full scientific certainty should not be used as a rationale to postpone action when there is a threat of serious or irreversible damage. The principle of *common but differentiated responsibilities* looks to the developed countries to take the lead in combating climate change. The principle of *sustainability* focuses on social and economic development and recognizes the need for increased energy consumption in developing countries. Climate change is seen as a *common concern of humankind,* but the *leadership* principle looks to the developed countries as the main source of the problem and of the resources to achieve solutions. The special needs of developing countries are recognized. The extent to which developing-country parties implement their commitments will depend on financial and technical assistance from the developed countries.

- Both developed and developing countries will adopt national programs for mitigating climate change and will develop strategies for adapting to its impacts. They will promote technology transfer and the sustainable management, conservation, and enhancement of greenhouse gas sinks and reservoirs. They will take climate change into account in their relevant social, economic, and environmental policies; cooperate in scientific, technical, and educational matters; and promote education, public awareness, and the exchange of information related to climate change.

- Annex 1 countries commit to adopting policies and measures aimed at returning their greenhouse gas emissions to specified amounts by specified dates between 2008 and 2012. Several states may together adopt a joint emissions target.

- Annex 2 countries will fund the full cost incurred by developing countries for submitting national communications. These cannot be redirected from developmental aid funds. Annex 2 countries will also help finance other projects, and they will promote and finance the transfer of, or access to, environmentally sound technologies, particularly for developing-country parties. Other "flexibility mechanisms" for meeting emissions goals are provided for, as are programs for partially reaching goals through best forestry management practices.

- The supreme body of the climate change regime is the Conference of the Parties (COP). The COP comprises all the states that have ratified the convention. It promotes and reviews implementation of the convention. It will periodically review existing commitments in light of the convention's objectives, new scientific findings, and the effectiveness of national climate change programs. The COP can adopt new commitments through amendments and protocols.

- A secretariat makes arrangements for sessions of the convention bodies, assists parties in implementing their commitments, provides support to ongoing negotiations, and works with the secretariats of other international bodies, notably the Global Environment Facility (GEF) and the Intergovernmental Panel on Climate Change (IPCC).

- Financial mechanisms provide funds on a grant or a concessional basis.

Assessment: Physical Parameters

Most observers conclude that full implementation of the Kyoto Protocol is insufficient to control the negative effects of change. More significant, however, are the data in Table 4.2, demonstrating that critically important nations are not meeting even their 2008–2012 goals under the modest targets, sometimes missing by giant margins. Furthermore, unless the term is to be stripped of any common meaning, the goal of "demonstrable progress" by 2005 is not met. Beyond these official data are numerous scientific observations and anecdotes related to the physical assessment: the disappearance of glaciers, blooming trees and flowers during autumns in the temperate zone, the lengthening of the growing season in some regions, the early arrival of migratory birds.

In areas where there have been emission reductions and deceleration of emissions increases, these have not uniformly been linked to the effect of law. For example, Russia and other former Soviet states experienced an immense economic downturn in the reporting periods.

The relationships between goal-setting for climate change and the actual atmospheric results are so complex that we can draw very few convincing conclusions, but it is clear that progress, if that term can be applied at all, is limited. To be fair, some of the emissions increases were set in place before the regime was conceptualized. Also, changes in the Kyoto part of the regime are possible and are generally predicted; of 75 participants in a high-level meeting on climate change, fewer than 10 saw the Kyoto Protocol as the final agreement on greenhouse gas controls, and most expected a future replacement measure (Pew Center on Global Climate Change n.d.).

**TABLE 4.2. Performance of Kyoto Protocol Participants
Selective Illustrative Data**

Region	Total emissions in tons of CO_2 or CO_2 equivalent in 1990 and in 1998	Percentage change
Asia	from 1,631 million tons to 2,466 million tons	+50.0%
Latin America	from 922 million tons to 1,222 million tons	+32.5%
Australia	from 423,237 Gg to 484,699 Gg	+15.0%
United States	from 4,844 million tons to 5,410 million tons	+11.7%
Japan	from 1,048 million tons to 1,128 million tons	+ 7.6%
Germany	from 1,208,807 Gg to 1,019,745 Gg	−16.0%
European Union	from 3,320 million tons to 3,327 million tons	+ 0.2%
United Kingdom	from 741,484 Gg to 679,850 Gg	− 8.0%
Russia	from 2,299 million tons to 1,415 million tons	−38.5%
Africa	from 599 million tons to 729 million tons	+21.7%
China	from 2,389 million tons to 2,893 million tons	+21.1%

Sources: United Nations FCCC, Subsidiary Body for Implementation, "National Communications from Parties Included in Annex I to the Convention: Green Gas Inventory Data from 1990 to 1998," 11 October 2000, plus newspaper coverage for some developing regions. COP-6 reported that 20 countries reported increases from 1990 through 1998.

Assessment: The Contribution of International Environmental Law

In considering the climate change case, I address a regime that includes the law of the FCCC and of the Kyoto Protocol and its refinements in numerous Conferences of the Parties. The regime has recognized the need in international environmental law for innovations in compliance promotion. These include allowing the involvement of NGOs, providing financial and other economic incentives for participation, emphasizing education, and recognizing that for many nations self-interest ultimately will call for the control and management of global warming. Innovations offered include the flexibility devices. Market mechanisms are generously recognized. Furthermore, the regime attracts the participation of many nations by requiring little of them and provides for their reporting before they need to commit to controls.

The Secretariat has performed in a professional manner, and the Conference of the Parties strategy has been able to respond to some, although not all, challenges to ongoing cooperation. It recognizes the need in international environmental law for indefinite iterations among countries to resolve differences. Overall the COP approach reflects a general ability of even large numbers of nation-states to work over long periods of time toward cooperative outcomes. The regime has credible and impressive links to the evolving scientific information base. There is an appropriate adoption of principles of soft law, including the precautionary principle and that of common but differentiated responsibilities of countries. Definitions are relatively clearly articulated, and a financial mechanism is being provided. Furthermore, the design builds on an evolving acceptance by the private sector of the problem and the alternatives to its control.

Yet there are very large weaknesses. Ease of entry is countered by ease of exit, as the decisions by the United States and later Australia to abandon the Kyoto process demonstrated dramatically. Emission limitations are both unrealistic in the short run and inadequate in the long run. It is not clear what ultimately will be done to enforce obligations, reflecting a desire to avoid difficult choices about what must be done. The same can be said for the consideration of regulatory measures and for what many consider inevitable, a global carbon tax. Some acceptable approaches under the flexibility devices may be in conflict with international trade law.[35]

Most fundamentally, the regime has not evolved to influence sufficiently, through any means, consumption by the billions of sources of greenhouse gases, and it lacks an acceptable position on equity in seeking changes in consumer patterns. Climate change affects people differentially in terms of location, age, and income (Miller, Sethi, and Wolff 2000). Unless there are compensatory strategies generated for the effects of cutbacks on the poor, the very young and very old, and certain geographic groups, opposition to across-the-board requirements to limit consumption could be significant.[36]

CONCLUSION: LESSONS LEARNED, COMPONENTS OF EFFECTIVE LAW

The overall assessments presented in the beginning of this chapter and the five case studies suggest the immense challenges that international environmental law faces. They also reveal the diversity of analyses of the effectiveness of the law. Conclusions about the elements that make an international legal instrument effective reflect both absence of consensus on goals and differences as to the paths or influences to realize them.

There is some convergence, however, on what might be called factors linked to successful environmental law. Of course, effectiveness can mean many things. Most simply, but most ambitiously, it denotes a solution of the environmental problem that brought together the lawmakers. It can focus on changing behavior in relevant ways. It may translate to realizing declared objectives (short of or different from quantified environmental improvements) or to creating correspondence between institutional outputs and expert advice. It can mean improving environmental quality over some hypothetical state of affairs (Levy, Keohane, and Haas 1993).

However defined, the list of factors linked to effectiveness is almost embarrassingly long. Credible analysts do offer the following more manageable list. A fair amount of scientific consensus about the existence and causes of the international problem is fundamental, as is political support within the participating nations. The organizational capabilities of the secretariat and other implementing institutions should be supported. The secretariat needs to have resources and information. The regime institutions must be able to create ad hoc alliances among themselves, and the regime must have an understandable and legitimate dispute resolution process. It should be open to public and scientific input. NGO involvement of a clearly determined type is important. A modest entry commitment should suffice for nation-state participation. A compliance-promoting mechanism, whether a taxing capacity or a subsidy or trust fund, and recognition of varying capacities of developed and developing nations are essential.

The regime should be based on consensual understandings of clear policy objectives. It should ensure to all stakeholders, including NGOs and the public, open communication and access to relevant information. It should establish and strengthen norms for cooperation, implementation, and compliance. These should be promulgated by a legitimate, competent, recognized authority with a willingness and ability to interpret treaty terms and to enforce them. Questions of liability and sanctions should be answered clearly. The institutions involved should foster collaboration and cooperation in agenda setting, negotiating, and bargaining. Public participation should be encouraged not only during policy formation but also in implementation. The treaty regime should embody consensus-building mechanisms and provide for an ongoing forum to manage issues. Finally, the regime's organizations must have sufficient human and financial resources.

5. INTERNATIONAL ENVIRONMENTAL LAW: EXPECTATIONS AND RECOMMENDATIONS

This chapter lays out conditions that are expected in the policy world in which international environmental law evolves. They address the functions of science in the law, the roles of private industry, and perspectives on how to attain desirable international outcomes. The chapter then presents a set of recommendations for improving the effectiveness of the law, recognizing the considerable challenges of fostering change in complex systems.

By several criteria the development of international environmental law has been impressive. Increasingly sophisticated instruments have been drafted. Much of the world community has accepted principles that reflect progressive, scientifically based understandings of environmental protection. Several regimes have focused on ways of successfully implementing principles of protection. Compliance-promoting ideas have been offered and employed.

Despite these overall positive conclusions, as elaborated in the last chapter, the record is rather mixed. For every few successes (reductions in whaling and in the production of ozone-depleting substances, for instance), there is a failure or at least a relatively weak initiative, such as BSEP or the Forestry regime. Principles are often co-opted to favor interests incompatible with environmental protection. Some instruments are ratified but very incompletely implemented. Other initiatives, possessing characteristics of effective law, are insufficiently funded.

An evaluation of the success of international environmental law must include an analysis of effects on the physical environment itself, the concrete challenge that is the subject of the initiatives. When so understood, the question is empirical, one that in most cases is not sufficiently modeled and understood. Results come from assessments of physical parameters and from expert judgments, the former being the most significant benchmark. As Chapter 4 noted, it is a benchmark that also is difficult to quantify adequately, and tracing its roots to various phases in the evolution of a legal regime is a task filled with uncertainties.

There is nonetheless a growing understanding that, even by the most rigorous criteria, a more effective law can be realized. Here I highlight characteristics needed to achieve that goal. I first lay out conditions that are expected in the world of policy-making in which the law evolves. There is an evolving appreciation that green is good, that environmental management achieves important national and corporate objectives, and that multinational organizations will increasingly accept these understandings.

Unfortunately, talking green is also good, so there has been an adoption of terminology associated with environmental protection independent of changes in performance. Expectations for the conditions in which law will be made include a greater incidence of democratic participation at the international level, greater convergence in the science that is the background for the consideration of treaties, and some convergence in the assessment of the effectiveness of international environmental instruments. I also expect more widely shared understandings of what needs to be done to create effective legal regimes. Each of these conditions has implications for the design and reform of international environmental law.

This chapter then moves to my recommendations, several of which account for changes expected in international policy-making and others that I consider necessary independent of anticipated changes. I address regulatory techniques, alternative enforcement and compliance-promoting strategies, involvement of NGOs, procedural reform, organizational changes linked to successful implementation, and incentives and sanctions including trade sanctions. The recommendations recognize the challenge of linking law, often soft law, to behavior that is established and entrenched. Some recommendations are specific to a class of global environmental problems. Others generalize to most all attempts to use law to protect world resources and the environment.

EXPECTATIONS

The Greening of Geopolitics

Expect new environment-friendly concepts and worldviews to enter the everyday discourse of international activities, including politics, trade, and development.

The significance of international environmental protection is increasingly recognized. There is no dearth of concepts on which to build meaningful international environmental regimes, and the concepts are moving ever more quickly into the official statements of institutions that matter. Societal conditions are creating a strong public interest in the environment, including ecosystem survival and its relationships to the health of the world population. A greening of geopolitics has been made possible by the collapse of the Soviet Union and the recognition of the limits of armed resolution of conflicts. As former Norwegian prime minister Brundtland noted, "already, a new awareness of global ecological interdependence is filling the political space which used to be occupied by divisive Cold War concerns" (Shabecoff 1996, 115).

An overall assessment of this potential requires an analysis of the interests that international environmental law serves. Many of the new understandings will be implemented within a policy-making world that will not change dramatically over a short period of time. Forces that generated decades-old institutions likely will not respond much to the discovery of new conceptual understandings, or speculations, or models of how the world operates. These often are offered by academics, members of NGOs, and others who are usually at the periphery of actual decision making. Mostafa Tolba said after the Stockholm Declaration that governments "need to change gears. We need a change of heart" (Shabecoff 1996, 45). Such changes come, if at all, slowly and with considerable cost. Also, discourse can change dramatically without an air shed being saved, a river cleaned, a species returned from the brink of extinction.

An underlying set of premises within the newer environmental law no doubt reflects the same interests that underscored the major environmental and economic policies of previous decades. Nonetheless, themes such as sustainable development, environmental management, privatization, and ecosystem analysis will continue to enter the vocabulary of regional and global environmental strategies.

The meteoric rise of the concept of sustainability is a case in point. The United Nations Conference on Environment and Development, through Agenda 21 and the Rio Declaration, brought the concept to the international community in an explicit way. Much earlier the groundwork was laid (without the exact term being used) for its emphasis in domestic and international affairs. It is at the very basis of UNEP by its constituent act, U.N. General Assembly Resolution 2997 (27), which stressed the need "to assist developing countries to implement environmental policies and programs that are compatible with their development plans" (Timoshenko and Berman 1993, 39). In 1983 UNEP's role in pursuing sustainability was recognized by the World Commission on Environment and Development (the Brundtland Commission), which gave the term general use. The idea was to reorient major international organizations through improved coordination and cooperation toward sustainable development (Timoshenko and Berman 1993). Brundtland defined this as "development that meets the needs of the present without compromising the ability of future generations to meet their own needs." UNEP in its fifteenth Governing Council attempted to clarify the idea: "Progress towards national and international equity, as well as the maintenance, rational use and enhancement of the natural resource base that underpins ecological resilience and economic growth."

UNEP introduced the concept into planning for environmental law. The first long-term Programme for the Development and Periodic Review of Environmental Law (the Montevideo Programme) was prepared by a meeting of senior government environmental law experts in 1981 (Timoshenko and Berman 1993, 40). After Rio, the United Nations Commission on Sustainable Development was created with the power to recommend policies to the U.N. Economic and Social Council. Nation-states have also institutionalized efforts to adopt sustainability as a policy anchor. The United States, for example, formed the 25-member President's Council on Sustainable Development. In 1988, 22 directors of U.N. agencies and programs met to plan and to coordinate their activities to promote sustainability (Caldwell 1990, 82).

The 1992 Biodiversity Convention defines sustainable development in its biological context: "The use of components of biological diversity in a way and at a rate that does not lead to the long-term decline of biological resources, thereby maintaining its potential to meet the needs and aspirations of present and future generations." Both it and the Climate Change Convention can be seen as making sustainability part of positive law. The WTO's constitutional instrument refers to "optimal use of the world's resources in accordance with sustainable development" (Uruguay Round 1994).

The sustainability concept avers that "the environment and economic growth need not be in conflict . . . without protection of ecological systems, global economic decline . . . [is] inevitable. Conversely, without economic progress, elimination of poverty, satisfaction of the material wants of people of the developing countries, and extension of human rights, efforts to protect nature and the earth's life-support systems . . . [are] doomed to failure" (Shabecoff 1996, 4).

Notions of sustainability will continue to motivate the development of international law, but whether they will help create effective law will depend on whether common meanings linked to making the environment a priority are adopted. As used so far, there has been considerable skepticism. Howard Mann argues that all international law should "be seen as being for sustainable development, rather than having the legal community struggle to define a new, separate or overarching branch of law—international law of sustainable development" (Sands 1995b, 67). Sustainable development, furthermore, is a concept that can invite "an overly anthropocentric and instrumental interpretation," which can lead to a "development-oriented view of environmental resources" (Handl 1994, 312, fn 43). It can be applied politically: "sustainable" means based on participation of local interests, but those interests may or may not conserve resources for future generations. The literature on indigenous resource exploitation suggests that these forms may generally be more sustainable, but the record is not clear. Some indigenous patterns are environmentally destructive, and "local" participation no longer equates with "indigenous" in many parts of the world (Sirola 2001). Locals may be among those most focused on short-term gains that derive from exploitation. Articulating high-sounding terms such as "sustainability" may also divert international efforts to achieve consensus on more practical matters, matters backed by science and politically acceptable, which can be effectively implemented in the mid-run. The most severe critique of sustainability holds that the environmental movement can be the handmaiden of forms of polluting development based on assertions that such development is green.

Nonetheless, different meanings of sustainability need not counter effective international environmental actions based on law. Doughman (1999), in a study of the use of the term by multilateral development banks, governments, NGOs, and the private sector in regard to water infrastructure projects in Mexico, suggested that variations may promote communication and, eventually, cooperation. There are more direct implications for an international environmental law. Critical analysis of such phrases ("ecosystem-based analysis," "privatization," and "environmental management" are similarly imprecise) is essential and is available in work by NGOs and in the academic literature. These general terms are a starting point for discussions of specific choices by states; they can be a means of bringing negotiators together at a high level of generality. They can provide ideas for joint setting of a research agenda, and they may stimulate consideration of specific strategies that environmental law can promote.

Participation of Nongovernmental Organizations

Expect that international environmental legal regimes will embrace forms of participation that will promote greater compliance.

The continued involvement of new actors with interests that counter an environmentally destructive status quo can be expected. In Rio and in Johannesburg, large numbers of people with strong environmental agendas participated in the conventions and in their parallel people's versions and influenced official actions. Since that time, hundreds of environmental action groups have been formed in every region of the world. In North America under the NAFTA institutions, the number of submissions brought by NGOs and private entities is striking when contrasted to the few consultations and arbitral panels assembled by the parties themselves. Green parties at the domestic level have played notable roles in promoting national legislation. They were influential in the collapse of the environmentally destructive Soviet regimes, and they have earned considerable legislative power in the United States and in Europe.

As it relates to the effectiveness of law, however, this expectation must be tempered. As recently as 1996, Koskenniemi could write, "non-governmental organizations (NGOs) do not play an official role in compliance review in any field of international law" (244). That is no longer precisely accurate in the international field, but environmental NGOs generally have limited roles in official proceedings. Where they are active, an international environmental law also needs to recognize that although NGOs can be productive players in treaty making, their contributions are not always positive. Many NGOs have objectives inconsistent with global environmental protection. Some are not particularly democratic, and rules for involving them in international proceedings may themselves be undemocratic. Motivations for participation include sustaining an organization independent of its impact on treaty evolution. Furthermore, competence is low in some NGOs, and even when objectives are clear and philosophical positions compatible with global stewardship, logistically it can be difficult to include large numbers of participants in the mundane tasks of instrument preparation and implementation.

Cooperation Based on Science

Expect science to establish causal links sufficiently compelling that nation-states will more readily accept inroads into sovereignty.

Science will continue to move toward consensus in some areas that inform the design of international law. Epistemic communities of scientists will grow in number and influence. International organizations, such as UNEP, will promote activities furthering agreement through collaborative meetings of scientific and technical bodies (UNEP 1999).

The function of science is important in creating agreement, in decreasing uncertainty, and in suggesting policy responses to global degradation. Some observers, however, have exaggerated its role. They choose to select unrepresentative examples of scientific findings that led to international policy initiatives, or they fail to consider cases where scientists disagree in fundamental ways about the importance of information. An example involved negotiations over the treaty on persistent organic pollutants (POPs). Some environmental groups, focusing on scientific information on ecological threats, called for global termination of production and use of DDT, but 400 medical researchers countered with data suggesting that DDT helps control malaria, which has approximately 3 million victims each year (*International Environment Reporter*, 15 September 1999, 745). Both groups are correct scientifically, but the issue is larger than finding the best data. Science cannot determine which objectives of an international environmental policy are most important.

Another example involves genetically modified crops and organisms. Here serious disagreements are found between the north and south, among the Western industrialized nations and within them. Scientific issues may over time be more amenable to empirical investigations rather than conclusions about values and priorities, but sorting one from the other is not easily done in the politically charged world of trial crops, square tomatoes, giant vegetables, and enhanced meat, poultry, and fish products.

True, the dominant scientific view internationally is that the risks of development and use of genetically modified crops and organisms are small and manageable. A type of biotechnology—plant hybridization—has a long and benign history. Critics, including some scientists, however, counter that the behavior of viral sequences encoded on plants is not well understood, that DNA migration through ecosystems has not been well studied, that secondary metabolite or protein toxins could result from gene manipulation, that the level of uncertainty in predictions of some results of experiments is very high, that risk assessment criteria are not a matter of scientific consensus, and that resistance of some crops could undesirably spread to weeds (Hunter, Salzman, and Zaelke 1998). Furthermore, the science that forms the basis for the conclusion that genetic modification is safe from a broad human and environmental health perspective does not offer the last word on "the broader cultural, social, and economic dimensions that are of wide concern to the public and many NGOs" (Nelkin, Sands, and Stewart 2000, 526). Laboratories that seek to learn more about the dynamics of genetic modification may be controversial when sited in developing nations without environmental impact assessment guidelines.

These and other disagreements, including skepticism about the existence of objective science when economic and regulatory implications of results are great, help explain the very different domestic laws on the regulation of genetically modified organisms.[1]

The dynamic among science, policy, and law may be more complex in the context of certain environmental problems. As Levesque (2000), following Litfin, explained for the function of scientific information in transboundary resource management between Canada and the United States:

"the power of competing knowledges—likely to be decisive of scientific uncertainty—was the critical factor" [in the outcome of the global ozone regime] (Litfin 1994, 178). Atmospheric science did not provide a foundation of objective, value-free facts that resulted in international cooperation. Instead, scientific knowledge "was framed in light of specific interests and pre-existing discourses so that questions of value were rendered as questions of fact, with exogenous factors shaping the political salience of various modes of interpreting that knowledge" (Litfin 1994, 5–6). Litfin's study demonstrates that scientific knowledge, as opposed to epistemic communities of scientists, was critical to the outcome of the negotiations. It highlights the fact that ability of scientific knowledge to foster cooperation was mediated by how scientific information was interpreted and framed as well as by whom the knowledge was interpreted and framed.

As to the origin and development of a regional conservation initiative (Yellowstone to Yukon), Levesque observed:

Y2Y does not derive its power from the guidance of a consensus-based epistemic community of scientists or from the ability to coordinate consensual action based on a body of objective, value-free facts. Instead, the network's power is derived from its ability to achieve consensus-based collaboration by interpreting and framing scientific information and knowledge in ways that reinforce and support network interests, identities and goals.

Other than the idiosyncratic Montreal Protocol, there are few examples of science driving international action, although in many more instances science has played a large role in promoting new official actions.

Diplomats do rely on scientists, including government-appointed experts, to undertake risk assessments and to relate policy options to effective risk management (Weiss 1992). Putting it more gently than some critics, Weiss noted that "on the one hand, this gives governments confidence in the outcomes, which is essential; on the other it may invite what has been termed 'negotiated science,' a matter about which some of the international scientific community have been particularly critical."

Negotiations for the climate-change convention illustrate some of the processes of science and policy interaction. From the perspective of international environmental lawmaking, two expectations about scientific consensus need to be critically addressed. First, the science on climate change's causes, its effects, and approaches to successful intervention will continue to converge. Second, science will drive an effective international legal response.

Convergence is occurring for some of the science. Recent independent studies confirm that there are changes in the earth's outgoing long-wave radiation spectrum, that there is a warming trend in the surface temperature over the past 20 years, that ocean temperatures are rising, that the thickness of Arctic sea ice is declining, that the Greenland ice sheet is melting, that the ice-free season has gotten longer in the past century, and that the Himalayas are warming.

The Third Assessment Report in 2001 made several reaffirmations of the IPCC's earlier work and added new findings. It characterized its results with qualitative descriptions of their certainty. The panel stated with high confidence (i.e., with a 67–95 percent judgmental estimate) that recent regional changes in temperature have had discernible effects on many physical and biological systems and that some social and economic systems have been affected by the increasing frequency of floods and droughts.

Other IPCC conclusions also suggest convergence but underscore considerable gaps in knowledge that relates to policy response. There was high confidence in the prediction of a significant disruption of ecosystems. Large-scale changes in oceans will include increases in sea surface temperature and mean global sea level, decreases in sea ice cover, and changes in salinity, wave conditions, and ocean circulation. Heat waves in urban populations, increased stress on coral reefs, and increases in the transmission of malaria and dengue–two vector–borne infections will be experienced.

Some quantitative projections are beyond respectable challenge, but some scientists criticize the IPCC 3 results as rushed and unconvincing (Revkin 2000a), and certain assessments related to law are made with very limited confidence. In sections they are obvious; they would not advance policymakers' inclinations to change their international obligations drastically. A few noted scientists continue to insist that there is not "any evidence that this is a serious problem."[2]

Scientific consensus about predictions of effects can be achieved while scientific consensus about means to address global warming remains elusive. "Regulatory uncertainty" (E. D. Elliott 1992) is as much a constraint on policy choice as is scientific uncertainty. For example, COP-6 (at The Hague in November 2000), faced with the question of how to account for the removal and storage of carbon from the atmosphere by forest sinks, was stymied by a split between parties who viewed knowledge as complete enough to include sinks in emissions reduction calculations and those who read the science either as incomplete or as identifying serious problems with reliance on sinks. Economic science also fails to converge on the value of models that describe proposed effects of different strategies, from taxes to subsidies and from trade programs to regulation. Scientific consensus likely will continue to grow, but it will constitute only one factor in choices among politically controversial control options and implementation strategies.

One can debate the notion that pure scientific findings exist and still recognize attempts to politicize science to achieve one or another end—not necessarily a less environmentally stringent end—in international environmental law and policy. Maurice Strong has said (begging the question but certainly giving understandable reasons for the absence of effective worldwide efforts at controlling environmental pollution), "Environmental problems are like a cancer spreading insidiously through the body. They will probably kill us eventually, but the symptoms are not acute enough to prod us into saving ourselves" (Shabecoff 1996, 140–141).

Some environmentalists argue that a scientific explanation of the environmental threat is qualitatively different from that of other subjects of legal control and that it demands a different kind of international respect. Even where scientific consensus is not complete, dramatic new centralized international initiatives are warranted because ecosystem collapse and related environmental disasters suggest the compelling need for the precautionary principle. Others consider this position not only unjustified but also unscientific and dangerous, pointing as Nespor (2000–2001) does to the history of poor prediction in the environmental policy arena. Nespor's examples include miscalculation of coal and oil reserves, gross underestimation of food production, overly dire statements about deforestation and the contribution of chemicals to carcinogenesis, as well as exaggerated assessments of the process of desertification. Furthermore, advocacy of particular lifestyles may be driving interpretations of data and decisions on environmental policy. Aggressive precaution with costly side effects on economics and other social goals may follow.

Still, science may lead to greater cooperation in international environmental matters in another way. Although the science on a particular question may not be compelling, the entry into public discussion of scientific considerations of environmental problems has been dramatic; it may suggest a more general interest in actions to preserve environmental resources than either the scientific community or governments actively promote. In tracing the impressive growth of a sector of world society concerned with the environment, the "rise of scientific discourse and association has been central. It universalized and legitimated earlier and narrower conceptions of the environment as the locus of either sentiment or particular resources" (Meyer et al. 1997, 645). States may be pushed farther into international cooperation despite the mainline objectives of preserving sovereignty that they would seek absent popular domestic concern.

The implications of these observations are straightforward. In the limited number of circumstances of clear and consensual scientific appreciation of an environmental impact link, law will be able to guide nation-state movement to select among control strategies. In other situations, negotiators will face choices where values other than environmental protection are salient and where science is the basis of competing, not converging, advocacy.[3]

Corporate Advocacy of Green Management

Expect the business sector to advocate less need for regulation because of green management strategies.

As elaborated in Chapter 3, for several reasons major private sector enterprises have recognized the value of promoting environmental protection policies. To a certain extent, green management of the kind espoused by Ford, DuPont, and major German and Scandinavian companies reflects the values of company executives, but the expectation articulated here is based on the more systemic factors that I discussed earlier. Green management can save money, it can enhance a firm's relations with its customers, it is a wise marketing technique, and it can improve a company's relationships with insurers and with domestic and international regulators.

As a case example, industry will continue to assert that climate stability can be achieved if business takes a leadership role. Strong initiatives on the part of major multinational corporations to pursue technology-trading approaches, serious commitments by leading CEOs to fundamental production changes, and consumer-driven changes in product types will be seen.

Some corporations will identify solutions to specific climate-altering problems, and markets will disseminate the innovative approaches that they identify. Ford, DuPont, Mitsubishi, BP Amoco, Royal Dutch Shell, United Technologies, and others will see the benefits of taking anticipatory measures to combat climate change.

Major European and other industrialized wealthy nations will continue to hold the position that the private sector must be deeply concerned about the environmental threat of climate change and can profit by being an early adopter. A case in point was the surprising response to the World Bank's Prototype Carbon Fund. It closed its first subscription period (15 January to 10 April 2000) with $35 million more than expected, almost $135 million in contributions. The fund sponsors projects designed to produce emission reductions consistent with the Kyoto Protocol. Private companies and government investors will receive a share of the reductions as credits. Canada, Finland, the Netherlands, Japan, Sweden, and Norway have led the way on this initiative (*International Environment Reporter,* 4 May 2000, 352). In the United States the private Joyce Foundation has funded an innovative experiment in trading greenhouse gases by the Chicago Climate Exchange.

Increasing availability of critical information will make the misuse of green discourse risky, and over time the positions that a company publicizes will become part of its culture, driving the decisions and actions of new employees. A related expectation nonetheless persists: the underlying consumption-promoting ethos of the multinational corporation will be at the heart of certain types of environmental degradation. A cleaner Ford continues to affect land patterns and use natural resources in ways ultimately antithetical to climate stabilization, sustainable development, and related environmental goals.[4]

The implications of these corporate orientations for international environmental law are twofold. Policymakers will see an ever-expanding inventory of strategies that focus on business's contributions to global environmental stewardship. At the same time, critics will question the actual performance of these approaches and contrast them with potential results of regulation and other government-guided interventions. Policymakers will need to make difficult decisions about the nature of the legal provisions that focus on industry.

Innovations in Compliance Mechanisms

Expect greater innovation in pursuing compliance with international environmental law.

As summarized in Chapter 2, legal scholars, policy analysts, and government officials offer many compliance-promoting mechanisms, and several have been introduced into international instruments. They range from establishing participatory mechanisms for making treaties to identifying funds and other economic incentives, to creating ongoing compliance committees. Managerial approaches to achieving international environmental goals will be more widely advocated as criticism of regulatory strategies mounts.

This focus on compliance will nonetheless confront implementation challenges, complicated in the national arena (Pressman and Wildavsky 1973) and much more difficult at the supranational level—both under traditional environmental diplomacy and under the managerial innovations.

In introducing innovations, the translation of concepts into dozens of languages across hundreds of countries is an enormous challenge. Where agreement is reached about meaning of terms at one level of abstraction, making the terms significant on the ground can be difficult. Beyond these relatively cosmetic differences are serious and enduring cultural disagreements about the best practices for reaching goals under a rule of law and without developed legal systems (Sievers 2001). Funding may also be an obstacle to implementing innovative ideas, such as fostering NGO participation or creating compliance accounts, not only because some countries lack money but because of shifting priorities in national budgets. Furthermore, those who commit to implementing a regime must communicate needed changes to numerous agencies, regulated entities, and the public. This is not easily done in many countries.

Some implementation difficulties derive from federalism. Subfederal levels of government may have strong conflicting positions on international treaties, and in some jurisdictions those governments can block effective implementation. Witness the struggle of commonwealth versus state authority in Australia over the question of how to respond to global climate change. In Canada, the full impact of NAAEC has not been realized in part because some provincial governments have not adopted the side agreement.[5]

These expectations—a growing rhetoric about and some commitment to a sustainable physical environment (to greening international law), a growing consensus in some global environmental science, a greater convergence of private sector goals and the public interest in environmental protection, and increasing knowledge about ways to achieve compliance—underscore the recommendations I offer for the next generation of international environmental law.

RECOMMENDATIONS FOR THE STRUCTURING OF INTERNATIONAL ENVIRONMENTAL LAW

Within the context set out above and the context of a pluralistic world of international policy, what can be done to enhance law's role in reaching global preservation? Among the array of available tools, which ones should the international community of sovereign nations select, promote, use, and enforce? Based on experience with successes, based on disappointment with failures, which characteristics of lawmaking and implementation should be emphasized?

Not all of the recommendations address each of the challenges summarized in this book. As developed in chapters 1 through 4, these range from attempts to control separate nonmalicious actions of millions of people to measures against a few individuals who destroy natural resources to achieve a financial or military advantage (international arson on oil fields, illegal movement of toxic materials). Groups of states or individual countries create harm outside their regions, on a single nation downstream or a large air shed that covers many countries. Some destruction, such as burning of the forests in Indonesia or Brazil, involves the deliberate but legal activities of small groups of people or a few nations. Some, such as dumping from cruise ships, comes from daily violations of many people. Some manifests itself immediately in clear and dramatic ways (loss of another species of once abundant fish). Some, such as global warming, will take years if not decades to register as insults.

The history of the performance of international environmental law is one of common characteristics, but it is not explainable by a single dynamic (Flores 2002). Remarkably particular at times, generally applicable at others, are factors that promote successful treaty making and implementation. Some are unique to the environmental circumstances, so that addressing them in policy for a different problem will not be useful. Others—those identified by managerial and participation-centered analyses of why nations comply, those of the regime theorists among political science, and those from organizational theory—are relevant to many efforts to influence complex behaviors. Their insights combine to approximate a midlevel theory (Merton 1967) of effectiveness of international environmental law. That theory generates some shared recommendations.

Recommendations build on knowledge of what works in the international community. These are not particularly ambitious. The most ambitious strategies are not only unrealistic but are also, in many cases, undesirable. Some should not be implemented. For example, I do not advocate creation of centralized supranational authorities with strong powers. Prerequisites for them to be effective and fair do not exist internationally. Citizens must be watchful of centralizing authority in their own states, and they need to be triply concerned about delegating authority upward to organizations that do not possess records that merit assumption of such power. Unfortunately, some elements of the less effective United Nations agencies remain cases in point.

Considerable progress has already been made. It provides the backdrop for evaluating just how much change recommendations require. As Edith Brown Weiss (1992, 11–12) wrote, "The provisions in the new agreements are generally more stringent than in the previous ones; the range of subject matters is broader; and the provisions for implementation and review are more sophisticated. One encouraging observation from this experience is that the learning curve demonstrated in international environmental law is unexpectedly steep."

Although learning by nations has been smooth, implementation has not. Furthermore, each successive attempt to assure implementation and compliance will be scanned with ever more vigilance; nations wonder if the benefits of entering international regimes are worth the sacrifices. The U.S. Senate's Byrd-Hagel resolution (U.S. Senate 1997) during the Kyoto negotiations is instructive. It opposes U.S. signing of climate change instruments if developing countries are not also required to limit emissions or if they would harm the U.S. economy.

The mammoth proliferation of international environmental law suggests that the international community should have a greater experience in its workings before making large and fundamental additions to its corpus. Less frequent adoption of new instruments and more effective implementation of those that exist are needed:

> International lawyers . . . should have a special interest in avoiding environmental legal window-dressing or fictitious law making: Legislation without concern for the effectiveness of the norms enacted, or the commitments states enter into, is self-defeating. More time and effort must be spent on strengthening monitoring of compliance and implementation of already existing commitments. Unless international environmental law on the whole . . . remains credible, no progress toward that goal [sustainable development] will be possible. (Handl 1994, 331)

There are a few other points of departure. First, international environmental law contributes to fixing a set of norms and then influences by sanctions and incentives those entities that deviate in some significant way for some significant time from those norms. Second, although there are sound arguments against centralized lawmaking, in select areas it has been effective. The conditions for such action (peacemaking in the former Yugoslavia, selective intervention in Africa) have been particular and special. Occasionally they may exist in the environmental arena. Third, many nonlegal instruments—from environmental education to green management—show promise for achieving environmental protection. To focus on the law is not to deny the utility of other methods. Rather, my purpose here is to highlight where the law has a unique function and to demonstrate how law can be used to channel some of the most effective elements of other instruments. They can then work in parallel to influence collective action. Law is not everything. It is not the only thing. Nor is it impotent (as some have argued in treatments of its deficiencies in general). It is a separate, identifiable institution that influences behavior, even very complicated behavior that creates climate change, destroys the protective ozone shield, and threatens the existence of a species.

Participation-Centered Global Lawmaking

Fundamental to the creation of effective global green law is participatory agreement making by nation-states. A further orientation toward an ongoing, egalitarian, interactive environmental diplomacy is called for. Countries thereby will learn about each other's priorities, not only as those are set out in policy briefings but in face-to-face deliberations. Values will be communicated and interpreted. Negotiators will reach conclusions about the accuracy and trustworthiness of information that is supplied by their peers. Disputes over provisions can be mediated in processes equitable to participants with vastly different international negotiating capabilities.

A discourse with few if any parallels in complexity needs to evolve: it touches on subjects as diverse as tools for monitoring pollutant emissions and effects, human rights, and specified levels of consumption and comfort. Communications must be orchestrated among large numbers of people with different professions, languages, and world views.

Despite globalization, including in communication, the amount of misunderstanding, ignorance, and misinterpretation of the positions of people on the other side of boundaries is significant. Perceived differences jeopardize the creation of a common understanding of treaty and other instrument choices. Transactive processes and joint participatory efforts are indispensable to the movement toward consensus in law, as in many other areas of international commerce and policy.

It can be surprising how different cultural perceptions are about the need for international intervention. At the 1999 Seattle meeting on global trade, some delegates from developing countries believed that the U.S. government was responsible for the violent street demonstrations, choreographed to justify the American position on a need for links between trade and environment and labor objectives. Also startling to Western NGOs was the position of some academics and NGO leaders from Africa, Asia, and Latin America that culminated in a statement opposed to including environmental and labor issues. Third World representatives asserted that these goals were promoted for economic gain by the wealthier nations, selectively targeting the developing world.

The tuna embargo against Mexico; the shrimp controversy involving the United States on one side and India, Pakistan, Malaysia, and Thailand on the other; the controversy over contaminants in gasoline involving Venezuela and Brazil as exporters; the concern, principally of the United States, with toxic inhalation hazards associated with inadequately packaged materials; Sweden's assessment of risks associated with transport of hundreds of millions of airbag items; France's ban on chrysotile asbestos, citing a risk of cancer at any exposure; the value of flexibility mechanisms to combat climate change; the need for regulation of genetically modified organisms—each involved strongly held cultural and national differences on subjects of international environmental law.

Ignoring such differences is a formula for treaty stillbirth. Joint and iterative articulation of the nature of an international environmental problem, joint analysis of the strategies that might be used in addressing it, transactional generation of ideas on successful implementation and compliance-promoting activities are essential. Treaty making must involve both governmental negotiators open to learning (including through joint fact finding) as well as teaching and civil society. As the Salzburg Initiative noted, treaty making should implement a "bottom-up" approach to "aggregating increasingly larger clusters of countries" into coalitions that can articulate important negotiating points (Susskind 1994a).

Social science provides some theoretical basis for advocating cooperation (Gehring 1994; Keohane 1995; Haas et al. 1994). "It is a central insight of almost all approaches to international regimes that actors may cooperate and establish international regimes *without* having to sacrifice the pursuit of their own interests" (Gehring 1994, 482). Gehring's work may be subject to some criticism because the cases he studied do not provide solid support of his theory (Mitchell 1995); nonetheless, the rationale is convincing (Gehring 1994, 483–484):

> During negotiations the actors gradually develop similar interpretations of recognized facts. Their appraisal of the desirability of certain options for action converges, and coincident expectations of appropriate behaviour emerge on this basis. Common interpretations, views and expectations are the result of a communication process during which understanding is reached. The result is collectively accepted by the actors involved and has already passed the coordination mechanism of the regime. . . . The gradual development of collectively agreed views of a social problem and its appropriate solution transforms a group of participating actors into a community.

In a process that aims to exchange information, rather than impose a position, what seems obvious to one side at the beginning becomes, under certain negotiating scenarios, more open to understanding by the other side. Compliance with a requirement is influenced by the presence or absence of an actor's participation in articulating norms and rules. This is among the most lasting findings of social psychological and organizational research (DiMento 1976, 1986). It helps to explain compliance with international law by nation-states, which on the ground must participate as people in groups (Allison 1971). Dynamics of norm internalization occur and generalize, spread among the nested small groups in an organization, within the institutions in the nations, and within the international organization or regime. Many leading students of international law have described the dynamics of norm creation, internalization, removal of barriers linked to ignorance, and creation of legitimacy. The legal scholar Harold Koh (1997) further develops the understandings made in part by professors Chayes and Fisher in the international context, offering what he calls "the missing causal element," transnational legal process:

> Such a process can be viewed as having three phases. One or more transnational actors provokes an interaction (or series of interactions) with another, which forces an interpretation or enunciation of the global norm applicable to the situation. By so doing, the moving party seeks not simply to coerce the other party, but to internalize the new interpretation of the international norm into the other party's internal normative system. The aim is to "bind" that other party to obey the interpretation as part of its internal value set. Such a transnational legal process is normative, dynamic, and constitutive. The transaction generates a legal rule which will guide future transnational interactions between the parties; future transactions will further internalize those norms; and eventually, repeated participation in the process will help to reconstitute the interests and even the identities of the participants in the process.

Much of the research on participatory dynamics involves problems addressed at the small group and community levels. Application internationally, however, is merited for several reasons. First, the international arena is composed of dynamic aggregations of smaller-scale levels. Negotiations take place among groups and communities of experts. Second, domestic policy and lawmaking are more mature than in the international community, but they are similar in several fundamental ways. Entities that have chosen to come together to control themselves for common benefit are seeking the best ways to do so, with imperfect information and often different cultural understandings. There is a need to establish or reaffirm legitimacy. There is a need to create understandability and clarity.

These appreciations not only provide a rationale for participation-based international law but also generate tool kits and instruments of active management (Koh 1997; Chayes and Chayes 1991, 1993, 1995).

They include transparency, reporting and data collection, mechanisms of verification and monitoring aids, dispute settlement fora, capacity building, and strategic review and assessment. Other helpful conditions include iterative functionalism. Feldman (1995, 188) defines it as "the replication and gradual refinement of procedures, rules, and obligations negotiated by nation-states in previous agreements in larger, more complex contexts." Supportive circumstances include a comparable voice among countries, an equitable commitment of resources, a careful selection of activities determined on the basis of organizational consensus and expertise, and an earned trust by a secretariat and its subsidiary bodies.

This checklist provides some of the bones of a skeleton of a lawmaking mechanism and a body of law. It needs to be fleshed out with details: What does transparency mean in the CITES context? What data collection is most important in the Black Sea international legal regime? How is confidence created among such a large number of representatives, often changing even within a nation, in a Conference of the Parties on climate change or transboundary hazardous waste?

Not only will the body of resulting law reflect achievable substantive goals, but it will also have the important additional element of implementability. Lipschutz (1992, 23) asks about some of the activities: "The key question is: Can all of these efforts, taken together, substitute completely for international agreements on environmental cooperation? No, but it is possible that they can form the basis for systems of implementation of those agreements."

Advocating participatory treaty making in a world of billions of people may sound unrealistic. It is clear that some daunting challenges to this model exist for some international environmental goals. In confronting problems that affect hundreds of nations, using different languages, accepting responsibility differentially, emphasizing drastically different values, in facing a task that requires addressing a large number of issues, effective process models are not obvious. It is not that the Climate Change Secretariat does not know how to structure meetings, negotiations, and interactions to assure cooperative resolution; it is that no one is confident about how to do that for unprecedented environmental problems.

The November 2000 Conference of the Parties of the global climate change regime represented to some a learning process. To others it was a failure. *New York Times* columnist Andrew Revkin (2000b) explained a part of the challenge:

Part of the problem was also a cultural rift, negotiators on both sides said. The European Union, where Green Party politics is a driving force, never found a way to compromise with the United States, where the environmental movement is increasingly working with industries to influence change. "It is extremely difficult to negotiate between groups where political cultures are so different," Dominique Voynet, the French Environment Minister and a Green Party member, told the plenary sessions.

It is clear, however, that interacting with people over time in structured settings entered to achieve a generally accepted outcome is more useful for creating common understandings of how to get to goals (or how to refine them) than, say, having small groups in hierarchical situations dictate ends and means through resort to their own views. The numbers of people who must be influenced are in the tens of thousands. To the extent that all regions wisely use and coordinate resources, meet regularly, focus on leading environmental problems, and mutually choose strategies that can influence behavior, a relatively small percentage of the world population can be significant. "Interaction breeds loyalties both to persons and more often to causes that may transcend a particular representative's instructions and especially the vaguely expressed directives that emanate from most governments in respect of international political enterprises far from home" (Szasz 1992, 74).

Conversely, small numbers of powerful actors who choose not to participate in lawmaking can seriously counter environmental protection. The global climate treaty and the treaty on the international banning of land mines are important illustrations. Realpolitik analyses consider these efforts weak in the face of U.S. refusal to engage actively. For some law challenges it remains an open question whether progress is possible without a reorientation of a treaty-making style that aims to impose and persuade rather than to cooperate and create.

Command and Control and Regulatory Systems

There remains a selective, customized role for regulatory systems. *Global Environment Outlook* (1997) concluded that one form, called command-and-control standards in domestic settings, is "effective in many cases in terms of short-term environmental improvements," although costs of implementation, enforcement, and compliance are high and may hinder economic development. Although such policies have proven effective for pollution control, they are less useful for resolution of problems associated with management, protection, and conservation of natural resources, "particularly when a large number of different groups and people use these resources." Part of the reason the applicability of command and control is seen as limited is that environmental issues are said to have developed from "simple (local, attributable, quantifiable, easy-to-solve, low-risk, and with short time horizons) to complex (global, non-attributable, non-quantifiable, difficult-to-solve, high-risk, and with long time frames)" (131). The comparison may be too stark and incomplete, but this conclusion (simple to complex) is useful for sorting out the approaches that work under specified conditions and for specified environmental problems. Many environmental problems in the past clearly were high risk and had long time horizons measured by environmental impact perseverance. Also, some were not easily attributable; witness the morass in assigning liability under the U.S. Superfund law. It serves little purpose to say that today's environmental problems are nonattributable. As I have tried to demonstrate in this book, they are not all attributable to the same sources, but attribution can be made. Further, many of the problems to be addressed manifest themselves not globally but in transboundary and regional contexts.

Mainstream regulatory efforts have long histories in domestic settings and in a few international settings.[6] They provide certain advantages in selective and strategic applications where states have sufficiently agreed on objectives. As Downs and his colleagues remind us, we know quite a bit about the impact of enforcement coupled with managerial variables such as transparency. They contrast this knowledge with "ideas and relative prices," which are not well-specified strategies that direct policymakers to ways to increase compliance. "We know relatively little about how to use ideas to change preferences about discount rates, consumption versus savings, or the environment" (Downs, Rocke, and Barsoom 1996, 398).

One must look critically at the wholesale rejection of regulatory approaches. Where do they originate? To what are they compared? They arise in part from frustration with implementation, but implementation is often attempted by agencies that have excessive mandates and limited resources. Problems are not always inherent in the strategy itself. Sometimes command and control is theoretically contrasted with economic incentives, self-regulatory activities, environmental management, and managerial thinking, which have limited histories and lack evaluation with real world complexity.

Certain international problems cannot avoid regulatory solutions. Ozone depletion and species extinction would not have lessened without rules and sanctions. Should the dominant understanding of the causes and controls of climate change continue, a greater commitment to a regulatory regime seems inevitable. Some nations will adopt self-controlling rules without the need for supranational requirements, but others will not. External pressure will be necessary, including providing national leaders with support for a decision that (although essential) is unpopular domestically.

Even in a climate stabilization system characterized primarily by flexibility mechanisms, market force, and trading, there remains a need for some kinds of sanctions and liability rules if reports on greenhouse gas emission reductions are not accurate (Nanda 1999). Other initiatives include requiring signatories to enforce effectively their environmental laws that already regulate carbon emissions or to pursue vigorously regulatory strategies provided for but not yet implemented in domestic law.

Whether typified as regulatory or otherwise, there is a need to clarify several elements of the system for climate stabilization. We must still determine time tables, further define terms (What is a forest? Under what circumstances does it qualify as a sink?), decide percentages of commitments that can be met by alternative means, and determine who will monitor and certify emissions reductions. Finally, however characterized, rates for taxation strategies must be established, monitoring must be done, and penalties must be assessed for failure to pay.

Certainly reliance on centralized top-down control, including through a supranational authority, should be limited. Sir Crispin Tickell, a former ambassador to the United Nations from the United Kingdom, foresaw a world police force operating under the authority of the Security Council "to compel environmental rectitude," although he concedes that the thought "is somewhat distasteful" (Shabecoff 1996, 118). It also is highly unrealistic and fraught with serious problems of value differences and implementation challenges and should not be a part of a regulatory model. In 1989 at The Hague, the prime ministers of France, Norway, and Holland suggested considering the creation of a world environmental legislative body to draw up global regulations and impose sanctions on noncompliers. The idea did not go forward because most governments were unwilling to cede important sovereign powers. Even the sponsoring nations were confident they would never have to be bound by their own ideas (Shabecoff 1996, 121). There may be extremely exceptional circumstances that justify suggestions such as Shabecoff's (118): "Military forces may increasingly be deployed to defend global security. Not only would the military engage in a precautionary role of monitoring and research but could also be called on to carry out its traditional 'coercive' function to protect the global commons from destruction and to enforce international environmental treaties." Rare, indeed, are scenarios that indicate the latter actions.

An international environmental agency within the United Nations with power and authority along the lines of the International Labor Organization has also been proposed (Esty 1994; G. Palmer 1992). It would rule in a super treaty system that sets environmental standards of international applicability by a two-thirds majority, and it would promote compliance. In light of the considerable power of trade and commercial enterprises, including the WTO, the proposal has some appeal. A world environmental organization could balance the excessive focus on progress measured in narrowly defined economic terms and seen as mainly linked to free trade. It could have substantial symbolic value, much like a constitutional provision for environmental protection in a domestic legal system. It could bring environmental interests nearer to an equal footing with commercial interests.

Such an organization, however, could not be effective until a consensus develops about its need, including recognition that the benefits of trade must be put into a context of localized costs. Second, it might well mushroom into a large bureaucracy that would operate heavily according to narrow political considerations, as many other international organizations do. Once established, it likely would not be sufficiently funded. This treatment would further erode the credibility of international environmental law. Furthermore, conflict with evolving and fragile but promising regional bodies is probable. A major question is what would be included and what would be outside the jurisdiction and subject matter of the organization. The parallel but much less ambitious environmental regime, the NAFTA Commission for Environmental Cooperation (CEC), in excluding several significant enterprises from the definition of environment, disappointed many initial supporters.

Command, Control, and Enforcement

The question of how compliance with the regime is to be fostered remains, whatever strategy is emphasized. Means range widely. They include domestic NGOs empowered to hold governments accountable for their actions or inactions, trade measures, citizen submission processes, direct private actor liability with subsidiary state liability invoked when a private operator cannot meet the obligation, financial guarantees such as bond posting, an international claims commission, procedural rules developed to ease barriers to effective enforcement, alternative dispute resolution techniques, and (in very limited settings) mandated criminal sanctions.

Focusing first on the most draconian choice, criminal sanctions have only a very circumscribed role in international environmental law. Nonetheless, a recognizable history of its consideration and advocacy exists. A major United Nations effort resulted in several research reports and a request to the Secretary General. This encouraged the incorporation, where appropriate, of international environmental law provisions by which states would be expected to enact sanctions under national criminal law and to examine the possibilities "of further harmonization of the provisions of existing international instruments entailing penal sanctions under national criminal law" (Resolution 45/121, 14 December 1990).

Many environmental conventions include penal provisions (Cho 2001). Some, such as the Basel Convention, require parties to take appropriate measures to ensure the application and the punishment of infractions. A second type, exemplified by the Convention for the Preservation of Fur Seals in the North Pacific, requires parties to enact and enforce necessary legislation to make effective the provisions "with appropriate penalties for violation." A third type makes violations punishable under national law. The Convention on the Physical Protection of Nuclear Materials is an example. A fourth approach focuses on legislation and other measures necessary "for the purpose of giving effect" to the agreement. There are also numerous bilateral, regional, and multilateral agreements of this kind, including a 1973 agreement to protect polar bears (Cho 2001). The Convention on the Protection of the Environment Through Criminal Law of the Council of Europe would obligate signatories to impose financial sanctions or imprisonment for illegal movements of hazardous waste and would apply extraterritorially. Nonetheless, few examples can be found of actual use of criminal sanctions outside domestic law, and there is no significant international environmental community that is a pressure group for criminal law enforcement.

Some hope to create an international criminal forum that would reach environmental violations. In 1998 the United Nations Diplomatic Conference of Plenipotentiaries on the Establishment of an International

Criminal Court (the Rome Conference) adopted the Rome Statute of the International Criminal Court. The statute's preamble affirmed "that the most serious crimes of concern to the international community as a whole must not go unpunished and that their effective prosecution must be ensured by taking measures at the national level and by enhancing international cooperation." Article 1 established an International Criminal Court at The Hague that "may exercise its functions and powers . . . on the territory of any State Party and, by special agreement, on the territory of any other State" (article 4).

Crimes within the jurisdiction of the court are limited to the most serious international offenses, such as genocide. War crimes (article 8) for which the court has jurisdiction include, as relevant to the environment, "extensive destruction and appropriation of property, not justified by military necessity and carried out unlawfully and wantonly" and "intentionally launching an attack in the knowledge that such attack will cause incidental loss of life or injury to civilians or damage to civilian objects or widespread, long-term and severe damage to the natural environment which would be clearly excessive in relation to the concrete and direct overall military advantage anticipated."

Among the laws that the court will consult are applicable treaties and the principles and rules of international law, including the established principles of the international law of armed conflict. In certain circumstances it will also apply general principles of law derived by the court from national legal systems, including, as appropriate, the laws of states that would normally exercise jurisdiction over the crime. This language could encompass domestic environmental crime statutes.

Certainly, some actions merit response with criminal sanctions. The application of penal law philosophically and from a policy perspective needs to be treated seriously for general deterrence purposes in cases of repeated violations.

The symbolic value of the criminal sanction can be immense. As it does at the domestic level, it can communicate the importance to the international community of deliberate destruction of environmental resources. It can set out lines beyond which no civilized nation or one of its constituent entities or one of its residents can go. One such line is in the draft articles of the International Law Commission, which includes criminal responsibility for "a serious breach of an international obligation of essential importance for the safeguarding and preservation of the human environment." Another factor equates serious deliberate environmental degradation with a violation of human rights. In the human rights sphere, there is close to consensus that criminal sanctions are appropriate for punishment of violations.

Use of the criminal sanction internationally must be viewed with very modest expectations. Among the few instances where international law has resorted to criminal sanctions, only a small number have been successful. In certain limited circumstances the world community can mobilize itself to locate alleged perpetrators of heinous international environmental crimes, achieve jurisdiction over them, subject them to fair and impartial trials, and apply meaningful criminal sanctions if the accused are found guilty. Strategies should be contextual. For deliberate destructive actions aimed at securing an unfair advantage or at meeting a military strategic objective, resort to a seated or an hoc criminal tribunal is merited. But those conditions will be rare.

For other enforcement goals, continued movement toward civil liability is more advisable. There have been some promising steps. UNEP encourages states to develop a civil liability regime. The 1982 Jeddah Regional Convention on the Protection of the Red Sea and the Gulf of Aden Environment introduced its consideration. The Law of the Sea Convention, in article 235(3) of the 1982 UNCLOS, has gone perhaps as far as any international instrument in this area:

> With the objective of assuring prompt and adequate compensation in respect of all damage caused by pollution of the marine environment, States shall co-operate in the implementation of existing international law and the further development of international law relating to responsibility and liability for the assessment of and compensation for damage and the settlement of related disputes, as well as, where appropriate, development of criteria and procedures for payment of adequate compensation, such as compulsory insurance or compensation funds.

In 1997 the Institute of International Law adopted a resolution declaring that the "breach of an obligation of environmental protection established under international law engages responsibility of the State (international responsibility), entailing as a consequence the obligation to reestablish the original position or to pay compensation." It called for environmental regimes "to include specific rules on responsibility and liability" and "strict liability of operators as the normal standard."

Once adequate substantive liability rules are put into law, they must be accessible. In 1960 the Paris Convention and in 1963 the Vienna Convention required victims of nuclear damage to make claims in fora extremely far from the point of damage. [By their terms they do not clearly allow for claims for environmental damage, although increased acceptance of that view has been noted (Sands 1995a, 161).] In the Bhopal disaster, releases of a toxic chemical from a Union Carbide factory in India led to the death of thousands and injury to hundreds of thousands. There legal liability and access to justice were problems in India and the United States.

In general, movement toward a more formal understanding of the responsibilities of nations and the private sector adds an element of seriousness to the statements countries sign about the environment. Required is (Sands 1995a):

> The establishment of procedural safeguards, presumptions, rules of evidence and interpretation which define the legal process, including the notions of fault, accountability and blameworthiness. . . . Such settlement may be weak in that there are no police to enforce it. But as it inevitably creates a norm (instead of applying one) . . . (quoting Sir Robert Jennings) "A plea that X is depleting the ozone layer may be legally less effective than a plea that, in so doing, X is not only depleting the ozone layer but also, being in breach of the 1985 Vienna Convention on the Ozone Layer, is in breach of the general international law of treaties and of its cardinal principle of pacta sunt servanda."

Hortatory approaches to increase compliance also deserve further use. These small steps can have a greater potential to be effective in certain circumstances than that of sanctioning efforts. For example, if a member of the International Labor Organization fails to carry out a recommendation of the commission, the International Labor Conference may take any action "it may deem wise and expedient to secure compliance therewith." Reports may be required from the members and examined by a committee of experts. The experts may note with "concern" or "regret" the implementation status of a country. Annually, a committee of experts may single out serious cases of noncompliance or violation. This negative publicity holds promise for improving the behavior of a member state—and even a nonmember state (Koskenniemi 1996, 246).

Hortatory statements when emphasized by respected spokespeople or energetic diplomats can also make a difference in the world's reactions to suggested legal reforms. The leadership styles of Mostafa Tolba of UNEP and Maurice Strong are effective. Personality cannot be cloned, but it is worthwhile to seek and to support committed leaders who prioritize compliance with international agreements. Persistence and charisma effects generalize to the largest global arenas.

NGO Involvement

A proper role for NGOs must be created, but what status should non-governmental organizations be granted in negotiating treaties and in meetings of the parties?[7] How formal a role in implementation should they assume? The amount of authority given to nonofficial actors is an important international policy matter.

Since citizen participation became widespread in the sixties in the War on Poverty in the United States, it has become a goal impossible to deny. It has meant creating roles for individuals and groups who do not have official governmental positions so that they can become involved in decision making. Citizens engage in activities ranging from commenting in public hearings to serving on committees that have specified governmental authority. Examples of the use and misuse of this approach are legion in both the social and environmental movements.

In the newer generation of activities, organized private citizens with interests in the international environment and NGOs or environmental NGOs have places at the table with negotiators and decision makers. They (1) advise representatives to treaty making in written and verbal forms, (2) introduce scientific background materials, and (3) engage dispute resolution processes by bringing actions against parties or entities within parties for failure to meet the objectives of a treaty.

Unofficial actors may help official representatives recognize and build on innovative strategies for policy development and implementation. They may be active locally in suggesting and implementing policies that are state treaty responsibilities. They may influence green attitudes toward risky behavior and promote consumer practices that enhance the viability of legal instruments (Drumbl 1999). NGOs may offer examples for national and international action. Greenpeace and other environmental NGOs have for several decades suggested policies outside the boundaries of official national positions, but they are influential in making countries' positions more environmentally aggressive. Internal politics may constrain the stances taken by nation-states at international meetings. Politics may be short-term and shortsighted and not representative of even the subject country's interests. The posture of the United States during the Earth Summit negotiations was a "textbook illustration that the *realpolitik* that motivates participants in international negotiations is not necessarily or even usually the interests of their nation. Their positions are frequently driven instead by the narrow and immediate partisan political needs of whoever is in power" (Shabecoff 1996, 136). NGOs can take positions that transcend the routine output of individual administrations. They can also be a force to prevent backsliding by a nation-state, to counter its free-riding (benefiting from a multilateral agreement that it does not support), and to expose instances of noncompliance (Cameron, Werksman, and Roderick 1996).

NGOs have played important roles in several international spheres. At the Rio meeting, their presence was invaluable for realizing elements of an agenda that some states had characterized as too aggressive. Organizations active at Rio were the Third World Network and the Environmental Liaison Center for the developing-country NGOs, the U.S. Citizens Network, the Consortium for Action to Protect the Earth, Friends of the Earth, the Sierra Club, the Environmental Defense Fund, the Natural Resources Defense Council, the National Wildlife Federation, the National Audubon Society, the European Environment Bureau, and the Congress of NGOs (which has United Nations consultative status) (Shabecoff 1996, 150). NGOs were visible and involved in negotiations for the Montreal Protocol in a way modeled on CITES, which strongly endorses their participation. At the global climate change Conferences of the Parties, NGOs from all over the world are advocating positions and providing assessments of scientific information and recommended strategies. They number in the hundreds. and there is a rational process for their recognition. Officially under the regime, the Conference of the Parties or the Secretariat can utilize NGO services, cooperation, and information [FCCC article 7(2)(1)], admit NGOs to sessions [FCCC article 7(6)], engage "legal entities" to work on emission reduction programs [Kyoto Protocol article 6(3)], and coordinate expert review teams that include NGO representatives (Kyoto Protocol article 8). NGOs can comment on the scientific basis for a recommendation. They sit as observers of all open meetings at the conference and have regular contact, including in environmental NGO briefings.

The Land Mines Treaty is another example of effective NGO involvement. Among the factors linked to success of this initiative (in addition to clearly specified deadlines and outcomes realizable in a reasonable period of time) was the strategic coalition of nongovernmental groups that came together with national entities; they undertook a campaign-style diplomacy that overcame the staid diplomatic resistance of some states.

NGOs can contribute distinctive skills and resources that promote international cooperation, and they may enhance the abilities of states to regulate globally (Charnovitz 1998b), but the "long-term effects of NGO participation on the international system are not clear. Wider participation is not an unmitigated good. While NGO participation eases political pressures (often from the same groups) and enhances the ability of states to create and maintain international regulatory rules, such participation brings with it dangers of capture, missed opportunities, and slower, more complex negotiations" (Raustiala 1997a, 737). In short, for environmental lawmaking, "civil society is not inherently 'good' and state power 'bad.'" (726).

Several other caveats exist. NGO participation usually heightens influence of the developed nations to the further disadvantage of the Third World. Purely logistically the large numbers of NGOs may be difficult to accommodate. Where not prohibitively numerous, NGO commentary may be irrelevant or it may displace useful negotiation by states. Accommodating numerous NGO positions may result in "least common denominator" policy positions or harmonization downward of international rules (Raustiala 1997b). Sometimes NGO presence does not add fresh and necessary perspectives; rather, certain NGOs exist for exclusionary or nationalistic purposes. Others, especially in regions with immense competition for limited external resources, work mainly to promote their own goals. They may, as in the Caspian Sea region, effect a "negative civil society" that is no more than a "counter-productive welfare program" (Sievers 2001, 394). Nearby, BSEP head Laurence Mee stated (in UNDP et al. 1998, iii):

> Where are the Black Sea NGOs in all of this? Sadly, their role is often as weak as the governmental agencies. In many cases, they are disconnected from the "grass roots" of society and have become special interest "clubs" of individuals who huddle together shielding themselves from the outside world. . . . It sometimes surprises me . . . that so much energy is put into meetings rather than "hands on" activities.

If international law is to behave more like other law, NGOs should not be decision makers. Their views should be solicited, and they should be given adequate time, within reason, to present to official bodies. But NGOs are self-appointed and not necessarily democratically representative, although they must respond to the values and concerns of their members. They should not be able to bootstrap themselves into positions filled by people who must meet the stringent appointment and review processes of international law. Where NGOs promote interests not otherwise represented, however, their roles in treaty making and implementation should be more central and stronger. Third parties can legitimately and effectively represent the interests of nature and its species. Although details remain as to who should be chosen to represent, these can be addressed, as Christopher Stone (1993) has attempted to do in his call to establish a system of guardians to defend the global commons.

NGOs played an appropriate role during discussions of the Montreal Protocol. The protocol was negotiated under a "polycentric model of decision making" (Shabecoff 1996, 125). "Environmentalists, scientists, corporate executives, and other outside interests, including the media, were integral parts of the process, pressing their own points of view . . . a more open, democratized diplomacy, vastly different from the diplomacy of traditional *realpolitik.*"

NGOs can also be influential in decisions *not* to participate, as they were in response to a 1999 invitation by the Organization for Economic Cooperation and Development to discuss exemptions of certain waste shipments from the Basel Convention. They reasoned that by being involved they would be a part of a process undermining the Basel waste trade ban (*International Environment Reporter,* 10 November 1999, 919).

Finally, international law can promote productive activities among NGOs, even if these are only of an advisory nature. Just as collaboration among nation-state representatives fosters appreciation of strongly held, but previously not understood, positions of other nations, NGO interactions can foster understandings needed to create and implement international law. Models include formal government-funded groups, such as the Joint Public Advisory Committee of the CEC, and more informal processes, such as that associated with the Black Sea Environmental Program or Yellowstone to Yukon described in Chapter 4 (Levesque 2000).

Environmental Impact Assessment

Environmental impact assessment (EIA) should be undertaken at several steps of regime creation. International circumstances are sufficiently distinctive to merit advocacy of analysis of proposed projects that can have a major environmental effect, despite deserved criticisms in regard to domestic law use.

Some critics consider EIA to be overly focused on process, to give to citizens the appearance of involvement in decision making while limiting their actual substantive effect, to be expensive, and to be insufficiently controlled to make a difference. However, influencing decision makers through information presentation, turning a focus to environmentally controversial projects, calling attention to the differential environmental effects of projects across boundaries, and adding new sources of data to the decision-making record are important functions. EIA can channel discussion of highly charged international issues into manageable fora. President Clinton's November 1999 executive order, requiring environmental review of proposed trade agreements, is an example. Written reviews, undertaken early in both bilateral and multilateral negotiations, were to be monitored by both the Council on Environmental Quality and the Office of the U.S. Trade Representative and made widely available for public comment (*International Environment Reporter*, 24 November 1999, 948). The World Bank's attempts to address environmental impacts associated with its lending is another step toward making the bank's actions more transparent and thus more subject to evaluation (*International Environment Reporter*, 29 September 1999, 798).

Some scholars conclude that EIA is already an element of customary international law (Hunter, Salzman, and Zaelke 1998), and regional impact assessment regimes exist in a small number of settings (Knox 2002). Experiences with EIA in the Economic Commission for Europe, OECD, the European Community, and NAAEC have been promising. The analytical framework for the latter was developed collaboratively by the parties, subjected to rigorous expert review, and customized to make application realistic. It is being applied progressively to various environmental stressors. The concept has been adopted in the Protocol on Environmental Protection to the Antarctic Treaty (annex 1, at Madrid, 4 October 1991) and is the subject of the Convention on Environmental Impact Assessment in a Transboundary Context, done at Espo, Finland, in 1991 (30 ILM 800, signed 25 February 1991). That treaty would require each party to establish an EIA process that permits public participation, to undertake an EIA for listed projects that are likely to have adverse transboundary impacts, and to notify affected parties of proposed activities. Conversely, the climate change regime fails to undertake adequate environmental impact assessment of proposed policy choices (Taylor 2000–2001). Needed is more assessment of policy alternatives, including technology-based approaches and those based on new economic and ecological strategies.

Guidelines that parallel those developed by nation-states are necessary: what is a major action that affects the quality of the regional or world environment? It is also necessary to alter the rules "widely provided" that the state proposing is the only determinor of the likelihood or seriousness of adverse impact and that the conclusion of the source state is final (Okowa 1997, 284). Broad access to the creation of the assessments and broad dissemination of results, including to the public, should be provided. To build a strong EIA process internationally, other questions need to be considered,[8] but they do not raise insurmountable negotiating issues.

EIA procedures and knowledge-based strategies build on the public's right to know and to have access to relevant information about environmental issues that affect it. The embryonic Aarhus Convention holds some promise. Aarhus provides as its objective:

> In order to contribute to the protection of the right of every person of present and future generations to live in an environment adequate to his or her health and well-being, each party shall guarantee the rights of access to information, public participation in decision-making, and access to justice in environmental matters in accordance with the provisions of this Convention.

The recommendation of more widespread use of environmental impact analysis reemphasizes the obligation of countries to consult when they are considering major actions that can have substantial environmental effects across borders.

Secretariat Design

Administrative entities for multilateral environmental agreements (MEAs) must be custom designed to help solve specific global environmental problems. Ultimately law, domestic or international, is implemented by organizations created by legislation or treaties, funded and staffed by political actors. A focus on institutional characteristics is essential for effective international environmental law. Proper design avoids excessive routinization of international law, an outcome that has taken place in some national environmental agencies. At the same time it is also important to provide for needed processes and standard operating procedures. Some routine is necessary for law to achieve credibility. Without predictability there will be very little trust in a new international entity.

One element of design is the size of international institutions; this dimension has been addressed in relationship to performance. Largeness does not necessarily indicate waste, inefficiency, mismanagement, and corruption, as developed countries have often said about the United Nations. The developing countries have raised similar concerns about the Bretton Woods organizations: the World Bank, the International Monetary Fund, and the former GATT (Gosovic 1992). At times, however, size does correlate with complacency and inflated rhetoric about improving environmental quality. Environmental law's agents, as any other type of growing human enterprise, should be subjected to systematic analysis and evaluation.

Another issue in organizational development is whether integration or differentiation best reaches stated goals. Some analysts advocate secretariats that administer multiple environmental treaties. Except, for example, with the integrated Law of the Sea negotiations, international environmental agreements have generally followed a pattern of differentiation that has provided flexibility and efficiency. One cost of organizational differentiation is absence of coordination and treaty congestion. Sjoberg (1996, 161–162) suggests, however,

> Should the Conventions decide to use the GEF as an integrated financial mechanism for global environmental problems, the contours of an entirely new type of regime emerge. . . . A regime established along these lines preserves the flexibility that has been the hallmark both of the process whereby legal agreements have been created and the evolution of the GEF. Rather than create a formal organization, this regime is more decentralized and builds on linkages between units with different purposes. Its design is in line with findings in organizational theory which suggest that while a hierarchical model works well in a stable environment, an organic and decentralized form is most appropriate in areas and times of change.

GEF itself may be a controversial choice. Many nations consider its priorities narrow or biased toward the West. In any event, further consideration of a 1991 UNEP recommendation on coordination is merited. Enhancing policy clarity and consistency is one goal, but there are others. The UNEP director proposed the creation of an intersecretariat coordinating committee to promote more effective monitoring and information dissemination, including through reports on means of improving verification activities. Also suggested was establishing monitoring systems even where agreements do not call for them. This idea was deferred and has limited application to instruments initiated through the United Nations, but it is a relatively promising means of increasing knowledge about implementation of international law.[9]

The suggestion that secretariats should be merged and that functions should be integrated across environmental treaties comes from conclusions that some secretariats are working at cross-purposes with others, that efficiencies in allocation and use of financial resources can be achieved with integration, and that learning about systemic elements of international environmental degradation can be fostered by proximity of staffs and scientific advisors and consultants. Oil pollution's effects, fisheries knowledge, seabed resource exploitation, and conservation should be considered as one challenge, not as independent phenomena.

In theory, the suggestion is persuasive; however, a few secretariats are sufficiently successful (such as that of the Montreal Protocol) that to require a change in direction would jeopardize further progress. Moreover, the science needs to be improved before organizations are merged on the basis of understandings of the synergies in environmental degradation and repair, such as between climate change and ozone depletion. Finally, efficiencies linked to integration of functions may best come with new ideas for secretariats; otherwise there may be a tendency to duplicate, rather than to streamline organizational elements. Pluralism and competition are healthy in this early period of international environmental law and policy.

When a secretariat is professional and fair and is moving the global environmental agenda, its authority should be enhanced. This is the case, for example, with the CEC. Because of the need for political oversight, strengthening should be subject to a periodic review at the ministerial level with the default on failure to evaluate being continuation of the authority. Strengthening a secretariat involves, as for the United Nations generally, providing for a professional, independent, and motivated staff and adequate independent financing that will reduce dependence on major donors (Gosovic 1992, 211).

In secretariat design a balance must be struck between the public's right to know and incentives to encourage national cooperation to assure that data supplied to meet treaty goals are protected. The FCCC adequately addresses this concern in article 12. The aim of some reforms is to assure that information exchange is full, open, and prompt, but secretariats must earn the reliance that nation-states put on them to care properly for sensitive and proprietary information (Susskind 1994b).[10]

Although a single world environmental organization is not useful, international environmental law can be strengthened by organizational improvements. Existing secretariats, part of a regime of law, need to convert their missions to concrete actions that address environmental quality. To do so, several secretariat characteristics are important. Flexibility in responding to environmental problems and to changing information is high on the list. Perceived legitimacy of the secretariat is important—by those who must be managed whether they be nations, oil companies, farmers, tourists, or ordinary daily consumers of environmentally sensitive products. Openness to public input and transparency of decision making are significant attributes. Operational capability (the wherewithal, in human and economic terms, to carry out a program) is essential as well. Without those resources the best designs can be stymied. Good professionals without considerable financial resources are more effective overall than inexpert professionals with flush resources. Ultimately, given the immense challenges of cleaning world oceans, stopping global warming, saving endangered species, and preventing waterborne environmental health disasters, both accomplished people and considerable funds are necessary.

Creating effective secretariats admittedly is a tall order. Limitations and gaps are typically not the fault of staff or a function of mistakes in design. The issue is much larger than individual personalities or elements of organizational structure.

Effective models are not known for confronting challenges that affect hundreds of nations, using different languages, accepting responsibility differentially, emphasizing drastically different values, in facing a task that requires addressing multiple issues. To be sure, theorists have offered approaches to dealing with uncertainties, ambiguities, knowledge gaps, varying risk assessments, and other characteristics of complex problems. They speak of "future-responsive-societal-learning" (Michael 1973) and transactive management. As recommended earlier, some of these strategies need to be tried, but there is little empirical review of them, and as Italian Nobel prizewinner Carlo Rubbia noted, "there is not a mature decision-making structure that is capable of governing global environmental emergencies, to make decisions in the interests of all." [11]

A focus related to organizational design is on the growth of the international law itself. No doubt there will be discoveries and realizations that call for new international laws. POPs is a recent example. But the international community needs to attend to making existing laws effective, to improving them, and to coordinating their implementation. Edith Brown Weiss (1992, 12) focuses on administrative, monitoring, and financial provisions. She rightly says that it is time to slow the rate of negotiating international agreements, since resources needed to engage in global environmental diplomacy are burdening developing countries. The effective implementation of agreements already concluded is a priority, presaging greater reliance on soft law.

Treaty development is best facilitated after further work generates at least general agreement on priority problems. The field of biodiversity protection is both an example and a metaphor. Scientists have identified about two dozen areas, from California to the Caucasus, that they label hot spots for native species protection. These are defined, among other characteristics, as places with 1,500 or at least half a percent of the world's 300,000 plant species as native. Focusing efforts, including international legal efforts, on these areas makes the biodiversity crisis more manageable and may be preferred policy. Conversely, if the hot spots degrade further, a large proportion of global biodiversity will be lost regardless of success elsewhere (Stevens 2000). Protecting vertebrate and plant species is also said to protect insects and invertebrates.

Selectivity is attractive (perhaps essential) and generalizes theoretically to other foci of international environmental law. This idea must be analyzed critically, however. It can be abused to promote unneeded development, and it can create international environmental injustice if hot spots tend to be found only in certain regions.

Incentives for Cooperation

Most efforts at implementing international environmental law, whether generated by top-down or participatory mechanisms, benefit from the strategic use of economic and other incentives. These are of several types: subsidies, direct payments, loans, taxes, trading schemes, transfers, and innovative interpretations of global property rights.

Global Environment Outlook 2000 (141) points to a number of successes with their application at the regional level. Reporting obligations under the Montreal Protocol were met much more commonly after financial assistance was given to developing countries. The number of parties providing data rose to 73, well above the 18 that had reported by 1992. European Union law provides several incentives to promote cooperative movement toward environmental goals.[12] Elsewhere, the Convention on the Prohibition of Military or Any Other Hostile Use of Environmental Modification Techniques, the Barcelona Convention for the Protection of the Mediterranean Sea Against Pollution, and the Cartagena Convention for the Protection and Development of the Marine Environment of the Wider Caribbean Region offer new ideas on technology transfer and technical assistance for developing countries. They address the terms under which transfer is to take place, the role of patent and other intellectual property rights, and innovative development and enhancement of endogenous technologies of developing countries (Susskind 1994b, 123).[13]

A fully functioning environmental protection regime that exploits economic forces requires some changes in international property law under which it is now difficult to establish and protect rights. It will be necessary in climate change and in other areas of international commons regulation to develop structures to facilitate the exchange of rights in order to enforce rights (Esty 1999). The more difficult a problem is to comprehend and the broader the spread of harm, however, the more difficult it is to internalize externalities (a fundamental property goal) and to achieve collective action (1546). Thus environmental law and policy experts should emphasize incentives and property concepts that foster environmental improvements and technology transfer. Environmental education (including preambles to policy instruments) should recognize that developed countries are polluting out of proportion to their numbers, violating fundamental but not yet legally recognized property notions. Relevant is Garrett Hardin's conclusion about commons properties: for certain problems "mutual coercion mutually agreed upon" is essential. Customary law also provides that the "principle of permanent sovereignty over natural resources requires each state to respect all other states in the use of their natural resources, which inherently includes the obligation not to cause transboundary pollution" (Perez 1996, 1212).[14]

When the task is clear and depends less on major policy concerns of a state than on availability of resources, direct economic assistance is reasonable. Dependence on incentives, however, can communicate that nations have an obligation to comply with international environmental standards only if they are subsidized. Incentives without greater involvement in attempts to build capacity in developing countries can be counterproductive. The funding commitments in the Montreal Protocol, the FCCC, and the Biodiversity Conventions are narrow means of capacity building. Attempts to increase the number, strength, competence, and constellation of governmental and NGO actions; to make relevant information more available; and to foster institutional relationships are superior. "True capacity-building involves a reconfiguration of political, economic, and social institutions; in some cases, it may even require these institutions to be created outright" (Drumbl 1999, 304).[15]

Some environmentalists do not accept that the less developed countries must be subsidized for movement toward environmental protection; development patterns of the industrialized nations are not an entitlement of all nations. In fact, some say, they were a mistake. What is needed is not a guilt-ridden policy that fosters further global destruction; rather, programs should admit the failures of the past and move forward both in the first and third worlds with less destructive consumer and development patterns. Incentives, subsidies, and technology should nonetheless be made available through international legal instruments. There is some possibility that replication of destructive patterns will occur, but the next generation of international environmental protection must be aware of the limitations of law to influence behaviors that are among the most fundamental of the species. If Third World countries are forced to choose between economic development and environment, the economy will prevail. Movement in the direction of enhanced protection can come only through realistic steps that recognize a politics that is not driven (in the absence of egregious environmental disasters) by environmental concerns alone. Thus subsidies and other incentives should be parts of treaties. In return, the treaties should create expectations of increased contributions by the south and be contingent on measurable progress by those nations.[16]

Trade Sanctions

Powerful forces of the market should be recognized in creating and implementing multilateral environmental agreements. The relationship between economics and international environmental stewardship is nowhere more important than in consideration of the use of trade sanctions. They are implicated in global environmental law in two critical ways. Trade sanctions may be employed to reach environmental objectives (trade-related environmental measures, or TREMS), and they are employed in trade agreements to punish alleged misuse of environmental law.

At least 20 treaties authorize some form of trade sanction to influence members. CITES is based centrally on regulation of trade of protected species. It also provides that parties may adopt stricter measures regarding conditions of trade of species, both included in its appendices and not so included [article 14 (1)]. The provisions of CITES do not affect domestic measures or treaty obligations "relating to other aspects of trade," including those that address public health and other matters [article 14 (2)]. The convention does not affect regional actions that maintain or remove customs control insofar as they relate to trade among the region's members [article 14 (3)]. The Montreal Protocol penalizes nonparties by placing restrictions on their access to foreign markets. Noncompliance with prior informed consent requirements of the Basel Convention can lead to a ban on the importation of hazardous wastes. Other important environmental agreements with trade provisions are the Convention on Biological Diversity (1992), the FCCC (1994), the Rotterdam Convention on the Prior Informed Consent Procedure for Certain Hazardous Chemicals and Pesticides in International Trade (PIC 1998), and the Cartagena Protocol on Biosafety (2000). Despite these potential sources of trade sanctions, the United Nations reported at the end of 1999 that "fortunately, no formal dispute has yet occurred in the WTO over the use of trade measures contained in multilateral environmental agreements." [17]

Domestic law also may authorize trade sanctions. Under the 1971 Pelly Amendment to the Fishermen's Protective Act of 1967, the United States may use sanctions for environmental violations of exporting countries. Under the 1979 Packwood-Magnuson Amendment to the Fishery Conservation and Management Act of 1976, the U.S. Secretary of State must reduce a foreign state's fishing quotas in U.S.-controlled zones if the Secretary of Commerce certifies that the state is engaged in actions that diminish the effectiveness of the International Convention for the Regulation of Whaling. Without the threatened use of trade sanctions by the United States to enforce compliance with the United Nations resolution on high-seas driftnet fishing, Japan, South Korea, and Taiwan likely would not have stopped their destructive activities (Makuch 1996; Rollin 2000).

TREMS may directly affect violating companies. Trade bans jeopardize a firm's capacity to do business abroad. Limitation of access to major markets is a severe penalty for companies, which communicate their concerns to their governments. TREMS are controversial, however. Even if adopted, the question arises whether the penalty would actually be imposed, as opposed to becoming a symbol of a larger international relations disagreement. If imposed, the measure may not always influence actions of the noncomplying state in the direction desired. An unintended consequence is to solidify opposition to other parts of a multilateral environmental agreement.

Trade sanctions can also work at odds with environmental law. In some situations (such as GATT, its successor institution the WTO, and NAFTA), sanctions may be imposed if environmental standards are considered discriminatory trading behavior. A trading partner may allege that the environmental action is a disguised barrier to free trade, or an investor from one party can submit a claim that a putative environmental measure is a protectionist act or even an expropriation (chapter 11 of NAFTA).[18] This may have a chilling effect on lawmakers, inhibiting them from incorporating regulatory measures and other instruments. If the challenger prevails, environmental controls may need to be lifted or the challenging party compensated.

The Charter of the International Trade Organization, which was to provide the institutional home for GATT but never entered into force, specifically allowed countries to take measures pursuant to an intergovernmental agreement relating to the conservation of fisheries, migratory birds, or wild animals (Makuch 1996, 101). Later the WTO (established in 1995 subsequent to the 1993 Uruguay Round of trade negotiations) did take steps toward the inclusion of environmental protection and sustainable development within the world free-trade regime. For example, in the shrimp-turtles case, Thailand and other nations challenged the United States for imposing import limitations on shrimp from countries that had allegedly inadequate conservation measures for endangered turtles. The WTO's appellate body recognized the principle that unilateral measures aimed at environmental protection could be valid, although in that case the United States was initially found to have failed to meet WTO requirements.

The environmental exceptions to the requirement that a law inconsistent with trade rules must be withdrawn or changed are found in article 20 of GATT. A state wishing to use the exception must justify its use and select the least trade-restrictive measure available to achieve its objectives. Environmentalists assert that the WTO provisions on sanitary and phytosanitary regulations are too narrowly defined, that the Agreement on Technical Barriers to trade will force downward harmonization of environmental law, and that WTO dispute settlement procedures are not transparent and do not sufficiently recognize environmental interests.

The NAFTA regime takes some steps but does not go far enough in integrating trade and environmental goals with regard to phytosanitary provisions. On food and safety, NAFTA emphasizes the autonomy of each signatory to establish its own sanitary and phytosanitary standards and the right to vary them by region, provided the standards are based on "scientific principles" (chapter 7). Chapter 7 also requires an importer of goods from a less rigidly regulated region to prove with scientific principles that the imported goods meet the safety requirements of the more restrictive region. Other sections of NAFTA [chapter 9 and article 904(2)] extend the assurance of autonomy from sanitary and phytosanitary to more general environmental standards. In contrast to the former, other environmental standards need not be justified by scientific principles. NAFTA provides access to formal dispute resolution procedures for certain food and safety and environmental claims. Other articles (760, 762) encourage notification and cooperation among the three parties.

The European Union has quite environmentally friendly trade rules. It has well-developed institutions that allow NGO involvement and, based on qualified majority voting, permit nations with strong environmental policies to promote them aggressively in the face of free trade challenges (Steinberg 1997). The EU has allowed dozens of actions harmonizing sanitary and phytosanitary measures upward. It permits member states to ban imports not produced according to EU environmentally sensitive processes and production methods. In certain cases the ban may be mandatory.

The EU serves as an excellent model for future trade-environment agreements. I also recommend establishing objective panels (as objective as they can be in these matters) composed of both trade and environment experts who give their views on the environmental intervention. They can determine, for instance, whether a rule is based on the best available expertise in the environmental sciences. Is it as narrowly applied as possible to achieve its aims? The burden of proof should take into consideration all relevant factors, including the nation's environmental record. In rare situations where conflicts cannot be resolved, resort could be to the environmental chamber of the ICJ.

The link between trade and the environment must put greater emphasis on the environment. In a world where trade regimes now regularly trump environmental concerns, to call for greater coordination and parity between environment and free trade is impotent without a major new commitment of states to create that parity. To make this recommendation meaningful, environmental ministries must be raised to a status comparable to that of trade and commerce. Along the way, changes in international rules on investment may further the environmental agenda; they "could turn out to be the very tool for allowing policy makers to escape their 'prisoner's dilemma' and pave the way for solutions out of the race-to-the-bottom-scenario at the trade-and-environment-interface" (Deimann, 1999, 37). Finally, as more world citizens begin to understand trade organizations like the WTO, more balance with non-trade societal goals is needed. Trade law "must be interpreted in light of other rules of public international law" (Pauwelyn 2001, 577). Specifically the WTO should be pressed to pursue trade goals by emphasizing international negotiation over sanctioning (Oesterle 2001; Charnovitz 2001).

RECOMMENDATIONS IN CONTEXT

Application of these recommendations must be realistic about the potential for change among international law's many subjects, from the individual to the multinational organization. Patterns that have created global environmental degradation are entrenched and not readily changeable with either encouraging statements or commands without controls and enforcement.

Some degrading actions are rational responses to systems that do not sufficiently charge for violations. Others stem from poverty. As a Mexican environmental planner said, "It is not easy to sell local citizens on a dimly perceived environmental benefit, when the alternative can put food on the poor family's table. . . . A mature turtle is worth $50 to a poacher for its meat, skin, and eggs, and it takes him an hour of work in the cool night air to get one. To earn that much in another way, he'd have to work two weeks at minimum wage harvesting watermelons in the hot sun. What would you prefer?" (Kraul 1997). International environmental law must go beyond adjusting the perceived costs of a violation. It must create benefits of compliance as well.

Recommendations must also address capacity to promote consensus about ownership of global resources. As the tortuous negotiations over the Law of the Sea made clear, agreement on international property rules will not come quickly, but in areas as divergent as demarking zones of territorial control and addressing the effects of deregulation and privatization, understandings of ownership effects can assist a move toward international cooperation.

Building on the concept of resources of all humankind, a system is needed to delineate natural resources that are not national resources. Resources—fish, air, water, animals, plant materials—pass back and forth through nations. The early treaties on migratory birds can serve as models. That system will come slowly, and law cannot get too far ahead of prevailing understandings. As an example, customary law of territorial seas with its jurisdictional demarcation for fishing and economic zones fails to take into account that environmental effects occur without regard to that zoning. So, too, transboundary rivers have been subject to customary property law. Even its more progressive doctrine of limited territorial sovereignty does not solve environmental problems, including upstream. Rather, it creates other problems, such as effluents in a limited national area and degradation of the groundwater.

Some advocates of a stronger international property law are clear on what needs to be done. They argue for example that all commonpool freshwater resources (those that cross political boundaries and are subject to externality problems) should be placed under international regulation (Benvenisti 1996). The lakes, rivers, aquifers, and unrelated combined groundwater need to be viewed as international water resources. Recommendations for an evolving global law, however, must realize that major international players are not yet ready to go so far.

Finally, until a major shift occurs in geopolitics, one important element of effective international environmental law will remain absent: binding jurisdiction, the inability to walk away from a legal commitment if a party chooses not to comply. That major shift is in the balance of power of nations. As long as there are countries who can abide by the rules when they choose but fear no reprisals when they do not, international environmental law will be subject to some of the criticisms with which this book began. Balance of power in modern times, however, is not only a military question. There are many forms of global influence, as the nonhostile fall of the Soviet Union, the dependence of superpowers on resource-rich states, and the adoption of treaties without participation by the United States suggest. Coalition building can create conditions in which environmental law based on the principles articulated above can succeed. To be sure, coalition building can also stymie environmental law.

Verdicts about success of an international environmental law ultimately depend on definitions. Global environmental improvement is certainly a function in some part of international law within the set of all law. Improvement will be variously understood. As we have seen, it can be seen as cooperation aimed at improvements in environmental quality. It may be viewed as creating a learning system among nations with environmental improvement as the goal. It can be defined as consensus resulting in learning that actually leads to objective improvements, though blissful cooperative ignorance and deliberate avoidance of difficult decisions are at least logical alternatives. It can have higher standards: substantial implementation of cooperative mechanisms that result in improvements in the air, water, flora and fauna, and natural resources as measured by commonly accepted indices. From a global perspective it means improvements in all the areas addressed in this book: the world commons, regional challenges, and across borders. If this perspective is realized, law will have played a necessary role.

NOTES

Chapter 1. Worldwide Environmental Quality and the Role of Law

1. Press release from the Committee on Resources (Don Young, Chairman), U.S. House of Representatives, Washington, D.C., 15 October 1998, "Rhinoceros and Tiger Conservation Bills Sent to President Clinton." The Javan, Sumatran, and Indian rhino of Asia and Africa's black and hook-lipped rhinoceros are in serious danger, but in South Africa both black and white rhinos are flourishing through an interesting yet controversial program that includes privatizing their ownership (Stewart 2001). In some regions the tiger has made a comeback; in others the species are near extinction.
2. U.S. Senate, Senator Jeffords speaking on "Protecting the Earth's Soil Fertility, June 17, World Day to Combat Desertification," *Congressional Record* (17 June 1999), pp. S7238–S7239, "Today, dust bowls are occurring in more than 90 countries with an alarming annual loss of 10 million acres of productive agricultural land worldwide."
3. The first *Global Environment Outlook* (GEO) produced by the United Nations Environment Programme (UNEP), in 1997, concluded on p. 237 that "between 1700 and 1980, the amount of non-domesticated area decreased globally by more than one-third—from about 95 percent to about 65 percent . . . mainly due to the conversion of natural forests and grassland into cropland and pasture." The forest loss figures are from the same source, p. 238, and from the 2000 GEO. The expected extinction rate is a 1995 figure, also from the 1997 GEO, p. 237.

Chapter 2. Law Trying to Save the Earth: Strategies, Institutions, Organizations

1. Resolution 3436 (XXX) of 9 December 1975. The quantitative analysis of treaties suggests that the proliferation may be decelerating somewhat. Meyer and his colleagues (1997) concluded: "The total number of international environmental treaties has continued to rise in recent decades, but growth in the rate of treaty formation has slowed, reflecting the emergence of more official intergovernmental organizations. New issues are increasingly likely to be handled by the expansion of extant official organizations rather than by the signing of new, specialized treaties."

2. The Prince-Bishop of Basel and the King of France in 1781 entered a convention to protect game birds and forests (Van Heijnsbergen 1997).

3. "Bering Sea Fur Seals Arbitration" (*Great Britain v. United States*), reprinted in J. Moore, *International Arbitrations*. History, 755–961 (Washington, D.C.-Government Printing Office, 1898.

4. http://fletcher.tufts.edu/multi/chrono.html.

5. Formally called "Protection of Artistic and Scientific Institutions and Historic Monuments Treaty Between the United States of America and other American Republics" (http://fletcher.tufts.edu/multi/chrono.html).

6. Influential newspapers paid only modest attention. *New York Times,* 18 May 1938, 4 June 1938, 25 June 1938.

7. Churchill and Ulfstein (2000, 625), for example, speak of "autonomous institutional arrangements" that are distinct from intergovernmental organizations (IGOs) in that they are "more informal and more flexible, and often more innovative in relation to norm creation and compliance."

8. Sands et al. (1994, 25) categorize the history slightly differently, identifying "at least four distinct periods" of international environmental law: from bilateral fisheries treaties to 1945, from the creation of the United Nations to Stockholm, from Stockholm to 1992 and the UNCED, and thereafter "the period of integration: when environmental concerns should, as a matter of international law and policy, be integrated into all activities."

9. U.S. Constitution, Art II, sec 2, giving the president the power "by and with the consent of the Senate, to make treaties, provided two thirds of the Senators present concur."

10. The EU was formerly the European Community, created under the Treaty Establishing the European Economic Community, 25 March 1957, 298 UNTS 3 (1958), commonly called the Treaty of Rome. It became the EU by the Treaty of the European Union, Maastricht, 7 February 1992. The EC has international legal personality, and the EU encompasses it, the European Coal and Steel Community, and the European Atomic Energy Community. The EU also encompasses the Common Foreign and Security Policy and the Justice and Home Affairs (Jaquemont 2001).

11. The International Law Commission in 1994 prepared a draft statute for a Permanent International Criminal Court. In July 2002, enough nations had signed the resulting agreement made in Rome (discussed in Chapter 5) for it to enter force. There is little expectation, however, that this will be a common forum for environmental issues.

12. *Japan Whaling Ass'n v. American Cetacean Society,* 478 U.S. 221 (1986), pp. 229–230.

13. Some environmental regimes, as we shall see, bear little relationship to general international law. Compliance control replaces the more traditional processes of dispute settlement, violation, and sanction. Implementation is a financial or technical issue addressed through consultation and help, instead of being viewed normatively; blameworthiness and punishment are irrelevant. Although many environmental treaties, for example, contain a clause on the settlement of disputes, there is little belief that compliance can be ad-

dressed through a fault and attributability regime, such as under the legal doctrine of state responsibility. Criticisms of international law in general are well summarized by Koh (1997), who describes the attacks by many legal philosophers including Hans Kelsen, John Austin, and H. L. A. Hart. Koh also points out that in 1789 Jeremy Bentham coined the term "inter-national law," which rejected "the monistic vision of a single, integrated transnational legal system in favor of a notion that the public law of nations operates on a separate horizontal plane for states only" (2609).

14. Southern Bluefin Tuna (*Australia and New Zealand v. Japan*) http://www .worldbank.org/icsid//bluefintuna/award080400.pdf, 4 August 2000.

15. *Handelskwekerj GJ Bier v. Mimes de Potasses d'Alsace.*

16. A party may also register a declaration simply stating that despite acknowledging that convention procedures have been followed, it does not accept a regulation. Japan, Norway, and the former USSR used this entity to reject the zero whaling quotas of the IWC in the 1980s (Lyster 1985).

17. 29 November 1969, completed by a London protocol of 2 November 1973.

18. Compliance may not be truly significant in itself in all regimes. Some international agreements are entered only when a nation-state understands that it will be in its interest to, convenient to, easy to comply: "We do not know what a high compliance rate really implies. Does it mean that even in the absence of enforcement states will comply with any agreement from the set of all possible agreements, or does it mean that states only make agreements that do not require much enforcement" (Downs, Rocke, and Barsoom 1996, 383). Toward one major goal, environmental improvement, some observers conclude that low compliance with challenging standards is superior to high compliance with lesser standards (Victor, Raustiala, and Skolnikoff 1998; Mitchell 1996). Still others conclude that "even perfect compliance with a strong regime is . . . not a *sufficient* condition for achieving policy goals defined in terms of biophysical impact" (Miles et al. 2001, 7).

19. See Declaration by the Ministers of the Environment of the Region of the United Nations Commission for Europe (UN/ECE) and the Member of the Commission of the European Communities Responsible for the Environment, 7 para. 22.1 (30 April 1993).

20. The provisions of the treaty illustrate the sensitivity, caution, and deference to sovereignty with which international environmental treaties are written. Article 10(3) of the Vienna Convention reads: "The Parties shall make every effort to reach agreement on any proposed amendment to this Convention by consensus. If all efforts at consensus have been exhausted, and no agreement reached, the amendment shall as a last resort be adopted by a three-fourths majority vote of the Parties present and voting at the meeting, and shall be submitted by the Depository to all Parties for ratification, approval or acceptance." Article 8 of the Montreal Protocol walks softly as well: "Non-Compliance. The Parties, at their first meeting, shall consider and approve procedures and institutional mechanisms for determining non-compliance with the provisions of this Protocol and for treatment of Parties found to be in non-compliance."

Chapter 3. Law's Targets: Whose Behavior Needs to Be Influenced?

1. *United Paperworkers Int'l. Union v. Int'l. Paper Co.*, 985 F.2d 1190 (1993), noted in Rice (1993).
2. France's Ministry of Industry reported in 1999 that French companies favor by a large margin use of end-of-pipe technologies over investments in new clean technologies (*International Environment Reporter*, 1 September 1999, 733). Some elements of international property law need to be made more flexible if benefits based on widespread dissemination of green products are to be more fully effective. The WTO's Agreement on Trade-Related Aspects of Intellectual Property Rights (TRIPS) sets generous rewards for holders of intellectual property rights. For example, some rights including patent protection extend 20 years. In Chapter 5 I argue that liberal interpretation of the exception to TRIPS is necessary: members of the world body are not obligated to grant patents for products or processes where "the prevention . . . is necessary to protect . . . human, animal or plant life or health or to avoid serious prejudice to the environment."
3. The curve is named for the economist Simon Kuznets, who described the relationship between growth and economic inequality.
4. In May 2001, OECD countries pledged to phase out within a decade environmentally degrading tax exemptions and subsidies to the energy and agricultural sectors (Environment News Service, 17 May 2001).

Chapter 4. An Accounting: Successes and Failures in International Environmental Law

1. Nonetheless, Susskind gives "several reasons to be pessimistic about the prospects for achieving the level of cooperation required to manage shared (or common) resources like the ocean, space, Antarctica, the atmosphere, or the diversity of species" (1994a, 18). They are the north-south split on these issues, the persistence (he calls it "stubborn") of national sovereignty, and the lack of incentives for nations to bargain.
2. Others find overall assessment too difficult: "International environmental law is so many-sided that a simple description of its status is impossible. The picture is in fact rather contradictory; in some respects dynamic and innovative; in other respects extremely cautious and conservative. On some issues there have been important achievements; on others a frustrating inertia and even setbacks" (Bugge 1995, 53).
3. In a provocative conclusion, Hough states: "Thus the issue contradicts the traditional belief that regimes are established in order to maximize the interests of dominant actors and it appears that norms of behavior in international politics, on which regimes develop, can have their source in morality as much as in the priorities of the powerful."
4. Statement by David Hofmann, director of the Climate Monitoring and Diagnostics Lab in Boulder, Colorado, as cited in Environmental News Network, 7 October 1998: "According to the WMO/UNEP 1998 Assessment of Ozone Depletion . . . the Antarctic ozone hole will remain severe for the

next 10 to 20 years. Following this period a slow healing is expected with full recovery predicted to occur in the 2050 time frame. Climate change, which is predicted to include a colder stratosphere, will affect the rate of recovery, Hofmann said."

5. See also Landers (1997).

6. Excerpt from Center for International Earth Science Information Network (CIESIN 1996): "Trends in CFCs have shown a nearly constant increase at all monitoring locations. The vast majority of CFC production is in the Northern Hemisphere but, due to their stability, CFCs become well-mixed in the troposphere. CFC-11 and CFC-12 have been increasing globally at a rate of approximately 3.7 to 4.0 percent per year from the late 1970s through the late 1980s. . . . however, Elkins et al. (1993) indicate a slowdown in the increase of CFC-11 and CFC-12. Global rates have shown decreasing growth from 11 ± 1 parts per trillion per year (ppt/yr) during the mid 1980s to 2.7 ppt/yr for CFC-11, and 19.5 ± 2 ppt/yr in the mid 1980s to 10.5 $\pm$ 0.3 ppt/yr for CFC-12. These trends coincide with industry reports of decreased production of these compounds. If such trends continue, peak levels of chlorine in the stratosphere may be reached before the turn of the century and a downturn may follow."

7. Excerpt from CIESIN (1996): "The most widely used source of ozone data is the TOMS data set. In an analysis of 13 years of daily ozone measurements from 1979 to 1991, Stolarski et al. (1991) show statistically significant decreases in total column ozone at all latitudes outside the tropical regions in 'Total Ozone Trends Deduced from Nimbus-7 TOMS Data.' Greatest loss is observed at high latitudes due to the unique conditions that lead to polar ozone depletion. Losses in the Antarctic show a maximum downward trend of approximately 3 percent per year during the spring months over the course of TOMS observations. Ozone loss at mid-latitudes ranges from 0.2–0.8 percent decrease per year. More recent TOMS data analysis by Gleason et al. (1993) in 'Record Low Ozone in 1992' shows globally averaged ozone levels reached all-time lows during 1992. Measurements from the National Aeronautic and Space Administration's Stratospheric Aerosol and Gas Experiment (SAGE) and ozone sonde launches have indicated that depletion has occurred primarily at low stratospheric altitudes, between 17 and 25 km."

8. Early reports of pollution by heavy metals and pesticides are countered by the *Black Sea Transboundary Diagnostic Analysis,* which concludes that "the concentration of . . . pesticides and PCBs . . . was found to be rather low in most cases . . . [and] it is quite apparent that the Black Sea is not generally polluted by heavy metals" (Global Environment Facility 1997, 74).

9. Conclusions regarding the status of a species differ, and the 1997 BSEP Annual Report states that 33 species exist in the Black Sea, with 4 species providing 80.4 percent of the total catch.

10. Personal communication with Program Coordination Unit staff member, 28 August 1998. See also BSEP Annual Report. In late 2001 the European Union announced that Black Sea countries will voluntarily implement the EU's water directive (Environmental News Network, 2 November 2001).

11. Their foci ranged from biodiversity at Batumi, Georgia, to integrated coastal

zone management in Russia. A similar program coordinating national efforts has also been created for the Caspian Sea (Sievers 2001).

12. Specifically, article 67 of the Strategic Action Plan states, "By 1998, all Black Sea coastal states will adopt criteria for environmental impact assessments and environmental audits that will be compulsory for all public and private projects. The coastal states will cooperate to harmonize these criteria by 1999 and where possible, to introduce strategic environmental assessments."

13. Brunnee and Toope (1997, 47) conclude that "despite the numerous dispute settlement provisions included in international environmental treaties, these mechanisms are not widely employed. Dispute avoidance schemes linked to river commissions, such as consultation mechanisms and prior notification rules, have proven useful, but most third-party dispute settlement processes remain unused." The availability of domestic and international fora to parties outside the jurisdiction where the environmental problem occurred is a matter of international law addressed in a variety of ways. Under the NAFTA regime described in a later section, individuals, NGOs, and others may initiate a submission alleging that any of the three parties to the Environmental Side Agreement has failed to enforce its environmental law effectively. In the European Community, see Esty and Geradin (1997, 309) and the Treaty Establishing the European Community, 7 February 1992, OJ (c 224) 1 CMLR 573 (1992), article 169. In this regard a reported legal action by scientists from the Black Sea nations against Austria and Germany is illuminating. The action would challenge nitrogen discharges by the two countries into the Danube, more than 200 tons a year, which is 35 percent of the Black Sea total receipt. The discharges may violate the European Union's directives on wastewater and nitrogen and thereby embarrass nations that take pride in pursuing strong environmental protection policies within their own borders and in other international contexts. The decision to pursue a legal action was reportedly made by a group of scientists and religious leaders. There are conflicting views of what actually was proposed (Laurence D. Mee in UNDP et al. 1998).

14. The *Black Sea Transboundary Diagnostic* states that some of the remedial actions required at the national and regional levels are "to establish . . . legal basis for environmental NGOs' participation in policy-making, implementation and assessment; . . . to adopt . . . legislation providing for the possibility to submit a law suit against a State official or State organ; to adopt . . . rules obliging State officials to meet with the public on their request and to answer questions on environment; . . . to ensure . . . open access to judicial organs, also in transboundary context." Each of these remedial actions was to have been done by 1997.

15. The difference between the export and import figures is approximately 8 percent. The amounts reported for the previous year, 1997, were considerably smaller, but that is probably mainly a reflection of the fewer countries reporting. The total waste exported was 1,890,000 metric tons, and total waste imported was 2,171,000 metric tons. The 1998 export data do not account for the 7 percent of wastes remaining after disposal and recycling. The import data have a gap of 13 percent; reported was 14 percent for disposal

and 73 percent for recycling. The Secretariat also reported a difference of about 23 percent between the total quantities reported by exporting and importing parties for disposal operations and an 18 percent difference for recycling operations. Countries reporting varied in size, region, and economic conditions and did not include the United States.

In 1998 the countries listed in the Secretariat's Country Fact Sheets were Albania, Algeria, Andorra, Antigua and Barbuda, Argentina, Australia, Austria, Bahrain, Belgium, Benin, Bolivia, Brazil, Bulgaria, Burundi, Canada, Chile, China, Colombia, Croatia, Cuba, Cyprus, Czech Republic, Denmark, El Salvador, Estonia, Finland, Gambia, Germany, Greece, Hungary, Iceland, Indonesia, Iran, Ireland, Japan, Kuwait, Kyrgyzstan, Latvia, Lebanon, Lithuania, Luxembourg, Malawi, Malaysia, Micronesia (Federated States of) Moldova, Monaco, Mongolia, Morocco, Netherlands, New Zealand, Nigeria, Norway, Oman, Panama, Poland, Portugal, Republic of Korea, Romania, Russian Federation, Saint Lucia, Senegal, Seychelles, Slovakia, Sri Lanka, Switzerland, Thailand, Turkey, Turkmenistan, Uganda, United Kingdom, Uzbekistan, Viet Nam, and the former Yugoslav Republic of Macedonia.

16. For a discussion of the effects of nonratification of Basel, see Bradford 1997.
17. Trade with Canada and Mexico accounts for approximately one third of all U.S. exports and 27 percent of all U.S. imports (Simos and Triantis 1995).
18. See Ferretti 1992, especially regarding the imposition of U.S. risk-benefit analysis onto Canadian health and safety regulations.
19. For example, regarding SEM-98-002, the CEC ruled as follows: "On 23 June 1998 the Secretariat determined not to review the Submission because it did not refer to environmental law as defined by the NAAEC. The subject matter of the submission is a commercial forestry dispute under law that, because of its primary purpose (managing the commercial exploitation of natural resources), is expressly excluded from Article 14 review by the definition of environmental law in Article 45(2)(b) of the Agreement." In response to a submission alleging that Canada had "jeopardized the future of Canada's east coast fisheries" (SEM-97-004), however, the CEC made the following determination focusing on process: "Under the circumstances, the submission does not appear to have raised the issue of non-enforcement in a timely manner in light of the temporal requirement of Article 14(1) established by the use of the words 'is failing.' The significant delay between the time of the alleged failure to enforce and the filing of the submission contravenes the purpose and intent of Article 14(1) in light of the circumstances described below" (CEC 2000).
20. According to the CEC, the submission (SEM-99-002) alleges that the Migratory Bird Treaty Act implements four international treaties, including agreements with Canada and Mexico, aimed at protecting migratory birds, and in section 703 prohibits any person from killing or "taking" migratory birds "by any means or in any manner," unless the U.S. Fish and Wildlife Service issues a valid permit. The submission alleges that "the United States deliberately refuses, however, to enforce this clear statutory prohibition as it relates to loggers, logging companies, and logging contractors." The CEC

did not rule that this submission is beyond its purview; rather in December 1999 it requested a response from the United States.

21. As of June 2002, a total of 34 citizen submissions on enforcement matters had been filed with the CEC, and five factual records had been ordered. Three factual records had already been completed and released: SEM-96-001 "Cozumel," SEM-97-001 "B.C. Aboriginal Fisheries," and SEM-98-007 "Metales y Derivados." Submissions have varied considerably. As noted in the text, "Cozumel" involved challenges to the environmental evaluation process of a public harbor terminal for tourist cruises on the Island of Cozumel in Quintana Roo, Mexico. In the fisheries submission the submitters alleged that the Canadian government is failing to enforce a section of the Fisheries Act and to utilize its powers pursuant to another law to ensure the protection of fish and fish habitat in British Columbia's rivers from ongoing and repeated environmental damage caused by hydroelectric dams.

22. In June 2000 the council approved a new role for the JPAC in reviewing issues about the submissions process.

23. The conflict has arisen in a number of cases. One involved Canada's attempt to ban the cross-border movement of hazardous wastes, including PCBs. Operating under the provisions of NAFTA chapter 11, a dispute resolution panel indicated that Canada's regulation treated a U.S. business differently from Canadian investors. Another case involved the claim of a Canadian business, Methanex Corportation, that the United States must pay almost $1 billion because California planned to remove the toxic chemical MTBE (methyl tertiary butyl ether) from gasoline to prevent water contamination. A third involved U.S. attempts to regulate Mexican truck movement into the United States in a broad manner rather than on a case-by-case basis. Allegedly, the United States was limiting access for safety reasons. In yet another conflict, an American firm recovered millions in damages against Mexico for that country's attempts to regulate a waste disposal facility. See the discussion on trade and the environment in Chapter 5.

24. IPCC assesses scientific, technical, and socioeconomic information relevant for the understanding of the risk of human-induced climate change. It does not carry out new research or monitor climate-related data. It bases its assessment on published and peer-reviewed scientific technical literature. From "About IPCC," http://www.ipcc.ch, accessed 21 July 1999.

25. Carbon emissions per capita per year were 5.3 metric tons in the United States (the highest per capita carbon dioxide emission rate in the world), 1.0 metric ton in Argentina, and 0.1 metric ton in Paraguay. The average for industrial nations was 3.1 metric tons (Herber and Raga 1995, quoting World Resources Institute 1991).

26. The U.S. Energy Department has predicted that for the near future, U.S. emissions of carbon dioxide and other heat-trapping greenhouse gases from energy use will grow faster than previously expected (*New York Times,* 13 November 1997).

27. The distinction between trading and joint implementation arose after the first COP vowed to ban trading as a means of meeting quantitative commitments under the joint implementation provisions of the framework (Driesen 1998, fn. 181).

28. According to one estimate (International Energy Agency), this and related decisions suggested that by the beginning of the millennium U.S. emissions would be 16 percent higher than they were in 1990 (Driesen 1998).
29. From FCCC article 3.3: "The Parties should take precautionary measures to anticipate, prevent, or minimize the causes of climate change and mitigate its adverse effects. Where there are threats of serious or irreversible damage, lack of full scientific certainty should not be used as a reason for postponing such measures."
30. The 39 annex 1 parties include Australia, Austria, Belgium, Bulgaria, Canada, Croatia, Czech Republic, Denmark, Estonia, European Community, Finland, France, Germany, Greece, Hungary, Iceland, Ireland, Italy, Japan, Latvia, Liechtenstein, Lithuania, Luxembourg, Monaco, Netherlands, New Zealand, Norway, Poland, Portugal, Romania, Russian Federation, Slovakia, Slovenia, Spain, Sweden, Switzerland, Ukraine, United Kingdom of Great Britain and Northern Ireland, and United States of America.
31. Article 4.2(g): "Any Party not included in Annex I may, in its instrument of ratification, acceptance, approval or accession, or at any time thereafter, notify the Depositary that it intends to be bound by subparagraphs (a) and (b) above. The Depositary shall inform the other signatories and Parties of any such notification." See also article 12.4: "Developing country Parties may, on a voluntary basis, propose projects for financing, including specific technologies, materials, equipment, techniques or practices that would be needed to implement such projects, along with, if possible, an estimate of all incremental costs, of the reductions of emissions and increments of removals of greenhouse gases, as well as an estimate of the consequent benefits."
32. "Sinks" are locations or chemical configurations that result in effective removal of pollution from biological, chemical, and physical processes. For example, forests act as a sink for carbon dioxide.
33. Although the COP process replaced the INC, the INC continued to meet up until the first COP (COP-1) to facilitate start-up issues of the FCCC (Bodansky 1997b, sec 4.1.5).
34. The Kyoto Protocol specifies, among other requirements, that only projects that provide "a reduction in emissions by sources, or an enhancement of removals by sinks, that is additional to any that would otherwise occur" may be used to meet annex 1 reduction commitments (article 6.1.b).
35. Countries that provide subsidies for energy-efficient products could be in conflict with the Agreement on Subsidies and Countervailing Measures of WTO rules, although there is an environmental protection exception. Most-favored-nation treatment may be inconsistent with a multilateral regime allowing trading only among parties to the Kyoto Protocol. The regime's compliance rules can, however, be promoted in ways that are technically consistent with WTO principles. They can be designed so as to avoid being considered a "service" and to not be "differentiated by their country of origin." More satisfying and more compatible with progressive international law is the conclusion that efforts to promote climate stabilization are exempt from the WTO restrictions—even if they look like trade activities, which, were they not so motivated, may confront challenges (Wiser 1999; Campbell 2000b). Certainly this will require creation of some means of monitor-

ing CDM activity. More important, it will require some trust in nation-states that are asserting this exemption.

36. Domestic policies considered in national law that are promising include expansion of federal weatherization assistance, location-efficient mortgages, recovery of inefficient cars and appliances, expansion of emergency management agency activities, and federal provision of health insurance (Miller, Sethi, and Wolff 2000).

Chapter 5. International Environmental Law: Expectations and Recommendations

1. The Cartagena Protocol reads remarkably like the Basel Convention in assessments of benefits and risks of geneticallly modified organisms. Among its requirements is that importing countries would be given prior notification of movements of genetically modified crops and that the importing nation's right to regulate and to bar the organism would be recognized. Some examples of the conflict over risk assessment make comical fodder. A number of Greenpeace members, including a noble, were arrested in Norfolk, England, for using a mower to tear up a trial crop of maize. The crop was one of a number of government-supported genetic modification trials in England (*International Environment Reporter*, 4 August 1999, 660). Even the royal family disagrees within itself about the role of genetic modification in British agriculture.

2. Richard S. Lindzen of MIT, who is the Alfred P. Sloan professor of meteorology, argues, "We don't know what determines upper level water vapor," a factor he says is "crucial and central to the predictions of future climate change" (William Stevens, *New York Times*, 1 December 1997). Uncertainties about interactions between and among natural systems, human systems, and climate remain numerous (Revkin 2000a).

3. A logical possibility in some spheres is that science will discover that legal intervention is too late. Although researchers offered the example to encourage improved resource management, in 2001 scientists reported that overfishing historically was a major cause of ecological extinction of some marine megafauna. Part of the cause was already triggered in the late aboriginal stage (Lazaroff 2001).

4. In 2000, Ford announced major efforts to make mileage improvements in its sport utility vehicles. The fleet had been among the industry's most profitable, but Ford management concluded that greater company sales could make up profit differences between SUVs and more efficient vehicles and that the increased sales might evolve from a commitment to environmental improvement (*International Environment Reporter*, 2 August 2000, 448). Critics consider these initiatives much too modest: the average fuel economy of Ford SUVs was 16 miles per gallon at the time, and environmental organizations such as the U.S. Public Interest Research Group were advocating a standard of 45 miles per gallon (*International Environment Reporter*, 2 August 2000, 612).

5. As of June 2002, only Alberta, Manitoba, and Quebec had signed the NAAEC side agreement (personal communication with CEC, 25 June 2000).

6. What is regulatory is a matter of semantics. Some analysts include taxes; others do not. Weiner (1999) lists technology-based requirements, harmonized policies, pollution taxes, fixed performance targets, tradeable allowances, as well as command and control, property rules, etc.

7. The numbers of these organizations are impressive. Massam and Earl-Goulet (1997), limiting their scope to only fourteen Central and Eastern European countries, analyzed 1,700 environmental nongovernmental organizations. At about the same time (1994), the count of all intergovernmental organizations was about 1,700 (Meyer et al. 1997). Meyer put the count of nongovernmental organizations with liaison with the UNEP Environmental Liaison Center at more than 10,000 by the mid nineties.

8. Which projects are of international environmental concern? At what point is international notification required? How is a response to comments defined across nation-states? Is information readily available in a national context diplomatically sensitive in an international setting? How is "environment" to be defined? Are social elements of the environment to be included?

9. Designing means of coordinating IGO activities can itself be an organizational challenge. In 1978 the United Nations attempted to promote communication and information-sharing among its constituent environment-focused organizations. It created the DOEM (Designated Officials on Environmental Matters), but the results have done "little in the way of priority setting, program steering or implementation design" (Hempel 1996, 144). UNEP now is establishing the Division for Environmental Conventions (UNEP 1999).

10. It has never been confirmed, but some of the problems that led to the precipitous resignation and firings in the CEC Secretariat in 1998 may have had to do with information leaks or the creation of improper channels between Secretariat members and their native states.

11. Translated by the author, from *Corriere della Sera,* 27 November 2000: "Ma, nel frattempo, non e' maturata una struttura decisionate che sia capace di governare la globalizzazione delle emergenze ambientali, di prendere decisioni nell'interess di tutti."

12. The purchase price of new vehicles is dependent on their fuel-efficiency by means of a tax or subsidy. A system of tradable emissions credits allows car manufacturers more flexibility in reaching emission standards, providing for both trading and banking for future use (Koopman 1995, 56).

13. Private economic initiatives also can foster efforts at cooperation. The strategic use of wealth by major foundations, such as Packard, and megarich individuals, such as Ted Turner and Bill Gates, can provide the means to implement cooperation where law design has been accomplished but means are scarce (in the Black Sea, for example).

14. Other specific asserted property rights need to be addressed. Some are quite technical. Under the climate change regime, for example, countries such as Russia (with economies in transition) have generated what is called hot air. Hot air is the amount by which a Kyoto target exceeds its probable emissions in the target year without climate change policies and mechanisms. These countries had agreed to reduce their emissions by an assigned amount, but many of them experienced considerable slowdowns in their

economies. International law can help determine whether hot air is now property to which the transition nations are entitled. Furthermore, should the notion of hot air be generalized to developing nations because they have not been responsible for generating the climate change problems (Batruch 1999)? If hot air is property, how much should it be worth? What market should set the value? It is, in any event, highly unrealistic to think that Western nations would willingly create sufficient funds to funnel billions of dollars into Russia for this commodity (Raustiala 2000b). At COP-6 an Indian professor raised the issue of ownership of the atmosphere, which can be both sink and source; he wondered who might get credit if the lower parts were declared to be a sink for methane.

15. Choosing strategies that are driven by incentives does not obviate the need for several other important steps in international law. Terminology in the amendment to the Montreal Protocol illustrates that reliance on economic incentives creates its own set of implementation challenges: "The parties shall establish an Executive Committee to develop and monitor the implementation of specific operational policies, guidelines and administrative arrangements, including the disbursement of resources, for the purpose of achieving the objectives of the Multilateral Fund. The Executive Committee shall discharge its tasks and responsibilities, specified in its terms of reference as agreed by the Parties, with the co-operation and assistance of the International Bank for Reconstruction and Development (World Bank), the United Nations Environmental Programme, the United Nations Development Programme or other appropriate agencies depending on their respective areas of expertise."

16. Customary international law binds states to cooperate in the protection of the environment (Scovazzi and Treves 1992, 27) independent of economic exchanges. Principle 24 of the Stockholm Declaration declares, "International matters concerning the protection and improvement of the environment should be handled in a cooperative spirit by all countries, big or small, on an equal footing. Cooperation through multilateral or bilateral arrangements or other appropriate means is essential to effectively control, prevent, reduce and eliminate adverse environmental effects resulting from activities conducted in all spheres, in such a way that due account is taken of the sovereignty and interests of all States." The obligation to cooperate manifests itself as "a duty to act in good faith," to meet the mutual interests of the states directly concerned and the general interest of the international community. The North Sea Continental Shelf case, a judgment of the ICJ (Reports 1969, 47), held that the parties are under an obligation not merely to go through a formal process of negotiation but also to conduct themselves so that the negotiations are meaningful (Scovazzi and Treves 1992, 27).

17. The EU has called for trade sanctions against countries that do not ratify the POPs convention (Rollin 2000).

18. The U.S. Ethyl Corporation settled for $13 million a dispute with Canada wherein the company claimed that a Canadian fuels additive act was a blatant domestic protectionist measure. A NAFTA tribunal in November 2000

found Canada in breach of NAFTA's investment protection provisions for temporarily banning transboundary movement of wastes containing polychlorinated biphenyls. The ruling found that the Canadian regulation treated an American company differently from Canadian businesses (*International Environment Reporter,* 22 November 2000, 901) Earlier that year an arbitration panel ordered the Mexican government to pay almost $17 million to an American company. The firm's plans to build a hazardous waste facility in San Luis Potosí were blocked by Mexican officials' conclusion that the site was environmentally unsound (Brevetti and Nagel 2000). There have been a handful of other demands for compensation under the NAFTA regime (Deimann 1999).

BIBLIOGRAPHY

Abrams, David. 1990. Regulating the International Hazardous Waste Trade: A Proposed Global Solution. *Columbia Journal of Transnational Law* 28: 801–845.

Adede, Andronico O. 1993. *International Environmental Law Digest.* Amsterdam: Elsevier.

Adler, Emanuel, and Peter Haas. 1992. Conclusion: Epistemic Communities, World Order, and the Creation of a Reflective Research Program. *International Organization* 46(1): 367.

Adler, Julienne I. 1991. Neighbors in Garbage. *American University Law Review* 4:885. Cited in *International Environmental Law and Policy,* by David Hunter, James Salzman, and Darwood Zaelke. New York: Foundation Press, 1998.

Akehurst, Michael. 1993. *A Modern Introduction to International Law.* New York: Routledge.

Aldy, Joseph E., Peter R. Orszag, and Joseph E. Stiglitz. 2001. Climate Change: An Agenda for Global Action. Arlington, Va.: Pew Center on Global Climate Change.

Aleksandrov, Valentin. 1997. Ecological Problems of the Black Sea. *International Affairs* (Moscow) 43(2): 87–99.

Allen, Mark E. 1995. Slowing Europe's Hazardous Waste Trade: Implementing the Basel Convention into European Union Law. *Colorado Journal of International Environmental Law and Policy* 6(1): 164–182.

Allison, Graham. 1971. *Essence of Decision: Explaining the Cuban Missile Crisis.* Boston: Little, Brown.

Alter, Karen J. 1996. The European Court's Political Power. *West European Politics* 19(3): 458–487.

Alvazzi del Frate, Anna, and Jennifer Norberry, eds. 1993. *Environmental Crime, Sanctioning Strategies, and Sustainable Development.* Rome: United Nations Publications.

Anderson, Terry L., and J. Bishop Grewell. 2001. It Isn't Easy Being Green: Environmental Policy Implications for Foreign Policy, International Law, and Sovereignty. *Chicago Journal of International Law* 2:427–445.

Andreen, William. 2000. Environmental Law and International Assistance: The Challenge of Strengthening Environmental Law in the Developing World. *Columbia Journal of Environmental Law* 25:17–69.

Aritake, Toshio. 2000. Japan May List Goods Linked with Cuts in GHG Emissions on Commodities Exchange. *International Environment Reporter* 23, no. 19 (13 September): 719.

Armenteros, Mercedes Fernandez. 2000. The Negotiation of the Clean Development Mechanism at the COP-6: Precautionary versus Cost-Effective Policies. *Environmental Law Network International* 2:2–11.

Arrow, K., B. Bohlin, R. Costanza, P. Dasgupta, C. Folke, C. S. Holling, B. O. Jansson, S. Levin, K. G. Maler, C. Perrings, and D. Pimentel. 1995. Economic Growth, Carrying Capacity, and the Environment. *Science*, 18 April, 520–521.

Arsov, R., T. Gordanov, T. Guirguinov, et al., eds. 1996. *Environmental Protection Technologies for Coastal Areas*. Water Science and Technology Series 32(7). New York: Pergamon.

Ascherson, Neal. 1995. *Black Sea*. New York: Hill and Wang.

———. 1998. Can a Study Cruise and a Noble Scrap of Paper Save the Black Sea? Accessed 7 February 1998, www.hydowire.org/internat/internat10.03a.html.

Audley, John J. 1997. *Green Politics and Global Trade: NAFTA and the Future of Environmental Politics*. Washington, D.C.: Georgetown University Press.

Aydin, Sulkuf. 1995. Sustainable Development and Environment: A Theory in the Making. *Bogazici Journal Review of Social, Economic, and Administrative Studies* 9(2): 45.

Bakan, Gulfem, and Hanife Buyukgungor. The Black Sea. *Marine Pollution Bulletin* 41(1): 21–43.

Balkas, T., et al. 1990. State of the Marine Environment in the Black Sea Region. Regional Seas, Regional Seas Reports and Studies 124. Nairobi: UNEP.

Ballard, Robert D. 2001. Deep Black Sea. *National Geographic* 199(5): 52–69.

Barrett, Scott. 1994. Self-Enforcing International Environmental Agreements. *Oxford Economic Papers* 46(4): 878.

———. 1999. International Environmental Agreements, Compliance and Enforcement: International Cooperation and the International Commons. *Duke Environmental Law and Policy Forum* 10: 131–145.

Barrows, Susan. 1995. Creating Solutions through Multilateral Agreements: The Hazardous Waste Dilemma. *Georgetown International Environmental Law Review* 7:881–888.

Bartlett, Robert, et al. 1995. *International Organizations and Environmental Policy*. Westport, Conn. : Greenwood Press.

Basel Convention. 1998. Secretariat home page, www.basel.int/centers/cfs98.htm.

———. 1999. Compilation Part 1: Reporting and Transmission of Information under the Basel Convention for the Year 1997 (excluding statistics on generation and transboundary movements of hazardous wastes and other wastes). Geneva, October 1999. Basel Convention Series/SBC 99/011.

Batabyal, Amitrajeet A. 1996. An Agenda for the Design and Study of International Environmental Agreements. *Ecological Economics* 19:3–9.

Batruch, Christine. 1999. "Hot Air" as Precedent for Developing Countries?

Equity Considerations. *UCLA Journal of Environmental Law and Policy* 17:45–66.

Baumert, Kevin A., Ruchi Bhandari, and Nancy Kete. 1999. What Might a Developing Country Climate Commitment Look Like? World Resources Institute Climate Notes. www.wri.org/wri.

Beach, Heather W., Jesse Hamner, J. Joseph Hewitt, Edy Kaufman, Anja Kurki, Joe A. Oppenheimer, and Aaron T. Wolf. 2000. *Transboundary Freshwater Dispute Resolution: Theory, Practice, and Annotated References.* New York: United Nations Press.

Beard, James E. 1996. An Application of the Principles of Sustainability to the Problem of Global Climate Change: An Argument for Integrated Energy Services. *Journal of Environmental Law and Litigation* 11(1): 191–245.

Behan, Nanoon. 1990. Regional Policy and World Crises: An East European View. *Journal of Peace Research* 27(2): 211–219.

Belenky, Lisa T. 1999. Cradle to Border: U.S. Hazardous Waste Export Regulations and International Law. *Berkeley Journal of International Law* 17: 30–91.

Belsky, Martin H. 1985. Management of Large Marine Ecosystems: Developing a New Rule of Customary International Law. *San Diego Law Review* 22(4): 733–779.

Benedick, Richard Eliot. 1991. *Ozone Diplomacy.* Cambridge, Mass.: Harvard University Press.

Benson, Christina C. 1996. The ISO 14000 International Standards: Moving Beyond Environmental Compliance. *North Carolina Journal of International Law and Commercial Regulation* 22(1): 307–364.

Benton, L. M. 1996. The Greening of Free Trade? The Debate about the North American Free Trade Agreement (NAFTA) and the Environment. *Environment and Planning* A 28:2155–2177.

Benvenisti, Eyal. 1996. Collective Action in the Utilization of Shared Freshwater: The Challenges of International Water Resources Law. *American Journal of International Law* 90(3): 384–415.

Bergesen, Helge Ole, and Trond Botnen. 1996. Sustainable Principles or Sustainable Institutions? The Long Way From UNCED to the Commission on Sustainable Development. *Forum for Development Studies* no. 1:35–62.

Berle, Peter, Jon Plant, and John Wirth. 1999. The Coming Storm. *NAMI News* 24 (Fall-Winter): 1–2.

Bernauer, Thomas. 1995. The Effect of International Environmental Institutions: How We Might Learn More. *International Organization* 41(2): 351–377.

Berwick, Teresa A. 1998. Responsibility and Liability for Environmental Damage: A Roadmap for International Environmental Regimes. *Georgetown International Law Review* 10:257–267.

Bethlehem, Daniel, James Crawford, and Philippe Sands, eds. 2001. *International Environmental Law Reports, Vol. 3: Human Rights and the Environment.* Cambridge: Cambridge University Press.

Bettini, Romano. 1993. Efficacy of Law and Socio-Economic Change. In *European Yearbook in the Sociology of Law,* edited by Alberto Febbrajo and David Nelkin. Milan: Giuffre Publisher.

Biancarelli, Jacques. 1996. Does the Community Legal Order Have the Power to Institute Sanctions? In *What Kind of Criminal Policy for Europe?* edited by Mireille Delmas-Marty. The Hague: Kluwer Law International.

Biermann, Frank. 1998. Land in Sight for Marine Environmentalists? *Revue De Droit International* 1 (January–April): 35–65.

Birnie, Patricia, and Alan Boyle. 2002. *International Law and the Environment.* 2nd ed. Oxford: Oxford University Press.

Biuliano, Mario, Tullio Scovazzi, and Tullio Treves. 1991. *Diritto Internazionale.* Milan: Giuffre Editore.

Blackman, Allen. 2000. Small Is Not Necessarily Beautiful: Coping with Dirty Microenterprises in Developing Countries. *Resources* no. 141:9–11.

Blatter, Joachim. n.d. Explaining Cross-Border Cooperation: A Border-Focused and a Border-External Approach. Mimeographed.

Blatter, Joachim, and Helen Ingram, eds. 2001. *Reflections on Water: New Approaches to Transboundary Conflicts and Cooperation.* Cambridge, Mass.: MIT Press.

Boardman, Robert. 1981. *International Organization and the Conservation of Nature.* Bloomington: Indiana University Press.

Bodansky, Daniel. 1997a. Review of *The Climate Change Convention and Developing Countries: From Conflict to Consensus,* by Joyeeta Gupta. *American Journal of International Law* 192:172–174.

———. 1997b. The History and Legal Structure of the Global Climate Change Regime. PIK Report 21. Accessed 22 July 1999, www.pik-potsdam.de/dept/soc/e/reports/pr217.htm.

Boer, Ben, Ross Ramsay, and Donald R. Rothwell. 1998. *International Environmental Law in the Asia Pacific.* London: Kluwer Law International.

Booncharoen, Charlotte, and John Gase. 1998. International Commitment toward Curbing Global Warming: The Kyoto Protocol. *Environmental Lawyer* 3 (June): 917–942.

Borisenko, E., and I. Semenenko. 1997. Black Sea Economic Cooperation. *International Affairs* 19(2): 91–97.

Borman, Margaret. 2000. Can Governments Encourage a Reduced Fish Harvest to Allow Global Stocks to Regenerate Their Numbers? *Journal of Environmental Law and Litigation* 15:127–145.

Botterweg, T., and D. W. Rodda. 1999. Danube River Basin: Progress with the Environmental Program. *Water Science and Technology* 40(10): 1–8.

Boyle, Alan E. 1991. Saving the World? Implementation and Enforcement of International Environmental Law Through International Institutions. *Journal of Environmental Law* 3:229.

———. 1997. Dispute Settlement and the Law of the Sea: Problems of Fragmentation and Jurisdiction. *International and Comparative Law Quarterly* 46 (January): 37.

Boyle, Alan, and David Freestone, eds. 1999. *International Law and Sustainable Development: Past Achievements and Future Challenges.* New York: Oxford University Press.

Boyle, John. 1988. Cultural Influence on Implementing Environmental Impact

Assessment: Insights from Thailand, Indonesia, and Malaysia. *Environmental Impact Assessment Review* 18:95–116.

Bradford, Mark. 1997. The United States, China, and the Basel Convention on the Transboundary Movements of Hazardous Wastes and Their Disposal. *Fordham Environmental Law Journal* 8(2): 305–349.

Braninga, Susan. 2000. Pollution Releases Increase Slightly from U.S. Canadian Industries, CEC Says. *International Environment Reporter* 23, no. 12 (7 June): 453.

Brevetti, Rossella, and John Nagel. 2000. Arbitration Panel Awards Metalclad Corp. $16.7 Million in Trade Dispute with Mexico. *International Environment Reporter* 23, no. 19 (13 September): 710.

British Institute of International and Comparative Law. 1996. *The International Court of Justice: Efficiency of Procedures and Working Methods.* Report of the study group established by the institute as a contribution to the U.N. Decade of International Law. ICQL Supplement 45: S1–S5.

Brunnee, Jutta. 2000. A Fine Balance: Facilitation and Enforcement in the Design of a Compliance Regime for the Kyoto Protocol. *Tulane Environmental Law Journal* 13 (Summer): 223–270.

Brunnee, Jutta, and Stephen J. Toope. 1997. Environmental Security and Freshwater Resources: Ecosystem Regime Building. *American Journal of International Law* 91:2626–2659.

Bryner, Gary. 1991. Implementing Global Environmental Agreements. *Policy Studies Journal* 19(2): 1–25.

BSEP. 1996. Strategic Action Plan for the Rehabilitation and Protection of the Black Sea, 31 October. Istanbul, Turkey.

Bugeda, Beatriz. 1999. Is NAFTA Up to its Green Expectations? Effective Law Enforcement under the North American Agreement on Environmental Cooperation. *University of Richmond Law Review* 32 (January): 1591–1616.

Bugge, Hans Christian. 1995. International Environmental Law: Status and Challenges. In *International Environmental Law* 53, edited by Hans Christian Bugge and Erling Selvig. Oslo: Juridisk.

Burke, W. T. 1996. Importance of the 1982 U.N. Convention on the Law of the Sea and Its Future Development. *Ocean Development and International Law* 27(1–2): 1–4.

Burley, Anne-Marie Slaughter. 1993. International Law and International Relations Theory: A Dual Agenda. *American Journal of International Law* 87 (April): 205–239.

Burns, William C. G. 2001. From the Harpoon to the Heat: Climate Change and the International Whaling Commission in the Twenty-first Century. *Georgetown International Environmental Law Review* 13:335–359.

Butler, Jo Elizabeth. 1997. The Establishment of a Dispute Resolution–Noncompliance Mechanism in the Climate Change Convention. *American Society of International Law Proceedings:* 250–258.

Caldwell, Lynton Keith. 1990. *International Environmental Policy: Emergence and Dimensions.* Durham, N.C.: Duke University Press.

———. 1991. Law and Environment in an Era of Transition: Reconciling Domestic and International Law. *Colorado Journal of International Environmental Law Policy* 2(1): 1.

———. 1999. Is World Law an Emerging Reality? Environmental Law in a Transnational World. *Colorado Journal of International Environmental Law and Policy* (January 15–30): 1–12. Online symposium.

Cameron, James. 1999. Future Directions in International Environmental Law: Precaution, Integration, and Non-state Actors. *Dalhousie Law Journal* 19(1): 122–138.

Cameron, J., J. Werksman, and P. Roderick, eds. 1996. *Improving Compliance with International Environmental Law*. London: Earthscan.

Campbell, Laura. 2000a. Globalization, the Kyoto Protocol, and the Role of the Private Sector. *International Environment Reporter* 23, no. 20 (27 September): 768.

———. 2000b. WTO and Climate Change: Trade, Investment, and the Kyoto Protocol. *International Environment Reporter* 23, no. 17 (16 August): 654.

Cappel, Kirsten Michelle. 2000. Investigation of the Kyoto Protocol: Strategies for the Future. Honors paper, University of California, Irvine.

Carr, Christopher J. 1997. Recent Developments in Compliance and Enforcement for International Fisheries. *Ecology Law Quarterly* 24(4): 847–860.

Carr, Susan, and Roger Mpande. 1996. Does the Definition of the Issue Matter? NGO Influence and the International Convention to Combat Desertification in Africa. *Journal of Commonwealth and Comparative Politics* 34(1): 143–166.

Carroll, Christina M. 1999. Past and Future Legal Framework of the Nile River Basin. *Georgetown International Law Review* 12(1): 269–304.

Carroll, John. 1988. *International Environmental Diplomacy*. Cambridge: Cambridge University Press.

———. 1990. *The Management and Resolution of Transfrontier Environmental Problems*. New York: Cambridge University Press.

Cass, Valerie. 1997. The Greenhouse Challenge: Australia's Approach for Reducing Greenhouse Gas Emissions via Self-Regulation. Ph.D. diss., University of California, Irvine.

CEC. 1997. Final Factual Record of the Cruise Ship Pier Project in Cozumel, Quintana Roo. Montreal: Commission for Environmental Cooperation.

———. 1999. Assessing Environmental Effects of North American Free Trade Agreement (NAFTA): An Analytical Framework (Phase 2) and Issue Studies. Montreal: Commission for Environmental Cooperation.

———. 1999. Tracking and Enforcement of Transborder Hazardous Waste Shipments in North America: A Needs Assessment. Montreal: Commission for Environmental Cooperation.

———. 2000. Public Registry of Submissions on Enforcement Matters. Accessed 27 February 2000, www.cec.org.

Champion, David. 1998. Environmental Management: Spreading the Green. *Harvard Business Review* 76(6): (November–December): 20–21.

Charnovitz, Steve. 1994a. Green Roots, Bad Pruning: GATT Rules and Their Application to Environmental Trade Measures. *Tulane Environmental Law Journal* 7:299–352.

————. 1994b. The NAFTA Environmental Side Agreement: Implications for Environmental Cooperation, Trade Policy, and American Treatymaking. *Temple International and Comparative Law Journal* 8:257–314.

————. 1998a. Linking Topics in Treaties. *University of Pennsylvania Journal of International Economic Law* 19(2): 329–345.

————. 1998b. Participation of Nongovernmental Organizations in the World Trade Organization. *University of Pennsylvania Journal of International Economic Law* 17(1): 331–357.

————. 2000. World Trade and the Environment: A Review of the New WTO Report. *Georgetown International Environmental Law Review* 12:523–541.

————. 2001. Rethinking WTO Trade Sanctions. *American Journal of International Law* 95(4): 792–832.

Chase, Adam. 1994. Barriers to International Agreements for the Adaptation of Global Climate Change: A Law and Economics Approach. *Environmental Law Journal* 1:18–42.

Chasek, Pamela S. 2001. *Earth Negotiations: Analyzing Thirty Years of Environmental Diplomacy.* New York: United Nations University Press.

Chayes, Abram, and Antonia Handler Chayes. 1991. Compliance Without Enforcement: State Behavior under Regulatory Regimes. *Negotiation Journal* 7(3): 311–330.

————. 1993. On Compliance. *International Organization* 47(2): 175–205.

————. 1995. *The New Sovereignty: Compliance with International Regulatory Agreements.* Cambridge, Mass.: Harvard University Press.

Cho, Byung-Sun. 2000–2001. Emergence of International Environmental Criminal Law? *UCLA Journal of Environmental Law and Policy* 19(1): 11–48.

Choksi, Sejal. 1999. The Basel Convention on the Control of Transboundary Movements of Hazardous Wastes and Their Disposal: Protocol on Liability and Compensation. *Ecology Law Quarterly* 28:509–539.

Chomo, Grace V., and Michael J. Ferrantino. 2000. NAFTA Environmental Impacts on North American Fisheries. In *Environment and Trade Series.* Commission for Environmental Cooperation.

Choucri, Nazli, ed. 1993. *Global Accord: Environmental Challenges and International Responses.* Cambridge, Mass.: MIT Press.

Churchill, Robin R., and Geir Ulfstein. 2000. Autonomous Institutional Arrangements in Multilateral Environmental Agreements: A Little-Noticed Phenomenon in International Law. *American Journal of International Law* 94(4): 623–659.

Cicerone, Ralph J. 2000. Human Forcing of Climate Change: Easing Up on the Gas Pedal. *Proceedings of the National Academy of Sciences* 97(19): 10304–10306.

CIESIN. 1996. Measurements and Trends in Ozone and Chlorofluorocarbon Levels. Accessed 27 February 2000, www.ciesin.org/TG/OZ/trends.html.

————. 2001. Menu of Treaty Texts. www.ciesin.org/entri/ENTRIchron.html.

Clapp, Jennifer. 1997. The Illegal CFC Trade: An Unexpected Wrinkle in the Ozone Protection Regime. *International Environmental Affairs:* 259–273.

Clinard, Marshall, and Peter Yeager. 1980. *Corporate Crime*. New York: Free Press.

Coate, Roger A., F. Charwick, and Ronnie D. Lipschutz. 1996. The United Nations and Civil Society: Creative Partnerships for Sustainable Development. *Alternatives* 21(1): 93–122.

Coglianese, Cary. 2000. Globalization and the Design of International Institutions. In *Governance in a Globalizing World*, edited by Joseph S. Nye and John D. Donahue. Washington, D.C.: Brookings Institution Press.

Colnic, Dave. 2000. BECC and Sustainability: Community Assessments of Environmental Protection. Paper prepared for the annual meeting of the International Studies Association, 15–18 March, Los Angeles.

Comment. 1994. Developments in the Law: International Environmental Law. *Harvard Law Review* 107(5): 1099.

Cooper, Richard. 1998. Why Kyoto Won't Work. *Foreign Affairs* 77(2): 66–79.

COP-4. 1999. Report of the Conference of the Parties on Its Fourth Session, 2–14 November 1998, Buenos Aires. Addendum, Part 2: Action Taken by the Conference of the Parties at Its Fourth Session. United Nations, 20 January.

Cox, Robert, ed. 1970. *The Politics of International Organizations: Studies in Multilateral Social and Economic Agencies*. New York: Praeger.

Crane, Andrew. 1997. Rhetoric and Reality in Greening of Organizational Culture. In *Greening the Boardroom*, edited by Grant Ledgerwood. Sheffield: Greenleaf Publishing.

Cupei, Jurgen G. R. F., and Walter R. Lotz. 1998. Authorization and EIA of Industrial Installations: A Legal Comparison of France, Germany, and Switzerland. *Environmental Impact Assessment Review* 18:313–325.

Cusack, M. 1990. International Law and the Transboundary Shipment of Hazardous Waste to the Third World: Will the Basel Convention Make a Difference? *American University Journal of International Policy* 5:393–423.

D'Amato, Anthony, ed. 1994. *International Law Anthology*. Cincinnati: Anderson Publications.

D'Anieri, Paul. 1995. International Organizations, Environmental Cooperation, and Regime Theory. In *International Organizations and Environmental Policy*, by Robert V. Bartlett et al. Westport, Conn.: Greenwood Press.

Dauvergne, Peter. 1998. Globalisation and Deforestation in the Asia-Pacific. *Environmental Politics* 7(4): 114–116.

Davies, Peter G. G., and Catherine Redgwell. 1997. The International Legal Regulation of Straddling Fish Stocks. *British Yearbook of International Law*. Oxford: Clarendon Press.

Dbar, Roman, and Yuri Ryuhin. 1996. The Program of Integrated Monitoring of the Sea Environment: The Black Sea, Abkhazia. Mimeographed.

de Guijl, Frank R. 1995. Impacts of a Projected Depletion of the Ozone Layer. *Consequences* 1(1).

Deimann, Sven. 1999. Investing in the Environment: A Green Agenda for the Millennium Round. *Environmental Law Network International Newsletter* 21(99): 35–42.

Dellapenna, J. W. 1989. Water in the Jordan Valley: The Potential Limits of Law. *Palestine YBIL* 5:15–47.

DeSombre, Elizabeth. 2000. *Domestic Sources of International Environmental Policy.* Cambridge: MIT Press.

———. 2000–2001. The Experience of the Montreal Protocol: Particularly Remarkable and Remarkedly Particular. *UCLA Journal of Environmental Law and Policy.* 19(1): 49–82.

de Vries, Michael S. 1990. Interdependence, Cooperation, and Conflict: An Empirical Analysis. *Journal of Peace Research* 27(4): 429.

De Yturriaga, Jose A. 1997. *The International Regime of Fisheries: From UNCLOS 1982 to the Sea.* The Hague: Martinus Nijhoff Publishers.

Diamond, Jared. 2000. The Greening of Corporate America. *New York Times,* 8 January.

DiMento, Joseph. 1976. *Managing Environmental Change: A Legal and Behavioral Perspective.* New York: Praeger

———. 1986. *Environmental Law and American Business: Dilemmas of Compliance.* New York: Plenum.

———. 1995. Regional Hazardous Waste Management in the Middle East: Compliance and Confidence Building in Implementing Peace. In *Practical Peacemaking in the Middle East,* by Steven L. Spiegel and David J. Pervin. New York: Garland Publishing.

———. 1996. NAFTA and a North American Environmental Law. In *A World Survey of Environmental Law,* by Stefano Nespor et al. Milan: Giuffre Editore.

———. 1997. EIA and NAFTA. In *International Environmental Impact Assessment,* edited by Environmental Law Network International. London: Cameron May.

———. 2001. Black Sea Environmental Management: Prospects for New Paradigms in Transitional Contexts. In *Reflections on Water: New Approaches to Transboundary Conflicts and Cooperation,* edited by Joachim Blatter and Helen Ingram. Cambridge, Mass.: MIT Press.

DiMento, Joseph, and Francesco Bertolini. 1996. Green Management and the Regulatory Process: For Mother Earth, Market Share, and Modern Rule. *Transnational Lawyer* 9(1).

DiMento, Joseph, and Pamela Doughman. 1998. Soft Teeth in the Back of the Mouth: The NAFTA Environmental Side Agreement Implemented. *Georgetown International Environmental Law Review* 3 (Spring): 651–752.

DiMento, Joseph F. C., Helen Ingram, Richard Matthew, and John Whiteley, eds. 2001. A Symposium on International Environmental Law. *UCLA Journal of Environmental Law and Policy* 19(1): 1–291.

Docker, Englebert, and Ngo van Long. 1993. International Pollution Control: Cooperative Versus Non-Cooperative Strategies. *Journal of Environmental Economics and Management* 25(1): 13.

Doughman, Pamela Mae. 1999. *Discourse, Sustainable Development, Mexico, and Water.* Ann Arbor, Mich.: UMI Dissertation Services.

Downs, George, Kyle W. Danish, and Peter N. Barsoom. 2000. The Transformational Model of International Regime Design: Triumph of Hope or Experience? *Columbia Journal of Transnational Law* 38(3): 465–509.

Downs, George W., David M. Rocke, and Peter N. Barsoom. 1996. Is the Good

News about Compliance Good News about Cooperation? *International Organization* 50(3): 379–406.

Doyle, William N. 1995. United States Implementation of the Basel Convention: Time Keeps Ticking, Ticking Away. *Temple International and Comparative Law Journal* 9(1): 141–161.

Driesen, David M. 1998. Free Lunch or Cheap Fix? The Emissions Trading Idea and the Climate Change Convention. *Boston College Environmental Affairs Law Review* 26(1): 1–87.

———. 2000. Choosing Environmental Instruments in a Transnational Context. *Ecology Law Quarterly* 27(1): 1–40.

Drumbl, Mark A. 1999. Does Sharing Know Its Limits? Thoughts on Implementing International Agreements: A Review of National Environmental Policies. *Virginia Environmental Law Journal* 18:281–304.

Dubner, Barry Hart. 1998. On the Interplay of International Law of the Sea and the Prevention of Maritime Pollution: How Far Can a State Proceed in Protecting Itself from Conflicting Norms in International Law? *Georgetown International Environmental Law Review* (Fall): 137–161.

Duffield, John S. 1992. International Regimes and Alliance Behavior: Explaining NATO Conventional Force Levels. *International Organization* 46(4): 819–835.

Duina, Francesco. 1997. Explaining Legal Implementation in the European Union. *International Journal of the Sociology of Law* 25(2): 155–180.

Dunoff, Jeffrey L. 1994. Institutional Misfits: The GATT, the ICS, and Trade-Environment Issues. *Michigan Journal of International Law* 15(4): 1043–1128.

———. 1995. From Green to Global: Towards the Transformation of International Environmental Law. *Harvard Environmental Law Review* 19 (Winter): 241–301.

Duruigbo, Emeka. 2000. Reforming the International Law and Policy on Marine Oil Pollution. *Journal of Maritime Law and Commerce* 31:65–88.

———. 2001. International Relations, Economics, and Compliance with International Law: Harnessing Common Resources to Protect the Environment and Solve Global Problems. *California Western International Law Journal* 31:177–213.

Earth Negotiations Bulletin. 1996. High Level Segment of the COP-2 of the FCCC. *Earth Negotiations Bulletin* 12. Accessed 23 July 1999, www.iisd.ca/linkages/vol12/1238014w.html.

Economics and Trade Unit and the International Institute for Sustainable Development. 2000. *Environment and Trade: A Handbook.* United Nations Environment Programme, Division of Technology, Industry, and Economics.

Eisen, Joel B. 1999. From Stockholm to Kyoto and Back to the United States: International Environmental Law's Effect on Domestic Law. *University of Richmond Law Review* 32 (January): 1435–1502.

Ekins, Paul. 1996. Economic Implications and Decision-Making in the Face of Global Warming. *International Environmental Affairs* 8(3): 227–243.

El-Hindi, Jamal. 1990. Note: The West Bank Aquifer and Conventions Regarding Laws of Belligerent Occupation. *Michigan Journal of International Law* 11 (Summer): 1400–1423.

Elliott, E. Donald. 1992. Global Climate Change and Regulatory Uncertainty. *Arizona Journal of International and Comparative Law* 9(1): 259–266.

Elliott, Lorraine M. 1994. *International Environmental Politics: Protecting the Antarctic.* New York: St. Martin's Press.

Elwell, Christine. 2001. NAFTA Effects on Water: Testing for NAFTA Effects in the Great Lakes Basin. *Toledo Journal of Great Lakes Law, Science, and Policy:* 151–218.

Enders, Alice. 1996. The Europe Agreements and NAFTA: A Comparison of Their Ends and Means. *International Politik und Gesellschaft* no. 3:254–264.

Environmental Law Institute. 1993. *Protecting the Gulf of Aqaba: A Regional Environmental Challenge.* Washington, D.C.: Environmental Law Institute.

Environmental Law Network International. 1999. *Practical Implications of Environmental Law Principles.* Brussels: Bruylant.

Esty, Daniel C. 1994. *Greening the GATT: Trade, Environment, and the Future.* Washington, D.C.: Institute for International Economics.

———. 1999. Toward Optimal Environmental Governance. *New York University Law Review* 74 (December).

Esty, Daniel C., and Damien Geradin. 1997. Market Access, Competitiveness, and Harmonization: Environmental Protection in Regional Trade Agreements. *Harvard Environmental Law Review* 21:265–335.

Etzioni, Amitai. 2000. Social Norms: Internalization, Persuasion, and History. *Law and Society* 34:157–178.

European Union. 1985. *The Assessment of the Effects of Certain Public and Private Projects on the Environment.* Directive on Environmental Assessment 85/337, L175, OJ.

Farber, Daniel A. 1996. Stretching the Margins. The Geographic Nexus in Environmental Law. *Stanford Law Review* 48 (May): 1247–1278.

Farha, Alfred. 1990. The Corporate Conscience and Environmental Issues: Responsibility of the Multinational Corporation. *Northwestern Journal of International Law and Business* 10:379–396.

Farkas, Andrew. 1998. *State Learning and International Change.* Ann Arbor: University of Michigan Press.

Farr, Karen Tyler. 2000. A New Global Environmental Organization. *Georgia Journal of International and Comparative Law* 28:493–525.

FCCC. 1999. Secretariat Press Release, 11 June: Ministerial talks on climate change set for 2–4 November in Bonn.

Feldman, David Lewis. 1995. Interacting Functionalism and Climate Management Organizations: From Intergovernmental Panel on Climate Change to Intergovernmental Negotiating Committee. In *International Organizations and Environmental Policy,* by Robert Bartlett et al. Westport, Conn.: Greenwood Press.

Ferretti, Janine H. 1992. Statement on Behalf of Pollution Probe before the Standing Senate Committee on Foreign Affairs on the North American Free Trade Agreement and the Promotion of Sustainable Development. 25 February, 6–7.

Flores, Marcello. 2002. *Il Secolo-Mondo: Storia del Novecento.* Bologna: Il Mulino.

Fois, Paolo. 1992. Ambiente (Tutela Dell') nel Diritto Internazionale. *Digesto* 4(7): 3–13.

———. 1995. Il Diritto Internazionale Dell'Ambiente nel Nuovo Ordine Internazionale. *Rivista Giuridica Sarda* 2:541–552.

Foster, Mark Edward. 1998. Trade and Environment: Making Room for Environmental Trade Measures within the GATT. *Southern California Law Review* 71:393–443.

Fowler, Robert. 1995. International Environmental Standards for Transnational Cooperation. *Environmental Law* 25(1).

Francimi, Francesco, ed. 2001. *Environment, Human Rights, and International Trade.* Portland, Ore.: Hart.

French, Hillary. 1992. From Discord to Accord. *National Forum* 72(4): 37–39.

———. 1994. Strengthening International Environmental Governance. *Journal of Environment and Development* 3(1): 59.

Friedman, Thomas L. 1998. A Brazilian Ecosystem Meets Globalization. *International Herald Tribune,* 4 August.

Fritz, Jan-Stefan. 1991. *A Survey of Environmental Monitoring and Information Management Programs of International Organizations.* UNEP, Harmonization of Environmental Measurement.

Fuentes, Ximena. 1997. The Criteria for the Equitable Utilization of International Rivers. Pp. 337–412 in *British Yearbook of International Law,* edited by Ian Brownlie and James Crawford. Oxford: Clarendon Press.

Gaja, Giorgio. 1981. The European Community's Participation in the Law of the Sea Convention: Some Incoherencies in a Compromise Solution. *Italian Yearbook of International Law* 5:110–114.

———. 1987. A New Vienna Convention on Treaties between States and International Organizations or between International Organizations: A Critical Commentary. *British Yearbook of International Law* 58:253–269.

———. 1996. *Introduzione al Diritto Comunitario.* Rome: Gius, Laterza, e Figli.

———. 1998. Evoluzione e Tendenze Attuali del Diritto Internazionale Dell'Ambiente. Remarks presented at Ambiente e Diritto, 11 June, Florence, Italy.

Garcia-Johnson, Ronnie. 2000. *Exporting Environmentalism: U.S. Multinational Chemical Corporations in Brazil and Mexico.* Cambridge, Mass.: MIT Press.

Gardner, Royal C. 1998. Exporting American Values: Tenth Amendment Principles and International Environmental Assistance. *Harvard Environmental Law Review* 22:1–49.

Garvey, Jack I. 2000. A New Evolution for Fast-Tracking Trade Agreements: Managing Environmental and Labor Standards Through Extraterritorial Regulation. *UCLA Journal of International Law and Foreign Affairs* 5:1–51.

Gehring, Thomas. 1994. *Dynamic International Regimes: Institutions for International Environmental Governance.* New York: P. Lang.

George, Clive. 1997. Assessing Global Impacts at Sector and Project Levels. *Environmental Impact Assessment Review* 17:227–247.

Giampietro, Franco. 1998. Le Nuove Frontiere del Diritto Communitario Dell'Ambiente. *Ambiente* no. 3.

Glassner, Martin. 1993. Implementation of the Law of the Sea Convention through International Institutions. *Canadian Geographer* 37(3): 271.

Gleckman, Harris, and Riva Krut. 1998. *ISO 14001: A Missed Opportunity for Sustainable Global Industrial Development.* London: Earthscan.

Global Environment Facility. 1997. *Black Sea Transboundary Diagnostic Analysis.* Black Sea Environmental Program Coordination Unit, UNDP.

Global Environment Outlook. 1997. GEO Team, United Nations Environment Programme.

Global Environment Outlook 2000. 1999. United Nations Environment Programme. London: Earthscan.

Global Learn. 1996. The Black Sea. www.globalearn.org.

Golub, Jonathan. 1996a. Sovereignty and Subsidiarity in EU Environmental Policy. *Political Studies* 44(4): 606 725.

———. 1996b. State Power and Institutional Influence in European Integration: Lessons from the [EU] Packaging Directive. *Journal of Common Market Studies* 34(3): 313–339.

Gosovic, Branislav. 1992. *The Quest for World Environmental Cooperation: The Case of the U.N. Global Environment Monitoring System.* New York: Routledge.

Gow, H. F. B., and H. Otway, eds. 1989. *Communicating with the Public about Major Accident Hazards.* New York: Elsevier Applied Science.

Greenpeace. 1993. All Talk, No Teeth: NAAEC Sidesteps the Environment. Posted to electronic conference trade, library@conf.igc.apc.org. Summer.

———. 1994. Money to Burn: The World Bank, Chemical Companies, and Ozone Depletion. *Greenpeace Newsletter* 1:4.

Greenpeace International. 2000. Undermining the Kyoto Protocol: Environmental Effectiveness versus Political Expendiency.

Groom, A. J. R., and Paul Taylor, eds. 1988. *International Institutions at Work.* London: Pinter.

Grout, Deborah Zamora. 1999. The Benefits of Basel. *Environmental Forum* (January-February): 19–25.

Grubb, Michael, Christian Vrolijk, and Duncan Brack. 1999. *The Kyoto Protocol: A Guide and Assessment.* London: Earthscan.

Grundmann, R. 1998. The Strange Success of the Montreal Protocol: Why Reductionist Accounts Fail. *International Environmental Affairs* 10(3): 197–220.

Gudofsky, Jason L. 1998. Transboundary Shipments of Hazardous Waste for Recycling and Recovery Operations. *Stanford Journal of International Law* 24(2): 219–286.

Gupta, Joyeeta. 2000. North-South Aspects of the Climate Change Issue: Towards a Negotiating Theory and Strategy for Developing Countries. *International Journal of Sustainable Development* 3(2): 115–133.

Gupta, Joyeeta, and Matthijs Hisschemoller. 1997. Issue Linkage as a Global Strategy toward Sustainable Development. *International Environmental Affairs:* 289–306.

Guruswamy, Lakshman D., Geoffrey Palmer, and Burns H. Weston, eds. 1994. *International Environmental Law and World Order: A Problem Oriented Course Book.* St. Paul, Minn.: West Publishing.

Haas, Peter M. 1989. Do Regimes Matter? Epistemic Communities and Mediterranean Pollution Control. *International Organization* 43(3): 377.

———. 1990. *Saving the Mediterranean: The Politics of International Environmental Cooperation.* New York: Columbia University Press.

———. 1992. Introduction: Epistemic Communities and International Policy Coordination. *International Organization* 46(1): 1.

———. 2001. International Environmental Governance: Lessons for Pollution Control Since UNCHE. Prepared for publication in *Managing a Globalizing World,* edited by Chantal de Jonge Oudraat and P. J. Simmons. Washington, D.C.: Carnegie Foundation.

Haas, Peter M., and Ernst B. Haas. 1995. Learning to Learn: Improving International Governance. *Global Governance* 1(3): 255–284.

Haas, P., R. Keohane, and M. Levy. 1993. *Institutions for the Earth: Sources of Effective International Environmental Protection.* Cambridge, Mass.: MIT Press.

Haas, Peter, et al. 1994. *Complex Cooperation: Institutions and Processes in International Resource Management.* Oslo: Scandinavian University Press.

Hackett, D. 1990. An Assessment of the Basel Convention on the Control of Transboundary Movement of Hazardous Wastes and Their Disposal. *American University Journal of International Law and Policy* 5:291.

Hafetz, Jonathan L. 2000. Fostering Protection of the Marine Environment and Economic Development Article 121(3) of the Third Law of the Sea Convention. *American University International Law Review* 15(3): 583–637.

Hanafi, Alex G. 1998. Joint Implementation: Legal and Institutional Issues for an Effective International Program to Combat Climate Change. *Harvard Environmental Law Review* 22(2): 441–500.

Handl, Gunther. 1977. Compliance Control Mechanisms and International Environmental Obligations. *Tulane Journal of International and Comparative Law* 5 (Spring): 29–49.

———. 1994. Controlling Implementation and Compliance with International Environmental Commitments: The Rocky Road from Rio. *Colorado Journal of International Environmental Law and Policy* 5:305–331.

Handl, Gunther, and Robert E. Lutz. 1989. An International Policy Perspective on the Trade of Hazardous Materials and Technologies. *Harvard International Law Journal* 30(2): 351–374.

Hardin, Garrett. 1968. The Tragedy of the Commons. *Science* 162:1243–1248.

Harris, Jonathan M. 1991. Global Institutions and Ecological Crisis. *World Development* 19(1): 111.

Harris, Paul G. 1997. Affluence, Poverty, and Ecology: Obligation, International Relations, and Sustainable Development. *Ethics and the Environment* 2(2): 121–138.

Harvard Law Review. 1991. Developments in the Law: International Environmental Law. *Harvard Law Review* 104 (May): 1580–1609.

———. 1994. Discretion and Legitimacy in International Regulation. *Harvard Law Review* 107(5): 1099.

Hauselmann, Pierre. 1996. ISO Inside Out: No Useful Tool for Forestry Certification. *TAIGA-NEWS* (August).

Heimert, Andrew. 1995. How the Elephant Lost His Tusks. *Yale Law Review* (April): 1473–1506.

Heller, Thomas C. 1996. Environmental Realpolitik: Joint Implementation and Climate Change. *Indiana Journal of Global Legal Studies* 3(2): 295.

Hemminger, Pat. 2000. E-Commerce: Coloring It Green? *The Earth Times,* 27 November.

Hempel, Lamont. 1996. *Environmental Governance.* Washington, D.C.: Island Press.

Herber, Bernard P., and Jose T. Raga. 1995. An International Carbon Tax to Combat Global Warming: An Economic and Political Analysis of the European Union Proposal. *American Journal of Economics and Sociology* 54(3): 257–266.

Hey, Ellen, and Laurence Mee. 1993. The Ministerial Declaration: An Important Step. *Environment, Policy, and Law* (Regional Affairs Black Sea) 2315:215.

Higuero, Ivonne. 1999. Harmonizing Trade and Environment Rules. *Synergies* no. 1:6. United Nations Environment Programme.

Hogenboom, Barbara. 1998. *Mexico and the NAFTA Environment Debate: The Transnational Politics of Economic Integration.* Utrecht: International Books.

Hohmann, Harold. 1994. *Precautionary Legal Duties and Principles of Modern International Environmental Law.* London: Graham and Trotman/Martinus Nijhoff.

Holdgate, Martin W. 1996. Pathways to Sustainability: The Evolving Role of Transnational Institutions. *Environment* 37(9): 16–42.

Hooghe, Liesbet, and Gary Marks. 1996. Europe with the Regions: Channels of Regional Representation in the European Union. *Publius* 26(1): 773–791.

Hope, Kempe Ronald, Sr. 1996. International Trade and International Technology Transfer to Eliminate Ozone-Depleting Substances. *International Environmental Affairs* 8(1): 32–40.

Hough, Peter. 1996. Stemming the Flow of Poison: The Role of UNEP and the FAO in Regulating the International Trade in Pesticides. *International Relations* 13(1): 69–79.

Hovl, Jon. 1996. Tvistelesning I GATT og WTO (Dispute Settlement in GATT and in the WTO): Le Reglement des Conflits au Sein du GATT et de l'OMC. *International Politik* 54(3): 331–344.

Humphreys, David. 1996a. Regime Theory and Non-Governmental Organizations: The Case of Forest Conservation. *Journal of Commonwealth and Comparative Politics* 34(1): 90–115.

———. 1996b. The Global Politics of Forest Conservations since the UNCED. *Environmental Politics* 5(2): 231–256.

Hunt, Tamlyn. 2001. People or Power: A Comparison of Realist and Social Constructivist Approaches to Climate Change Remediation Negotiations. *UCLA Journal of International Law and Foreign Affairs* 6:265–311.

Hunter, David, James Salzman, and Durwood Zaelke. 1998. *International Environmental Law and Policy.* New York: Foundation Press.

Huntoon, Barbara A. 1989. Emerging Controls on Transfers of Hazardous

Waste to Developing Countries. *Law and Policy in International Business* 21(2): 247–271.

Hurlbut, David. 1993. Beyond the Montreal Protocol: Impact on Non-Party States, Lessons for Future Environmental Protection Regimes. *Colorado Journal of International Environmental Law and Policy* 4(2): 344–368.

Hurrell, Andrew, and Benedict Kingsbury, eds. 1992. *The International Politics of the Environment.* Oxford: Clarendon Press.

Hurrell, Andrew, and Anand Menon. 1996. Politics Like Any Other? Comparative Politics, International Relations, and the Study of the EU. *West European Politics* 19(2): 386–402.

Huygen, Nina. 1996. Towards a Permanent International Criminal Court. *Verfassung und Recht in Ubersee* 29(3): 292–308.

Ingram, Helen. 1995. *Divided Waters: Bridging the U.S.-Mexico Border.* Tucson: University of Arizona Press.

Ingram, Helen, and Suzanne L. Fiederlein. 1988. Traversing Boundaries: A Public Policy Approach to the Analysis of Foreign Policy. *Western Political Quarterly* 41(4): 725–745.

Ingram, Helen, and D. White. 1993. International Boundary and Water Commission: An Institutional Mismatch for Resolving Transboundary Water Problems. *Natural Resources Lawyer* 33(1–2): 153–177.

International Environment Reporter 22 and 23 (4 August 1999–22 November 2000). Bureau of National Affairs.

IPCC. 1995. The Second Assessment Synthesis of Scientific-Technical Information Relevant to Interpreting Article 2 of the UN Framework Convention on Climate Change.

IPCC Working Group I. 2001. Summary for Policy Makers: The Science of Climate Change. IPCC, Section 4.

IPCC Working Group II. 1995. Summary for Policymakers: Scientific-Technical Analyses of Impacts, Adaptations, and Mitigation of Climate Change.

IUCC. 1979. The First World Climate Conference. Geneva: Information Unit on Climate Change, UNEP.

———. 1999. Climate Change Information Sheet 17: The international response to climate change. UNEP.

IUCN (World Conservation Union). 2000. Carbon Sequestration, Biodiversity, and Sustainable Livelihoods.

Jacoby, Henry D., Ronald G. Prinn, and Richard Schmalensee. 1998. Kyoto's Unfinished Business. *Foreign Affairs* 77(4): 54–66.

Jaffe, Daniel. 1995. The International Effort to Control the Transboundary Movement of Hazardous Waste: The Basel and Bamako Conventions. *ISLA Journal of International and Comparative Law* 2(1): 123–137.

Jaquemont, Frederic. 2001. The EU and Climate Change: Is Clarification of EU Legal Competence Possible? *Environmental Law Network International Review* no. 1:30–35.

Johnson, Kirk. 2000. Global Warming Moves from Impassioned Words to First Modest Deeds. *New York Times,* 19 November.

Johnson, Pierce Marc, and André Beaulieu. 1996. *The Environment and*

NAFTA: Understanding and Implementing the New Continental Law. Washington, D.C.: Island Press.

Johnson, Stanley P., and Guy Corcelle. 1992. *The Environmental Policy of the European Communities.* London: Graham and Trotman.

Joyner, Christopher C. 1998. *Governing the Frozen Commons: The Antarctic Regime and Environmental Protection.* Columbia: University of South Carolina Press.

Judge, David, and David Earnshaw. 1994. Weak European Parliament Influence? A Study of the Environment Committee of the European Parliament. *Government and Opposition* 29(2): 262.

Jurgielewicz, Lynne M. 1995. International Regimes and Environmental Policy: An Evaluation of the Role of International Law. In *International Organizations and Environmental Policy,* by Robert V. Bartlett et al, Westport, Conn.: Greenwood Press.

———. 1996. *Global Environmental Change and International Law: Prospects for Progress in the Legal Order.* Lanham, Md.: University Press of America.

Kagan, Robert A., and Lee Axelrod. 2000. *Regulatory Encounters: Multinational Corporations and American Adversarial Legalism.* Berkeley: University of California Press.

Kakonge, John O. 1998. EIA and Good Governance: Issues and Lessons from Africa. *Environmental Impact Assessment Review* 18:289–305.

Kalas, Peggy R., and Alexia Herwig. Dispute Resolution under the Kyoto Protocol. *Ecology Law Quarterly* 27(1): 53–134.

Kamieniecke, Sheldon. 1993. *Environmental Politics in the International Arena: Movements, Parties, Organizations, and Policy.* Albany: State University of New York Press.

Kamo, Valerie. 1991. Protection of Endangered Gorillas and Chimpanzees in International Trade: Can CITES Help? *Hastings International and Comparative Law Review* 14(4): 989–1015.

Kaplan, Robert A. 1991. Into the Abyss: International Regulation of Subseabed Nuclear Waste Disposal. *University of Pennsylvania Law Review* 139: 769–800.

Kelly, J. Patrick. 2000. The Twilight of Customary International Law. *Virginia Journal of International Law* 40:449–541.

Kelly, Michael J. 1997. Overcoming Obstacles to the Effective Implementation of International Environmental Agreements. *Georgetown International Environmental Law Review* 9:447–488.

Keohane, Robert O. 1995. Against Hierarchy: An Institutional Approach to International Environmental Protection. In *Local Commons and Global Interdependence: Heterogeneity and Cooperation in Two Domains,* by R. Keohane and Elinor Ostrom. Thousand Oaks, Calif.: Sage Publications.

Keohane, Robert, and Joseph Nye, Jr. 1998. States and the Information Revolution. *Foreign Affairs* 77(5): 81–94.

Keppermans, Bart. 1996. Do Institutions Make a Difference: Non-Institutionalism, Neo-Institutionalism, and the Logic of Common Decision-Making in the European Unions. *Governance* 9(2): 217–240.

Kerr, Andrew. n.d. With a Gurgle and a Sigh, the Climate Change Threat Disappears into a Black Hole of Loopholes. *Daily Diary: The Road to Kyoto.* Web site, World Wildlife Fund.

Kerr, Suzi. 1995. Markets Versus International Funds for Implementing International Environmental Agreements: Ozone Depletion and the Montreal Protocol. Paper 95-12, Department of Agricultural and Resource Economics, University of Maryland at College Park.

Kibel, Paul Stanton. 1996. Justice for the Sea Turtle: Marine Conservation and the Court of International Trade. *Journal of Environmental Law* 15:57–81.

King, Richard J. 1996. Regional Trade and the Environment: European Lessons for North America. *Journal of Environmental Law* 14:209–245.

Kingsbury, Benedict. 1998. The Concept of Compliance as a Function of Competing Conceptions of International Law. *Michigan Journal of International Law* 19:345–372.

Kiss, Alexandre, and Dinah Shelton. 1993. *Manual of European Environmental Law.* Cambridge: Grotius Publications.

———. 2000. *International Environmental Law.* London: Graham and Trotman.

Kliot, Nurit, and Deborah Shmueli. 1997. *Institutional Framework for the Management of Transboundary Water Resources* 2. Edward and Anna Mitchell Family Foundation Water Resources Management Laboratory. Haifa: Technion, Israel Institute of Technology.

Kliot, Nurit, Deborah Shmueli, and Uri Shamir. 1997. *Institutional Framework for the Management of Transboundary Water Resources* 1. Haifa, Israel: Haifa Water Resources Institute.

Knauss, John A. 1987. The International Whaling Commission: Its Past and Probable Future. *Ocean Development and International Law* 26(1): 79–87.

Knox, John H. 2001. A New Approach to Compliance with International Environmental Law: The Submissions Procedure of the NAFTA Environmental Commission. *Ecology Law Quarterly* 28:1–122.

———. 2002. The Myth and Reality of Transboundary Environmental Impact Assessment. *American Journal of International Law* 96(2): 291–319.

Knudsen, Stale. 1995. Fisheries along the Eastern Black Sea Coast of Turkey: Informal Resource Management in Small-scale Fishing in the Shadow of a Dominant Capitalist Fishery. *Human Organization* 54(4): 437–448.

Koh, Harold HongJu. 1997. Why Do Nations Obey International Law? *Yale Law Journal* 106 (June): 2599–2659.

Kohler-Koch, Beate. 1996. Catching Up with Change: The Transformation of Governance in the European Union. *Journal of European Public Policy* 3(3): 359–380.

Koopman, Gert Jan. 1995. Policies to Reduce CO_2 Emissions from Cars in Europe. *Journal of Transport Economics and Policy* 29(1): 53–70.

Kopp, Mike. 2000. Second Amazonian Company Receives Certification by Forest Stewardship Council. *International Environment Reporter* 23, no. 24 (22 November): 911.

Korfmacher, Katrina Smith. 1998. Water Quality Modeling for Environmental Management: Lessons from the Policy Sciences. *Policy Sciences* 31:35–54.

Korten, David C. 1995. *When Corporations Rule the World*. Hartford, Conn.: Kumarian.

Koskenniemi, Marti. 1992. Breach of Treaty or Non-compliance: Reflections on Enforcement of the Montreal Protocol. *Yearbook of International Environmental Law* 3:123–133.

———. 1996. New Institutions and Procedures for Implementation Control and Reaction. In *Greening International Institutions,* edited by Jacob Werksmann. London: Earthscan.

Kraul, Chris. 1997. Mexico Gets Tough in Turtle Wars. *Los Angeles Times,* 13 November.

Krois, H. 1999. Water Protection Strategies: Critical Discussion in Regard to the Danube River Basin. *Water Science Technology* 39(8): 185–192.

Krueger, Jonathan. 1998. The Basel Convention and Transboundary Movements of Hazardous Wastes, Energy, and Environmental Programme. Briefing 45.

Ku, Charlotte. 1995. The Developing Role of Non Governmental Organizations in Global Policy and Law Making. *Chinese Yearbook of International Law and Affairs* 13:140–156.

Kublicki, Nicholas. 1994. The Greening of Free Trade: NAFTA, Mexican Environmental Law, and Debt Exchanges for Mexican Environmental Infrastructure Development. *Columbia Journal of Environmental Law* 19:59–140.

Kumar, Arad Lana, Jean Milner, and Annie Petsonk. 1996. The North American Free Trade Association. In *Greening International Institutions,* edited by Jacob Werksmann. London: Earthscan.

Kummer, Katharine. 1996. *International Management of Hazardous Wastes: The Basel Convention and Related Legal Rules.* New York: Oxford University Press.

Kuperman, K., and Jon S. Sutinen. 1998. Blue Water Crime: Deterrence, Legitimacy, and Compliance in Fisheries. *Law and Society Review* 32(2): 309–338.

Kurmos, Cyril, Brett Grosko, and Russell A. Mittermeier. 2001. US Participation in International Environmental Law and Policy. *Georgetown International Environmental Law Review* 13:661–693.

Kutting, Gabriella. 1994. Mediterranean Pollution: International Cooperation and the Control of Pollution from Land-Based Sources. *Marine Policy* 18(3): 233–247.

Kutting, Gabriella, and Gotthard Gauci. 1996. International Environmental Policy on Air Pollution from Ships. *Environmental Politics* 5(2): 345–353.

Lallas, Peter L. 2000–2001. The Role of Process and Participation in the Development of Effective International Environmental Agreements: A Study of the Global Treaty on Persistent Organic Pollutants. *UCLA Journal of Environmental Law and Policy* 19(1): 83–152.

———. 2001. The Stockholm Convention on Persistent Organic Pollutants. *American Journal of International Law* 95:692–708.

Landers, Frederick Poole Jr. 1997. The Black Market Trade in Chlorofluorocarbons: The Montreal Protocol Makes Banned Refrigerants a Hot Commodity. *Georgia Journal of International and Comparative Law* 26:457.

Lavelle, Marianne. 1994. Poisoned Waters. *National Law Journal,* 24 March.
Lazaroff, Cat. 2001. Historic Overfishing Led to Modern Ocean Problems. Environment News Service, 14 August.
Ledgerwood, Grant. 1997. *The Greening of the Boardroom.* Sheffield: Greenleaf Publishing.
Lee, Kai N. 2001. Searching for Sustainability in the New Century. *Ecology Law Quarterly* 27:913.
Levesque, Suzanne. 2000. From Yellowstone to Yukon: Combining Science and Activism to Shape Public Opinion and Policy. Ph.D. diss. University of California, Irvine.
Levy, Marc A., Robert O. Keohane, and Peter M. Haas. 1993. Improving the Effectiveness of International Environmental Institutions. Pp. 397–426 in *Institutions for the Earth: Sources of Effective International Environmental Protection,* by P. Haas, R. Keohane, and M. Levy. Cambridge, Mass.: MIT Press.
Lipschutz, Ronnie D. 1992. Local Action, Bioregional Politics, and Transnational Collaborative Networks in Policy Responses to Global Environmental Change. Paper presented to the annual meeting of the American Political Science Association, September 1992.
———. 1996. *Global Civil Society and Global Environmental Governance.* Albany: State University of New York Press.
———. 2000–2001. Why Is There No International Forestry Law? *UCLA Journal of Environmental Law and Policy* 19(1): 153–180.
Lipschutz, Ronnie D., and K. Conca. 1993. *The State and Social Power in Global Environmental Politics.* New York: Columbia University Press.
Litfin, Karen. 1994. *Ozone Discourses: Science and Politics in Global Environmental Cooperation.* New York: Columbia University Press.
Llobet, Gabriela. 1997. Trust But Verify: Verification in the Joint Implementation Regime. *George Washington Journal of Law and Economics* 31.
Loibl, Gerhard. 1996. Environmental Law-Making in the European Context and Its Relations to International Environmental Agreements. *ILSA Journal of International and Comparative Law* 2(3): 685–693.
Long, Bill. 1991. Managing the Environment. *OECD Observer* no. 168:4.
Lutz, Robert E., and George D. Aron. 1990. Codes of Conduct and Other International Instruments. In *Transferring Hazardous Technologies and Substances: The International Legal Challenge,* by Gunther Handl and Robert E. Lutz. London: Graham and Trotman.
Lyster, Simon. 1985. *International Wildlife Law.* Cambridge: Grotius Publications.
Mabry, Linda. 1999. Multinational Corporations and U.S. Technology Policy: Rethinking the Concept of Corporate Nationality. *Georgetown Law Journal* 87 (February): 563–673.
Machado, Pedro. 2001. Procedural Participation under the Environmental Impact Assessment Directive. *Environmental Law Network International Review* no. 1:3–14.
Maggio, Gregory F. 1998. Recognizing the Vital Role of Local Communities in

International Legal Instruments for Conserving Biodiversity. *Journal of Environmental Law* 16:179–226.

Makuch, Zen. 1996. The World Trade Organization and the General Agreement on Tariffs and Trade. In *Greening International Institutions,* edited by Jacob Werksmann. London: Earthscan.

Mancuso, Salvatore. 1997. La Convenzione di Bamako sui Rifiuti Pericolosi in Afrika. *Rivista Giuridica Dell'Ambiente* 12(3–4): 613–622.

Markel, David L. 2000. The Commission for Environmental Cooperation's Citizen Submission Process. *Georgetown International Environmental Law Review* 12:545–574.

Martin, Lisa L. 1992. Interests, Power, and Multilateralism. *International Organization* 46(4): 765.

Mastny, Bryan H., and Robert Earl-Goulet. 1997. Environmental Nongovernmental Organizations in Central and Eastern Europe's Contribution to Civil Society. *International Environmental Affairs* 9(2): 127–147.

Mathews, Jessica Tuchman. 1991. *Preserving the Global Environment.* New York: W. W. Norton and Company.

McAdams, Richard H. 1997. The Origin, Development, and Regulation of Norms. *Michigan Law Review* 96(2): 338–433.

McCaffrey, Stephen C. 2001. *The Law of International Watercourses: Nonnavigational Uses.* Oxford: Oxford University Press.

McKinsey and Company. 1994. The Corporate Response to the Environmental Challenge. In *Transnational Environmental Law and Its Impact on Corporate Behavior,* edited by Eric Urbani and Conrad P. Rubin. Irvington-on-Hudson, N.Y.: Transnational Juris Publications.

Mekaus, Susan. 1996. International Ecotourism and the Valuation of Tropical Rainforests in Costa Rica. *Journal of Environmental Management* 47:1–10.

Merton, Robert King. 1967. *On Theoretical Sociology.* New York: Free Press.

Metz, Bert, and Joyeeta Gupta. 2001. From Kyoto to the Hague: European Perspectives on Making the Kyoto Protocol Work. *International Environmental Agreements: Politics, Law, and Economics* 1(2).

Meyer, John W., David John Frank, Ann Hironaka, Evan Schofer, and Nancy Brandon Tuma. 1997. The Structuring of a World Environmental Regime, 1870–1990. *International Organization* 51(4): 623–51.

Michael, Donald N. 1973. *On Learning to Plan and Planning to Learn.* San Francisco: Jossey-Bass.

Miles, Edward L. 1998. Personal Reflections on an Unfinished Journey through Global Environmental Problems of Long Timescale. *Policy Sciences* 31:1–33.

Miles, E. L., Arild Underdal, Steinar Andresen, and Elane M. Carlin. 2001. *Environmental Regime Effectiveness.* Cambridge, Mass.: MIT Press.

Miles, Lee, and John Redmond. 1996. Enlarging the European Union: The Erosion of Federalism? *Cooperation and Conflict* 3(3): 285–309.

Milich, Lenard, and Robert G. Varady. 1998. Managing Transboundary Resources: Lessons from River-Basin Accords. *Environment* 40(8): 11–41.

Miller, Alan, and Mack McFarland. 1996. World Responds to Climate Change and Ozone Loss. *Forum for Applied Research and Public Policy* 11(2): 55–63.

Miller, K. Angie, Gautam Sethi, and Gary H. Wolff. 2000. *What's Fair? Consumers and Climate Change.* San Francisco: Redefining Progress.

Milner-Gulland, E. J., and Ruth Mace. 1991. The Impact of the Ivory Trade on the African Elephant *Loxodonta africana* Population as Assessed by Data from the Trade. *Biological Conservation* 58(2): 215–229.

Mitchell, Ronald. 1994. Regime Design Matters: International Oil Pollution and Treaty Compliance. *International Organization* 48(3): 425–458.

———. 1995. Review of *Dynamic International Regimes: Institutions of International Environmental Governance,* by Thomas Gehring. *International Environmental Affairs:* 189–190.

———. 1996. Compliance Theory: An Overview. In *Improving Compliance with International Environmental Law,* edited by J. Cameron and P. Roderick. London: Earthscan.

Molina, Mario, and Rowland, Sherwood. 1974. Stratospheric Sink for Chlorofluoromethanes: Chlorine Atomic-catalysed Destruction of Ozone. *Nature* 249:810–812.

Montini, Massimiliano, and Rene Seerden. 1998. Verso Uno Ius *Commune* Ambientale? Note a Margine Della Conferenza dell'Universita' di Maastricht sul Diritto Ambientale Comparato Nell'Unione Europea. *Rivista Giuridica Dell'Ambiente* 8(4): 161–165.

Moore, Molly. 2000. Is the Bosporus Taking on More Than It Can Handle? *International Herald Tribune,* 17 November.

Mounteer, Thomas R. 1991. Codifying Basel Convention Obligations into U.S. Law: The Waste Export Control Act. *Environmental Law Reporter* 21 (February): 10085–10098.

Mueller, John. 1989. *Retreat from Doomsday: The Obsolescence of Major War.* New York: Basic Books.

Mulenex, David. 1991. Improving Compliance Provisions in International Environmental Agreements. In *International Environmental Treaty Making,* edited by L. E. Susskind, J. Dolin, and J. W. Breslin. Cambridge, Mass.: Program on Negotiation.

Mumma, Albert. 2001. The Poverty of Africa's Position at the Climate Change Convention Negotiations. *UCLA Journal of Environmental Law and Policy* 19(1): 181–216.

Mumme, Stephen. 1993. Innovation and Reform in Transboundary Resource Management: A Critical Look at the International Boundary and Water Commission, United States and Mexico. *Natural Resource Journal* 33(1): 93–132.

———. 1999. NAFTA's Environmental Side Agreement: Almost Green. www.irc-online.org/borderline/1999/b160ib160naft.html.

Mumme, Stephen, and Pamela Duncan. 1998. The Commission for Environmental Cooperation and Environmental Management in the Americas. *Journal of Interamerican Studies and World Affairs* 39(4): 41–62.

Mumme, Stephen, and Terry Sprouse. 1999. Beyond BECC: Envisioning Needed Institutional Reforms for Environmental Protection on the Mexico-U.S. Border. In *Handbook of Global Environmental Policy and Administration,* by Dennis L. Soden and Bret S. Steel. New York: Marce and Dekker.

Mura, Loredan. 1998. Il Decreto del 28 Novembre 1997, Istitutivo del Parco

Dell'Asinata e la Normativa Internazionale Sulle Aree Protette. In *L'Isoa Dell'Asinata: L'Ambiente, Las Storia, Il Parco,* by Michele Gutieerez, Antonello Mattone, and Franca Valsecchi. Nuoro: Poliedro.

Murphy, Sean D. 1994. Prospective Liability Regimes for the Transboundary Movement of Hazardous Wastes. *American Journal of International Law* 88(1): 24–75.

Myers, Melvin L. 1979. *A Survey of International Intergovernmental Organizations: The Strategies That They Use to Abate Pollution.* Washington, D.C.: Environmental Protection Agency.

Nader, Ralph. 1993. *The Case Against Free Trade: GATT, NAFTA, and the Globalization of Corporate Power.* San Francisco, Calif.: Earth Island Press.

Nader, Ralph, Richard Brownstein, and John Richard, eds. 1981. *Who's Poisoning America: Corporate Polluters and Their Victims in the Chemical Age.* San Francisco: Sierra Club Books.

Nanda, Ved P. 1995. *International Environmental Law Policy.* Irvington, N.Y.: Transnational Publishers.

———. 1999. The Kyoto Protocol on Climate Change and the Challenges to Its Implementation: A Commentary. *Colorado Journal of International Environmental Law and Policy* 10 (Summer): 319–333.

Nelkin, Dorothy, Philippe Sands, and Richard Stewart. 2000. Genetically Modified Organisms: Forward, the International Challenge of Genetically Modified Organism Regulation. *New York University Environmental Law Journal* 8: 523.

Nelson, Paul J. 1998. Internationalizing Economic and Environmental Policy: Transnational NGO Networks and the World Bank's Expanding Influence. *Millennium* 26(3): 605–633.

Nespor, Stefano. 2000–2001. Environmentalism and the Disaster Strategy. *UCLA Journal of Environmental Law and Policy* 19(1): 211–230.

Nespor, Stefano, et al., eds. 1996. *Rapporto Mondiale Sul Diritto Dell'Ambiente: A World Survey of Environmental Law.* Milan: Giuffre' Editore.

Ni, Kuci-Jung. 2001. Contemporary Prospects for the Application of Principle 12 of the Rio Declaration. *Georgetown International Environmental Law Review* 14: 1–33.

Nicholson, Nigel, and Diana C. Robertson. 1996. The Ethical Issue Emphasis of Companies. *Human Relations* 49(1): 1367–1393.

Nickler, Patrick A. 1999. A Tragedy of the Commons in Coastal Fisheries: Contending Prescriptions for Conservation, and the Case of the Atlanta Blue Fin Tuna. *Boston College Environmental Affairs Law Review* 26(3): 549–576.

Nigeria-Italy Waste Trade. www.american.edu/ed/nigeria.htm.

Nollkaemper, A. 1996. The Contribution of the International Law Commission to International Water Law: Does It Reverse the Flight from Substance? In *Netherlands Yearbook of International Law* 27: 39–73.

Nordquist, J. 1995. *Corporations and the Environment.* Santa Cruz, Calif.: Reference and Research Services.

Oesterle, Dale Arthur. 1999. The WTO Reaches Out to the Environmentalists: Is It Too Little, Too Late? *Colorado Journal of International Law and Policy* (Fall): 1–32.

———. 2001. Just Say 'I Don't Know': A Recommendation for WTO Panels

Dealing with Environmental Regulations. *Environmental Law Review* 3(2): 113–130.

Okowa, Phoebe N. 1997. Procedural Obligations in International Environmental Agreements. In *British Yearbook of International Law,* edited by Ian Brownlie and James Crawford. Oxford: Clarendon Press.

Oldson, William O. 1997. Background to Catastrophe: Romanian Modernization Policies and the Environment. *East European Quarterly* 30(4): 517–529.

O'Neill, Kate. 1997. Regulations as Arbiters of Risk: Great Britain, Germany, and the Hazardous Waste Trade in Western Europe. *International Studies Quarterly* 41:687–718.

OPSEA. 1998. UNOPS Serving the Black Sea. www.unops.org/finance/wbsea.html.

O'Reilly, James T., and Lorre Barbara Cuzze. 1997. Trash or Treasure? Industrial Recycling and International Barriers to the Movement of Hazardous Wastes. *Journal of Corporation Law* 22(3): 507–534.

Ostrom, Elinor. 1990. *Governing the Commons: The Evolution of Institutions for Collective Action.* Cambridge: Cambridge University Press.

Otto, Dianne. 1996. Non-Governmental Organizations in the United Nations System: The Emerging Role of International Civil Society. *Human Rights Quarterly* 18(1): 107–141.

Ovink, John B. 1995. Transboundary Shipments of Toxic Waste: The Basel and Bamako Conventions, Do Third World Countries Have a Choice? *Dickinson Journal of International Law* 13(2): 281–295.

Oxman, Bernard Ho. 1998. International Decisions (Gabcikovo-Nagymaros Project). *American Journal of International Law* 92(2): 273–278.

Oye, Kenneth A., and James H. Maxwell. 1995. Self-Interest and Environmental Management. *Journal of Theoretical Politics* 6(4): 607–608.

Ozturk, E. Yuksel, and A. Tanik. 1999. Waste Water Management Strategies for the Black Sea Coast of Turkey. *Water Science Technology* 39(8): 169–176.

Pallemaerts, Marc. 1993. International Environmental Law from Stockholm to Rio: Back to the Future? In *Greening International Law,* edited by Philippe Sands. London: Earthscan.

Palmer, Alice. 1996. Hazardous Waste (Regulation of Exports and Imports) Amendment Act 1996. *Australian Business Law Review* 24(6): 465–467.

Palmer, G. 1992. New Ways to Make International Environmental Law. *American Journal of International Law* 86:259–283.

Panagia, Salvatore. 1993. *La Tutela Dell'Ambiente Naturale Nell Diritto Penale D'Impresa.* Milan: Casa Editrice Dott. Antonio Milani.

Papasavva, Stella, and William R. Moomaw. 1997. Adverse Implications of the Montreal Protocol Grace Period for Developing Countries. *International Environmental Affairs* (Summer): 219–231.

Parikh, Jyoti. 1995. Joint Implementation and North-South Cooperation for Climate Change. *International Environmental Affairs* 7(1): 22–41.

Park, Rozelia S. 1998. An Examination of International Environmental Racism through the Lens of Transboundary Movement of Hazardous Wastes. *Global Legal Studies Journal* 5(2): 659–709.

Parson, Edward A., and Karen Fisher-Vanden. 1999. Joint Implementation of Greenhouse Gas Abatement. *Policy Sciences* 32(3): 207–224.

Passini, Serena. 1988. Aspetti Istituzionali e Meccanismi di Decisione Nelle Convenzioni ONU Sulla Protezione Dell'Ambiente. *Rivista Giuridica Del l'Ambiente* 13(5): 781–818.

Pauly, Louis W., and Simon Reich. 1997. National Structures and Multinational Corporate Behavior: Enduring Differences in the Age of Globalization. *International Organization* 51(1): 1–30.

Pauwelyn, Joost. 2001. The Role of Public International Law in the WTO: How Far Can We Go? *American Journal of International Law* 95:535–578.

Pearce, Frank, and Steve Tombs. 1998. *Toxic Capitalism: Corporate Crime and the Chemical Industry*. Aldershot, England: Ashgate Dartmouth.

Pearson, Charles S., ed. 1987. *Multinational Corporations, the Environment, and the Third World*. Durham, N.C.: Duke University Press.

Perez, Frank X. 1996. The Relationship between "Permanent Sovereignty" and the Obligation Not to Cause Transboundary Environmental Damage. *Environmental Law* 26(4): 1187–1212.

Pergamon, Metropolitan John of. 1997. Speech presented at Religion, Science, and the Environment, Symposium 2: The Black Sea in Crisis. University of Thessaloniki, 28 September.

Perlez, Jane. 1999. World Court Leaves Fight Over Danube Unresolved. *New York Times*, 25 September.

Pershing, J., 2000. Common Approaches: Taxes, Trading, and Negotiated Agreements. Remarks presented at the Pew Center/RIIA Conference on Innovative Policy Solutions to Global Climate Change, April, Washington, D.C.

Petsonk, C. 1990. The Rise of the United Nations Environment Programme (UNEP) in the Development of International Environmental Law. *American Journal of International Law and Policy* 5:367–372.

Pew Center on Global Climate Change. n.d. www.perclimate.org.

Philbrick, Nathaniel. 2000. In a Gray Area. *New York Times Book Review*, 15 October.

Piaseki, Bruce. 1995. *Corporate Environmental Strategy: The Avalanche of Change Since Bhopal*. New York: John Wiley and Sons.

Pillitu, Paola Anna. 1992. *Profili Costituzionali Della Tutela Ambientale Nel l'Ordinamento Comunitario Europeo*. Perugia: Galeno Editrice.

Pineschi, Laura. 1992. Antarctica. In *World Treaties for the Protection of the Environment*, edited by Tullio Scovazzi and Tullio Treves. Milan: Istituto Per L'Ambiente.

Pollack, Mark A. 1997. Delegating Agency and Agenda Setting in the European Community. *International Organization* 51(1): 99–135.

Popiel, Brian R. 1995. From Customary Law to Environmental Impact Assessment: A New Approach to Avoiding Transboundary Environmental Damage between Canada and the United States. *Boston College Environmental Affairs Law Review* 22(2): 447–479.

Porter, Michael. 1990. *The Competitive Advantage of Nations*. New York: Free Press.

Posner, Eric A. 2000. *Law and Social Norms.* Cambridge, Mass.: Harvard University Press.

Powell, Frona M. 2000. The North American Commission for Environmental Cooperation's San Pedro Report: A Case Study and Analysis of the CEC Process. *Environmental Lawyer* 6 (June): 809–838.

Pressman, Jeffrey L., and Aaron Wildavsky. 1973. *Implementation: How Great Expectations in Washington Are Dashed in Oakland.* Berkeley: University of California Press.

Putnam, Robert D. 1993. *Making Democracy Work: Civic Traditions in Modern Italy.* Princeton, N.J.: Princeton University Press.

Ragaini, R. C. 1999. Environmental Security Issues in the Black Sea Region. Lawrence Livermore National Laboratory, University of California.

Raustiala, Kal. 1997a. States, NGOs, and International Environmental Institutions. *International Studies Quarterly* 41:719–740.

———. 1997b. The Participatory Revolution in International Environmental Law. *Harvard Environmental Law Review* 21:537–586.

———. 2000a. Sovereignty and Multiculturalism. *Chicago Journal of International Law* 1(2): 401–419.

———. 2000b. Compliance and Effectiveness in International Regulatory Cooperation. *Case Western Reserve Journal of International Law* 32(3): 387–440.

Rawls, John. 1999. *The Law of Peoples.* Cambridge, Mass.: Harvard University Press.

———. 2001. *Justice as Fairness.* Cambridge: Belknap Press.

Redgwell, Catherine. 1999. Protection of Ecosystems under International Law: Lessons from Antarctica. In *International Law and Sustainable Development: Past Achievements and Future Challenges,* edited by Alan Boyle and David Freestone. New York: Oxford University Press.

Reif, Linda C. 1994. Book Review: Multidisciplinary Perspectives on the Improvement of International Environmental Law and Institutions. *Michigan Journal of International Law* 15(3): 723–745.

Reilly, William K. 1992. International Cooperation on the Environment: The Cleanup of Eastern Europe. *Boston College Environmental Affairs Law Review* 19(3): 501.

Republic of Georgia. 1996. Verification of Compliance with International Environmental Accords. In *State of the Environment Georgia.* Tbilisi: Geoinformation Center.

Revkin, Andrew C. 2000a. Report Forecasts Warming's Effects. *New York Times,* 12 June.

———. 2000b. Climate Pact Eludes Major Players. *International Herald Tribune,* 27 November.

Rice, Faye. 1993. Who Scores Best on the Environment? *Fortune,* 26 July: 114.

Richards, Eric, and Martin McCrory. 2000. The Sea Turtle Dispute: Implications for Sovereignty, the Environment, and International Trade Law. *University of Colorado Law Review* 71 (Spring): 295.

Robinson, Nicholas A. 1992. International Trends in Environmental Impact Assessment. *Environmental Affairs* no. 19:591–621.

Rogus, LeeAnn. 1996. The Basel Convention and the United States. *New England International and Comparative Law Annual.*

Roht-Arriaza, Naomi. 1995. Shifting the Point of Regulation: The International Organization for Standardization and Global Lawmaking on Trade and the Environment. *Ecology Law Quarterly* 22:479–539.

Rollin, Sara Thuria. 2000. Industry, Government to Review Plan to Impose Trade Restrictions in Treaty. *International Environment Reporter* 23, no. 8 (12 April): 315.

Rose-Ackerman, Susan. 1995. *Controlling Environmental Policy: The Limits of Public Law in Germany and the United States.* New Haven: Yale University Press.

Rothwell, Donald R. 1996. The Law of the Sea in the Asian-Pacific Region: An Overview of Trends and Developments. *Chinese Yearbook of International Law and Affairs* 13:81–110.

———. 2000. The General Assembly Ban on Driftnet Fishing. In *Commitment and Compliance: The Role of Non-Binding Norms in the International Legal System,* edited by D. Shelton. Oxford: Oxford University Press.

Rowland, F. Sherwood. 2001. Atmospheric Changes Caused by Human Activities: From Science to Regulation. *Ecology Law Quarterly* 27:1261–1293.

Rubin, Alfred P. 1994. The Impact of Changing Institutions of Environmental Law and Corporate Responsibility. In *Transnational Environmental Law and Its Impact on Corporate Behavior,* edited by Eric J. Urbani, Conrad P. Rubin, and Monica Katzman. Irvington-on-Hudson, N.Y.: Transnational Juris Publications.

Rueda, Andres. 2000. Tuna, Dolphins, Shrimp, and Turtles: What about Environmental Embargoes under NAFTA? *Georgetown International Environmental Law Review* 12:647–692.

Safadi, R., and P. Low. International Policy Coordination and Environmental Quality. World Bank Discussion Paper 159.

Sakmar, Susan L. 1999. Free Trade and Sea Turtles: The International and Domestic Implications of the Shrimp-Turtles Case. *Colorado Journal of International Law and Policy,* 15 January. On-line forum.

Salzman, James. 1999. Beyond the Smokestack: Environmental Protection in the Service Economy. *UCLA Law Review* 47(2): 411–489.

———. 2001. Seattle's Legal Legacy and Environmental Reviews of Trade Agreements. *Environmental Law* 31(3): 501–548.

Sampson, Martin W. III. 1995. Black Sea Environmental Cooperation: States and "The Most Seriously Degraded Regional Sea." *Bogazici Journal Review of Social, Economic, and Administrative Studies* 9(1): 51–76.

———. 1996. Environmental Aspects of Migration in the Black Sea Region. Paper presented at the Conference on Migration and Security, September, Istanbul.

———. 1999. Black Sea Environmental Cooperation: Toward a Fourth Track. In *Protecting Regional Seas and Fostering Environmental Cooperation in Europe: Conference Proceedings,* 14 May, edited by Stacy D. Van Deveer and Geoffrey D. Dabelko. Saving the Seas: Developing Capacity and Fostering Environmental Cooperation in Europe. Woodrow Wilson International Center for Scholars.

Sanchez, Roberto. 1993. Public Participation and the IBWC: Challenges and Options. *Natural Resources Journal* 33 (Spring): 283–298.

Sand, Peter H. 1991a. Institutions for Global Change: Whither Environmental Governance? *Policy Studies Journal* 19(2): 93–102.

———. 1991b. Lessons Learned in Global Environmental Governance. *Boston College Environmental Affairs Law Review* 18:213–277.

———, ed. 1992. *The Effectiveness of International Environmental Agreements*. Cambridge: Grotius Publishers.

Sandberg, Mikael. 1992. *Baltic Sea Region Environmental Protection: Eastern Perspectives and International Cooperation*. Stockholm: Almqvist and Wiksell International.

Sandler, Deborah, Emad Adly, Mahmoud A. Al-Khoshman, Philip Warburg, and Tobie Berstein. 1993. *Protecting the Gulf of Aqaba: A Regional Environmental Challenge*. Washington, D.C.: Environmental Law Institute.

Sands, Philippe. 1991. European Community Environmental Law: The Evolution of a Regional International Environmental Protection Regime. *Yale Law Journal* 100:2510–2523.

———. 1993. *Greening International Law*. London: Earthscan.

———. 1995a. *Principles of International Law 1: Frameworks, Standards, and Implementation*. Manchester: Manchester University Press.

———. 1995b. International Law in the Field of Sustainable Development: Emerging Legal Principles. In *Sustainable Development and International Law*, edited by Winfried Lang.

Sands, Philippe, Richard Tarasosky, and Mary Weiss. 1994. *Documents in International Environmental Law*. Manchester: Manchester University Press.

Schachter, Oscar. 1991. The Emergence of International Environmental Law. *Journal of International Affairs* 457 (Winter): 457–493.

Schmitt, Michael N. 1996. Aegean Angst: A Historical and Legal Analysis of the Greek-Turkish Dispute. *Roger Williams University Law Review* (Fall): 1.

Schmitt-Roschmann, Verena. 2000. German Business Group Urges Promotion of Green Standards When Investing Abroad. *International Environment Reporter* 23, no. 24 (22 November): 909.

Schneider, William. 1996. The Basel Convention Ban on Hazardous Waste Exports: Paradigm of Efficacy or Exercise in Futility? *Suffolk Transnational Law Review* 20(1): 247–286.

Schram Stokke, Olav, and Davor Vidas, eds. 1997. *Governing the Antarctic: The Effectiveness and Legitimacy of the Antarctic Treaty System*. Cambridge: Cambridge University Press.

Scott, Gary L., and Craig L. Carr. 1996. Multilateral Treaties and the Formation of Customary International Law. *Denver Journal of International Law and Policy* 25 (Fall): 71–93.

Scovazzi, Tullio. 1992. *World Treaties for the Protection of the Environment, Supplement (November)*. Milan: Istituto Per L'Ambiente.

Scovazzi, Tullio, and Tullio Treves, eds. 1992. *World Treaties for the Protection of the Environment*. Milan: Istituto Per L'Ambiente.

Selden, Thomas M., and Daquig Song. 1994. Environmental Quality and Development: Is There a Kuznets Curve for Air Pollution Emissions? *Journal of Environmental Economics and Management* 27:147–62.

———. 1995. Neoclassical Growth, the J Curve for Abatement, and the Inverted U Curve for Pollution. *Journal of Environmental Economics and Management* 29:162–68.

Setear, John K. 2001. Learning to Live with Losing: International Environmental Law in the New Millenium. *Virginia Environmental Law Journal* 20:139–167.

Sezer, Duygu Bazoglu. 1997. From Hegemony to Pluralism: The Changing Politics of the Black Sea. *SAIS Review* 17(1): 1–30.

Shabecoff, Philip. 1996. *A New Name for Peace: International Environmentalism, Sustainable Development, and Democracy*. Hanover: University Press of New England.

Shanks, Cheryl, Harold K. Jacobson, and Jeffrey Kaplan. 1996. Inertia and Change in the Constellation of International Governmental Organizations, 1981–1992. *International Organization* 50(4): 593–627.

Sharma, Prasad. 1998. Restoring Participatory Democracy: Why the United States Should Listen to Citizen Voices While Engaging in International Environmental Lawmaking. *Emory International Law Review* 12 (Spring): 1215–1253.

Sharma, Shalendra. 1996. Building Effective International Regimes: The Case of the Global Environment Facility. *Journal of Environment and Development* 5(1): 73.

Shearer, C. Russell. 1994. International Environmental Law and Development in Developing Nations: Agenda Setting, Articulation, and Institutional Participation. *Tulane Environmental Law Journal* 7(2): 391–430.

Shelton, Dinah, ed. 2000. *Commitment and Compliance: The Role of Non-Binding Norms in the International Legal System*. Oxford: Oxford University Press.

Shevardnadze, Eduard. 1991. Governments Alone Won't Turn the World Green: Prospects for Ensuring the Success of a Global Environmental Movement. *New Scientist* 131(1784): 50.

Shuye, Henry. 1994. After You: May Action by the Rich Be Contingent upon Action by the Poor? *Global Legal Studies Journal* 1(2): 343–366.

Siegal, Charles T. 1998. Rule Formation in Non-Hierarchical Systems. *Temple Environmental Law and Technology Journal* 16(2): 173–243.

Sievers, Eric W. 2001. The Caspian, Regional Seas, and the Case for a Cultural Study of Law. *Georgetown International Environmental Law Review* 13:361–415.

Signaldsson, Herluf. 1996. The International Whaling Commission: The Transition From a Whaling Club to a Preservation Club. *Cooperation and Conflict* 31(3): 311–352.

Simmons, P. J., and Chantal de Jonge Oudrat, eds. 2001. *Managing Global Issues: Lessons Learned*. Washington, D.C.: Carnegie Endowment for International Peace.

Simos, Evangelos, and John E. Triantis. 1995. International Economic Outlook. *Journal of Business Forecasting Methods and Systems* 14(1): 30–33.

Sims, Holly. 1996. The Unsheltering Sky: China, India, and the Montreal Protocol. *Policy Studies Journal* 24(2): 201–214.

Sirola, Paula. 2001. When Rhetoric and Reality Don't Match: A Critical Analysis of Environmentalism in Indigenous Development Projects. Paper presented at The Greening X Conference, University of California, Irvine, 27 January.

Sjoberg, Helen. 1996. The Global Environmental Facility. In *Greening Environmental Institutions,* edited by Jacob Werksmann. London: Earthscan.

Sjostedt, Gunnar. 1993. *International Environmental Negotiation.* Newbury Park, Calif.: Sage Publications.

———. 1994. Looking Ahead. In *Negotiating International Regimes: Lessons Learned from the United Nations Conference on Environment and Development (UNCED),* by Bertram Spector et al. London: Graham and Trotman.

Slaughter, Anne-Marie. 1997. The Real New World Order. *Foreign Affairs* (September-October): 183–197.

Smith, Turner T., and Roszell D. Hunter. 1992. The European Community Environmental Legal System. *Environmental Law Reporter* 22(2): 10106–10130.

Socolof, Maria Leet, Richard E. Saylor, and Lance N. McCold. 1997. Replacement of Chlorofluorocarbons at the DOE Gaseous Diffusion Plants: An Assessment of Global Impacts. *Environmental Impact Assessment Review* 17:39–51.

Sohn, Louis B. 1973. The Stockholm Declaration on the Human Environment. *Harvard International Law Journal* 14:423–450.

Somsen, H., H. Sevenster, J. Scott, L. Krämer, and T. F. M. Etty. 2002. *Yearbook of European Environmental Law.* Oxford: Oxford University Press.

Soros, Marvin S. 1991. The Evolution of Global Regulation of Atmospheric Pollution. *Policy Studies Journal* 19(2): 115–125.

Spengler, Katherine. 2001. Expansion of Third World Women's Empowerment: The Emergence of Sustainable Development and the Evolution of International Economic Strategy. *Colorado Journal of International Environmental Law and Policy* 12(2): 303–346.

Spracker, Stanley M., Gregory M. Brown, and Annemargaret Connolly. 1993. Environmental Protection and International Trade: NAFTA as a Means of Eliminating Environmental Contamination as a Competitive Advantage. *Georgetown International Environmental Law Review* 5 (Summer): 669–704.

Stein, R., and B. Johnson. 1979. *Banking on the Biosphere? Environmental Procedures and Practices of Nine Multilateral Development Agencies.* Lexington, Mass.: Lexington Books.

Steinberg, Richard H. 1997. Trade-Environment Negotiations in the EU, NAFTA, and WTO: Regional Trade Trajectories of Rule Development. *American Journal of International Law* 91: 231–267.

Stenzel, Paulette L. 2000. Can the ISO 14000 Series Environmental Management Standards Provide a Viable Alternative to Governmental Regulation? *American Business Law Journal* 37 (Winter): 237–294.

Stevens, William. 2000. The Hot Spot Approach to Saving Species. *New York Times,* 14 March.

Stewart, Doug. 2001. The Rhinos are Baaack! *Smithsonian* March: 77–84.

Stone, Christopher. 1993. *The Gnat Is Older Than the Man: Global Environment and Human Agenda.* Princeton, N.J.: Princeton University Press.

———. 1999. The NAFTA Environmental Side Agreement. Pre-conference comments, Third Generation of International Environmental Law, UCI. Mimeographed.

Subedi, Surya P. 1999. Balancing International Trade with Environmental Protection: International Legal Aspects of Eco-Labels. *Brooklyn Journal of International Law* 25.

Suhre, Sarah. 1999. Misguided Morality: The Repercussions of the International Whaling Commission's Shift from a Policy of Regulation to One of Preservation. *Georgetown International Environmental Law Review* 12(1): 303–309.

Supanich, Gary P. 1993. The Legal Basis for Intergenerational Responsibility: An Alternative View, The Sense of Intergenerational Identity. *Yearbook of International Environmental Law* 3:94–101.

Susskind, Larry E. 1994a. *Environmental Diplomacy: Negotiating More Effective Global Agreements.* New York: Oxford University Press.

———. 1994b. What Will It Take to Ensure Effective Global Environmental Management? A Reassessment of Regime-Building Accomplishments. In *Negotiating International Regimes: Lessons Learned from the United Nations Conference on Environment and Development,* by Bertram Spector et al. London: Graham and Trotman.

Sweet, Alec Stone, and James A. Caporaso. 1998. From Free Trade to Supranational Polity: The European Court and Integration. *Revue Francaise de science politique.* 48:195–244.

Switzer, Jacqueline Vaughn, with Gary Bryner. 1994. *Environmental Politics: Domestic and Global Dimensions.* New York: St. Martin's Press.

Szasz, Paul C. 1992. International Norm-Making. In *Environmental Change and International Law,* edited by Edith Brown Weiss. Tokyo: United Nations University.

Tadros, Victor. 1998. Between Governance and Discipline: The Law and Michel Foucault. *Oxford Journal of Legal Studies* 18(1): 75–103.

Tagliabue, John. 2000. From Spotted Owls to Caviar: Industry Drains Its Very Lifeblood from Caspian Sea. *New York Times,* 30 December.

Taylor, Prue. 2000–2001. Heads in the Sand as the Tide Rises: Environmental Ethics and the Law on Climate Change. *UCLA Journal of Environmental Law and Policy* 19(1): 247–280.

Thieffry, Patrick, and Peter E. Nahmias. 1991. The European Community's Regulation and Control of Waste and the Adoption of Civil Liability. *Hastings International and Comparative Law Review* 14:949–971.

Thompson, Janna. 1995. Towards a Green World Order: Environment and World Politics (Ecology and Democracy). *Environmental Politics* 4(4): 31.

Timoshenko, Alexander, and Mark Berman. 1993. The United Nations Environment Programme and the United Nations. In *Greening Environmental Law,* edited by Philippe Sands. London: Earthscan.

Tiremann, Mary. 1998. Waste Trade and the Basel Convention: Background and Update. Congressional Research Service, Report for Congress 98-638 ENR. www.enie.org/nle/waste-26.html.

Tolba, Mostafa K., and Iwona Rummel-Bulska. 1998. *Global Environmental Diplomacy: Negotiating Environmental Agreements for the World, 1973–1992.* Cambridge, Mass.: MIT Press.

Townsend-Gault, Ian. 1999. Compliance with the United Nations Convention on the Law of the Sea in the Asia-Pacific Region. *University of British Columbia Law Review* 33: 227–241.

Tracey, Patrick. 2001. Ozone Depletion: Britain Faces Refrigerator Crisis under EU Law Requiring CFC Removal. *International Environment Reporter* 24, no. 25 (5 December): 1089.

Trask, Jeff. 1992. Montreal Protocol Noncompliance Procedure: The Best Approach to Resolving International Environmental Disputes? *Georgetown Law Journal* 80: 1973–2001.

Tromans, Stephan. 2001. EC Waste Law: A Complete Mess? *Journal of Environmental Law* 13(2): 133–156.

Tutchton, Jay. 1996. The Citizen Petition Process under NAFTA's Environmental Side Agreement: It's Easy to Use, But Does It Work? www.earthlaw.org/netwest/nafta.htm.

Underdal, Arild. 1995. The Study of International Regimes. *Journal of Peace Research* 32(1): 113–119.

UNDP, UNEP, the World Bank, Phare, and Tacis. 1998. *Black Sea Environmental Programme: 1997 Annual Report.* New York: United Nations Development Programme.

UNEP. 1987. Proposed Principles and Guidelines of Environmental Impact Assessment. UNGAOR, Session 42, Supp. 25 of U.N. Doc. A/42/25.

———. 1999. *Synergies: Promoting Collaboration on Environmental Treaties* 1 (October).

———. 2000a. UNEP and ICC Sponsor Millennium Business Awards for Environmental Performance. 30 September, United Nations Environment Programme.

———. 2000b. Background Study on Possible Components of the Programme for the Development and Periodic Review of Environmental Law for the First Decade of the Twenty-first Century. Nairobi: United Nations Environment Programme.

———. 2000c. Report of the Meeting of Senior Government Officials Expert in Environmental Law to Prepare a Programme for the Development and Periodic Review of Environmental Law for the First Decade of the Twenty-first Century. Nairobi: United Nations Environment Programme.

Upadhye, Shasbank. 2000. The International Watercourse: An Exploitable Resource for the Developing Nation under International Law. *Cardozo Journal of International and Comparative Law* 8 (Spring): 61–101.

Uram, Charlotte. 1990. International Regulation of the Sale and Use of Pesticides. *Northwestern Journal of International Law and Business* no. 10: 460–478.

Urbani, Eric J., Conrad P. Rubin, and Monica Katzman. 1994. *Transnational*

Environmental Law and Its Impact on Corporate Behavior. Irvington-on-Hudson, N.Y.: Transnational Juris Publications.

Uruguay Round. 1994. Agreement Establishing the Multilateral Trade Organization. Multilateral Trade Negotiations (the Uruguay Round), Dec. MTN/FA, 33 ILM.

U.S. Congress. 1993. Committee on Banking, Finance, Trade, and Monetary Policy. *Proposed Operations and Structure of a Permanent Global Environmental Facility.*

U.S. Department of State. 2000. USAID Sees Rapidly Expanding Overseas Markets for Climate Change Technologies and Services. 22 June, International Information Programs, usinfo.state.gov/topical/global/environ/climate/00062603.htm.

U.S. EPA. 1998. International Trade in Hazardous Waste: An Overview. Enforcement and Compliance Assurance (222A). November, EPA-305-K-98-001.

U.S. General Accounting Office. 1992a. *International Environment: International Agreements Are Not Well Monitored.* Washington, D.C.: GAO.

———. 1992b. *International Environment: Strengthening the Implementation of Environmental Agreements.* Report to Congressional Requesters. Microform. Washington, D.C.: GAO.

U.S. Initiative on Joint Implementation. 2000. New Projects in Africa and South America Approved to Promote Sustainable Development. 25 October.

U.S. Senate. 1997. The Byrd-Hagel Resolution, Article 235(3) of the 1982 UN-CLOS. 105th Cong., S. Res. 98.

U.S. Senate Committee on Commerce, Science, and Transportation. 1977. Treaties and Other International Agreements on Fisheries, Oceanic Resources, and Wildlife Involving the United States. Washington, D.C.: Government Printing Office.

Utton, Albert E., and Ludwik A. Teaclass. 1987. *Transboundary Resources Law.* Boulder, Colo.: Westview Press.

Van der Mensbrugghe. February 1990. Legal Status of International North Sea Conference Declarations. *International Journal of Estuarine and Coastal Law* 5(1): 15–22.

Van Heijnsbergen, P. 1997. *International Legal Protection of Wild Fauna and Flora.* Amsterdam: IOS Press.

Vaubel, Roland. 1996. The Constitutional Future of the European Union. *Constitutional Political Economy* 7(4): 317–324.

Vickers, Geoffrey. 1965. *The Art of Judgment: A Study of Policy Making.* New York: Basic Books.

Victor, David G. 2001. *The Collapse of the Kyoto Protocol and the Struggle to Slow Global Warming.* Princeton: Princeton University Press.

———. 2001. Piety at Kyoto Didn't Cool the Planet. *New York Times,* 23 March.

Victor, David G., with Abram Chayes and Eugene B. Skolnikoff. 1993. Pragmatic Approaches to Regime Building for Complex International Problems. In *Global Accord: Environmental Challenges and International Responses,* edited by Nazli Chourci. Cambridge, Mass.: MIT Press.

Victor, David G., Kal Raustiala, and Eugene B. Skolnikoff. 1998. *The Implementation and Effectiveness of International Environmental Commitments: Theory and Practice.* Cambridge, Mass.: MIT Press.

Vicuna, Francisco Orrego. 1992. State Responsibility, Liability, and Remedial Measures under International Law: New Criteria for Environmental Protection. In *Environmental Change and International Law,* edited by Edith Brown Weiss. Tokyo: United Nations University.

Vig, Norman J., and Regina S. Axelrod. 1999. *The Global Environment: Institutions, Law, and Policy.* London: Earthscan.

Vilcheck, Michelle M. 1991. The Controls of the Transfrontier Movement of Hazardous Waste from Developed to Developing Nations: The Goal of a Level Playing Field. *Northwestern Journal of International Law and Business* 11:643–674.

Vinogradov, Sergei. 1996. Transboundary Water Resources in the Former Soviet Union: Between Conflict and Cooperation, part 1. *Natural Resources Journal* 36(2): 393–415.

Wallace, Charles P. 1994. Asia Tires of Being the Toxic Waste Dumping Ground for the Rest of the World. *Los Angeles Times,* 23 March.

Warburg, Paul. 1995. Middle East Environmental Cooperation. *IGCC Policy Brief* 5:1–4.

Warren, H. 1997. Co-ordinated Action Is Key to Black Sea Pollution Strategy. *Lloyd's List International,* 2 January.

Wateron, Claire, and Brian Wynne. 1996. Building the European Union: Science and the Cultural Dimensions of Environmental Policy. *Journal of European Public Policy* 3(3): 421–440.

Waugh, Theodore. 2000. Where Do We Go from Here? Legal Controls and Future Strategies for Addressing the Transportation of Hazardous Wastes across International Borders. *Fordham Environmental Law Journal* 11:477–544.

Weale, Albert. 1996. Environmental Rules and Rule-Making in the European Union. *Journal of European Public Policy* 3(4): 594–611.

Weiner, Jonathan B. 1999. Global Environmental Regulation: Instrument Choice in Legal Context. *Yale Law Journal* 108:677–788.

Weinstein, Henry. 1993. Two Found Guilty of Exporting Toxic Waste. *Los Angeles Times,* 16 April.

Weinstein, Michael M., and Steve Charnovitz. 2001. The Greening of the WTO. *Foreign Affairs* 8(6): 147–156.

Weiss, Edith Brown, ed. 1992. *Environmental Change and International Law.* Tokyo: United Nations University.

———. 1993. International Environmental Law: Contemporary Issues and the Emergence of a New World Order. *Georgetown Law Journal* 81(3): 675–710.

Weiss, Edith Brown, and Harold K. Jacobson. 1998. *Engaging Countries: Strengthening Compliance with International Environmental Accords.* Cambridge, Mass.: MIT Press.

Weiss, Edith Brown, David B. Magraw, and Paul Szasz. 1999. *International En-*

vironmental Law: Basic Instruments and References, 1992–1999. Ardsley, N.Y.: Transnational Publishers.

Welford, R. J. 1998. Corporate Environmental Management, Technology, and Sustainable Development: Postmodern Perspectives and the Need for a Critical Research Agenda. *Business Strategy and the Environment* 7:1–12.

Werksman, Jacob, ed. 1996. *Greening International Institutions.* London: Earthscan.

Wettestad, Jorgen. 1999. *Designing Effective Environmental Regimes: The Key Conditions.* Aldershot: Edward Elgar Publishing.

Wettestad, Jorgen, and Steinar Andresen. 1991. *The Effectiveness of International Resource Cooperation: Some Preliminary Findings.* Lysaker, Norway: Fridtjof Nansen Institute.

Wiener, Marshall. 1980. *Environmental Cooperation in the North Atlantic Area.* Washington, D.C.: University Press of America.

Wilder, Margaret. 2000. Border Farmers, Water Contamination, and the NAAEC Environmental Side Accord to NAFTA. *Natural Resources Journal* 40:873–893.

Wilson, A. M., and M. E. Moser. 1994. *Conservation of Black Sea Wetlands: A Review and Preliminary Action Plan.* IWRB Publication 33. Slimbridge, Gloucester: International Waterfowl and Wetlands Research Bureau.

Winham, Gilbert R. 1994. Enforcement of Environmental Measures: Negotiating the NAFTA Environmental Side Agreement. *Journal of Environment and Development* (IR/PS, UCSD, La Jolla) 3(1): 29–30.

Wirth, David A. 1999. Teaching and Research in International Environmental Law. *Harvard Environmental Law Review* 23:423.

Wiser, Glen M. 1997. Joint Implementation: Incentives for Private Sector Mitigation of Global Climate Change. *Georgetown International Environmental Law Review* 9:747–767.

———. 1999. The Clean Development Mechanism Versus the World Trade Organization: Can Free-Market Greenhouse Gas Emissions Abatement Survive Free Trade? *Georgetown International Environmental Law Review* 11(3): 531–597.

Woodard, Colin. 1997. Black Sea Nations Wary of Russia's Big Oil Plans. *Christian Science Monitor,* 22 October.

World Bank. 1991. World Bank Operational Directive 401: Environmental Assessment. In *The World Bank Inspection Panel,* by Ibrahim F. I. Shihata.

World Resources Institute. 1996. *Ozone Protection in the United States: Elements of Success.* Excerpted on www.igc.apc.org/wri/climate/ozone/.

———. 2000. WRI report reveals export credit agencies fuel increases in greenhouse gases. 18 July. www.wri.org/press/eca.html.

WTO Secretariat. 1999. *Trade and Environment,* Special Studies 4. www.wto.org/wto/environ/environmental.pdf.

Wurzel, Rudiger. 1996. The Role of the EU Presidency in the Environmental Field: Does It Make a Difference Which Member State Runs the Presidency? *Journal of European Public Policy* 3(2): 272–291.

Yoshida, O. 1999. Soft Enforcement of Treaties: The Montreal Protocol's Noncompliance Procedure and the Functions of Internal International Institutions. *Colorado Journal of International Law and Policy* 10 (Winter): 95–140.

Young, Oran. 1977. *Resource Management at the International Level: The Case of the North Pacific.* New York: Nichols Publishing.

———. 1979. *Compliance and Public Authority: A Theory with International Applications.* Baltimore: Johns Hopkins University Press.

———. 1987. *The Intermediaries: Third Parties in International Crises.* Princeton, N.J.: Princeton University Press.

———. 1989. *International Cooperation: Building Regimes for Natural Resources and the Environment.* Ithaca: Cornell University Press.

———. 1989. The Politics of International Regime Formation: Managing Natural Resources and the Environment. *International Organization* 43(3): 349.

———. 1991. Political Leadership and Regime Formation: On the Development of Institutions in International Society. *International Organization* 45(3): 281.

———. 1993. International Organizations and International Institutions: Lessons Learned from Environmental Regimes. In *Environmental Politics in the International Arena,* by Sheldon Kamieniecki. Albany: State University of New York Press.

———. 1998. *Creating Regimes: Arctic Accords and International Governance.* Ithaca: Cornell University Press.

Young, Oran, George J. Demko, and Kilaparti Ramakrishna, eds. 1996. *Global Environmental Change and International Governance.* London: University Press.

Young, Oran, and G. Osherenko. 1993. *Polar Politics: Creating International Environmental Regimes.* Ithaca: Cornell University Press.

Zarsky, Lyuba. 1995. The Prospects for Environmental Cooperation in Northeast Asia. *Asian Perspective* 19(2): 103–13.

GENERAL INDEX

AUTHOR INDEX

CONVENTIONS INDEX

CASE INDEX